SIXTY YEARS OF AIRFIX MODELS

SIXTY YEARS OF AIRFIX MODELS

JEREMY BROOK

THE CROWOOD PRESS

First published in 2015 by
The Crowood Press Ltd
Ramsbury, Marlborough
Wiltshire SN8 2HR

www.crowood.com

British Library Cataloguing-in-Publication Data
A catalogue record for this book is available from the British
Library.

ISBN 978 1 84797 975 9

Note: Years given for models and kits in the captions refer to the
year in which the item depicted was purchased, which in some
cases is not the year of its original release.

Typeset by Shane O'Dwyer, Swindon, Wiltshire

Printed and bound in Malaysia by Times Offset (M) Sdn Bhd

Contents

Foreword

Airfix is one of those brands that gets under your skin.

It's hard to know why this is. Let's face it, it's only a box full of plastic parts, that by some miracle ends up being the perfect replica of the real thing! And when I say perfect, I mean perfect at any age. At eight years old, that Spitfire with the droopy wings and glue-damaged canopy was the perfect model of one of the world's greatest ever fighters, and even after taking over the dining table for what seemed like weeks, the whole family agreed too. That is what I believe is the magic of Airfix. It's the fact that it grows up with you, with some creating models that are even better than the real thing – well certainly in looks!

If you started Airfix modelling at a young age I think you'll know exactly what I mean, if not it's never too late to start, and Jeremy, who I've known for many years, takes you on an informative and enthusiastic tour in the following pages.

Darrell Burge

Glossary

Before the advent of multi-lingual and step-by-step diagrammatic instructions, the early Airfix instruction sheets had an 'exploded' diagram with a written description of each stage. As a child, I learnt many exotic words like 'nacelle', 'mizzen mast' and 'pitot tube', to name but a few, all from perusing the kit's assembly instructions. The young modeller of today relies on symbols and arrows to help him assemble the kit. Since we are told that 'a picture paints a thousand words', it means a kit can be made as easily by a child from Sweden as one from Swindon. I cannot help feeling, however, that modern youngsters are losing out on a chance to learn more about the subject they are modelling. Such 'technical' words are outside the scope of this book.

Several unusual words are used in connection with plastic construction kits in this book, and below are simple descriptions of some of the more frequently used ones.

After-market or 'cottage' companies: When a major kit company such as Airfix produces a new kit, there are several small companies out there which produce short-run components for advanced modellers to use to detail their kits or produce new variants. The parts are usually made out of resin or photo-etched metal. They tend to be available for a limited time. Some cottage companies produce whole kits in limited runs or detailed decal sheets for many kits.

Decals: The standard term for the markings on a sheet that are transferred to the painted model. They can be 'water-slide' or 'peel-off'. Older modellers grew up calling them 'transfers'.

Flash: Flash is the very thin plastic that sometimes surrounds a moulded part. It is usually seen on older kits where the mould is beginning to wear and the molten plastic is forced out between the two faces when they are closed together. It is very easily removed but can be difficult on very fine pieces.

K-resin: A harder compound polythene that Airfix has been using on its latest issue of the 1:32 figure sets. The earlier sets were produced in polythene, which whilst meaning the soldiers did not break, were very difficult for paint or glue to adhere to. K-resin is harder and seems to accept paint better, although bayonets are more likely to break off.

Polybagged: Originally many kit companies would swap moulds or lend moulds to another company to mould the kits. However, there is always scope for loss or damage in transit. Nowadays most companies run off a batch of kits, which are then put into polythene bags and sent to another company for them to add decals, boxes and so on. This is known as 'polybagging'. Hornby used several 'polybag' kits when it first took over Airfix to increase the range, but is now using primarily its own moulds.

Polyprop: This refers to the ready-assembled tanks and vehicles that Airfix introduced in its range, aimed more at the younger modeller. They are made of a more flexible polythene compound rather than the harder polystyrene used for standard kits.

Polystyrene: Pre-war and early toys and kits, such as the Ferguson Tractor, were usually made out of acetate, which was unstable and prone to warping. Polystyrene is a hard plastic, which when heated flows easily into cavities in a mould and shows the tiniest of details. Rejected runners can be ground down and used again. It does not seem to scour the mould, so the moulds can last for fifty or more years. Nowadays many early acetate toys have warped quite badly, whereas kits such as the original *Golden Hind* seem as good as new.

Runner: This is the correct name for the 'tree' or framework on to which all the parts are moulded. The early kits had the parts moulded either side of a straight runner, but later kits had a rectangular runner with the parts moulded inside. This afforded much more protection for the parts, and meant the runners fitted into the boxes better. They are often incorrectly referred to as 'sprues', and Hornby actually labels its runners as 'Sprue A', for example.

Sprue: The sprue is the point or 'gate' where the plastic flows from the runner into the individual parts. So when a modeller refers to 'sprue stretching' to produce thin plastic for rigging wires, for example, it should be 'runner stretching', but it doesn't sound as good!

Transfers: This was the old name, certainly in the UK, for the water-slide transfers that were applied to models. The markings were dipped in warm water, and after a few moments, slid off or 'transferred' to the kit. In the US they were known as decals. Nowadays 'decal' is the word applied to kits, and even full-size aircraft and vehicles use decals.

Vac-form: Most of us are familiar with the plastic trays that are included in food and other containers to keep parts separate. They are made of a thin plastic, which is drawn up into a mould to achieve the shape. It is known as vacuum-forming, as a vacuum is created to pull the plastic into the mould. The plastic sails on the large sailing ships are 'vac-formed' and cut out carefully by the modeller. Many of the military sets, such as the D-Day Assault Sets, contain a vac-form base on which to pose the models. They are, however, very thin and do not react well to being leant on!

Introduction

Sixty years ago, in 1955, as Britain was at last emerging from the post-war austerity that had prevailed since 1945, shoppers in branches of F. W. Woolworth & Co were pleased to note the appearance of a plastic construction kit of the most famous fighter of World War II, the Spitfire. It was produced by a small South London company that was perhaps better known for its range of plastic toys and, until recently, combs. The company was Airfix Products, and since the early 1950s they had been producing a small range of construction kits that were sold exclusively through Woolworths.

The early kits were mainly a selection of small sailing ships or vintage cars, but since interest in British war films and the war itself was very high, and the film of the famous Dambuster raids was packing cinemas, the decision by Airfix to manufacture its first aircraft kit, a Spitfire, was inspired. The aircraft range grew more quickly than any other, and soon made Airfix a household name. Within a few years 'Airfix' was to become the generic name for all construction kits, and its earlier products, like the combs, had almost been forgotten. It would go on to produce more toys, games, racing sets, trains, building, art and craft sets, but it will always be remembered for its kits. The kits were the only part of Airfix to survive intact the disastrous events of January 1981.

By the late 1970s, and bolstered by its own magazine, *Airfix Magazine*, which was the highest-selling modelling magazine at that time, it had produced the largest and most diverse range of construction kits in the world. Keen modellers could buy kits of dinosaurs, birds or steam engines as well as ships, figures and, of course, aircraft. In fact many people believed that the name 'Airfix' was taken from its range of aircraft construction kits, but that was just a happy coincidence!

The largest range of kits was, and still is, the range of aircraft kits, which cover scales from 1:144 through 1:72 and 1:48 to the giant 1:24 'Superkits' that Airfix pioneered. One of the early selling points of the Airfix range was its adherence to a 'constant scale' whereby every kit in a particular range was moulded to the same scale, so that a schoolboy's Messerschmitt could attack a Lancaster without looking out of place. Kits were also sold in numbered series, from one to twenty, depending upon complexity and size. So, for example, a Sopwith Camel would appear in Series 1, whilst a B-29 Superfortress was in Series 7, making it an ideal Christmas present for young modellers. Airfix strove to release a large aircraft kit just before Christmas, no doubt with the 'present' market in its sights.

Airfix also employed some of the finest artists to illustrate the box tops, believing that it was the picture that sold the kit. Who can forget those stirring Roy Cross paintings, like the Lancaster struggling to land with an engine on fire, or Brian Knight's Waterloo Highlanders in their bright red uniforms firing at the advancing French infantry? That was what sold the model to the countless numbers of schoolboys, and their fathers, who would regularly visit their local newsagents or nearby branch of 'Woolies' to see if the latest kit was out. It was the dream that sold the reality, and to this day the box tops tend to be what many older modellers remember with most affection. Many of the kits have not aged well over fifty or more years, but those stirring paintings still entice the would-be buyer to part with his money, and are in fact works of art in their own right.

Sixty years after the release of the first Spitfire, Airfix is once again releasing new kits at a rate not seen since the 1960s and 1970s. Many of those tired old kits from fifty or more years ago are now being replaced by new tools with an unprecedented level of detail. The history of Airfix has been well covered in the books written by Arthur Ward and in the back issues of *Constant Scale*, so I shall concentrate on the kits and models Airfix has released since the little *Golden Hind* over sixty years ago.

Kits were designed to be made; older modellers took their time and often never

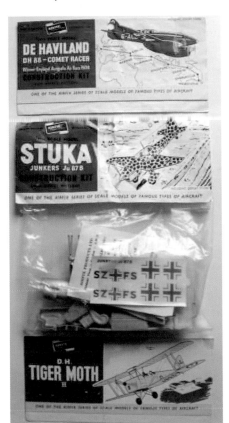

Early aircraft kits from the 1950s.

Late 1950s Series 2 headers.

Front and back cover of the first edition of the Airfix Catalogue, 1962.

Diesel Crane kit from 1961.

got round to starting some of the kits in their 'stashes', which would prove fortuitous to visitors of eBay today – but young modellers were very impatient. Typically, the latest kit was bought with your pocket money in the morning and assembled by early afternoon, and thanks to the introduction of 'one-hour' enamel paints they could be painted up before tea-time. Then you borrowed your mum's nail scissors, put some water in a saucer and applied the waterslide 'transfers' to your latest project. Once dry, or nearly dry, the fun would begin: battles were fought and war stories re-enacted, and when you tired of it (in those pre-Health and Safety days) you could buy some penny 'bangers' or load your air rifle and blow your model to bits. Most satisfying!

I started making Airfix kits when I was nine or ten, and still have most of the models I made. As you will see from the pictures herein, many bear the dust and dirt marks of thirty-five years or more in storage, and reflect my own modest modelling skills. I could never reach the standard of the super modellers one sees in magazines and at model shows, but I enjoyed making them and doing my best, and that is what it is all about. I learned a lot about aircraft, tanks and ships from making those models, and they encouraged me to find out more.

In those early days we spent hours with one of our dad's old razor blades clutched between our fingers, cleaning up the plastic on our kits and stretching plastic 'sprue' over a candle, inhaling the intoxicating

aroma of the plastic glue! I still have the scars from my early encounters with them.

We may have shot our models to pieces or blown them up in the back garden shortly after we'd made them, but we could always lie in bed with the latest Airfix kit catalogue and drool over all those wonderful paintings of the kits we had just destroyed. We could also dream that one day we might be able to complete a kit so that it looked like the ones on the pages. This is the story of those dreams.

Jeremy Brook

CHAPTER ONE

A Brief History of Airfix

1n 1938, a Hungarian Jew by the name of Miklos Kovesh arrived in Britain, whereupon he changed his name to Nicolas Kove. He had led an interesting life, having been sent to Siberia in World War I before, apparently, walking back home! Between the wars he moved with his family to Spain, where he set up a company employing cellulose-based plastics and patented a process for stiffening collars called 'Interfix'. With the threat of civil war in Spain looming, he moved to Italy; however, he found that Mussolini's strong connections to Hitler made Italy an unsafe base for a Jewish-run company. So he took his family and set off for a safer home.

The story of Airfix starts with his arrival in England. Upon arriving he set up a new company, probably in 1939, in the Edgware Road in London. He called his new company 'Airfix', which had nothing to do with aircraft models; the famous kits would not appear for another fourteen or so years. He chose the name 'Airfix' because he strongly believed that a successful company should appear at the front of a trade directory, and he also had an interest in trademarks ending in 'ix', which he had used to name his collar-stiffening process. Since one of his earliest products was to be air-filled mattresses, he felt 'Airfix' was appropriate since his product was 'fixed with air'. He has also been credited with inventing the Li-Lo air bed.

The war intervened, and despite his being a Jewish businessman, effectively a refugee, he is believed to have been interned on the Isle of Man for a short while. After the war, like many others, he found that materials were in very short supply and so he had to resort to finding materials wherever he could, even grinding down old fountain pens to produce plastic for his injection-moulding machines. He had been manufacturing utility lighters, but was always on the lookout for new markets and ways to keep his hungry machines busy. By this time the company logo read 'Airfix Products in Plastic', to reflect his growing dependence on plastic toys and articles.

Around 1947 he happened upon a new market. Windsor's had just produced the first plastic injection-moulding machine in the UK and were looking for someone

Four views of the Airfix toolroom in the 1940s.

to operate it. Islyn Thomas of Newark, USA, who ran Hoffman Tools and would supply Kove with his first mould for combs, was to introduce him to Windsor's. This fusion of needs resulted in Airfix operating the first injection-moulding machine in the country.

At that time combs were made of acetate and the teeth were cut using saws. Utilizing the moulds supplied by Hoffman Tools, Kove could provide combs made out of plastic, which were much stronger and cheaper than the old acetate ones. Within a short while, Airfix was the largest manufacturer of combs in the UK, and controlled the market. So keen was Woolworths, its principal customer, to get their combs that they frequently picked them up from Airfix rather than waiting to have them delivered! By the early 1950s, however, Airfix was facing increasing competition from other comb-making manufacturers, and so in 1951 or 1952, Airfix withdrew from the comb-making business.

The early days at Airfix were always somewhat chaotic, and it was very much a 'hand-to-mouth' existence. The man who was employed as the manager at Airfix before 1950 was John Dolan. He gave a very interesting and illuminating interview to the Plastic Historical Society in the late 1990s, shortly before his death. In it he describes many of the goings-on at Airfix whilst Nicolas Kove was running it. He tells of Kove's attempts to track down and acquire raw materials for

production, and of having to cut a hole in the first floor of the factory so that the injection-moulding machine could be lowered in!

Kove reputedly had a fiery temper, but he could also be very generous. His health was not too good, and much of the day-to-day running of the company was put into John Dolan's hands, and from 1950 into Ralph Ehrmann's. Nicolas Kove died in 1958, and in that year Airfix became a limited company with Ralph Ehrmann at its head.

Dolan claims to have invented the kitbag and header for the Ferguson Tractor and later kits, although he left Airfix in 1949, around the time that the tractor was first being produced. Whilst there is cause to doubt the veracity of some of his reminiscences, he does paint an interesting picture of a typical post-war small company, struggling to survive.

As the pioneer in injection moulding in the UK, Airfix had been making a range of toys and games that were becoming increasingly popular. This expertise is probably the reason that Airfix was approached by Harry Ferguson in the late 1940s to produce a promotional model of his new TE20 tractor, which was entering production in Coventry. He wanted a made-up model that his sales force could show and give to prospective customers. The finished tractor was to 1:20 scale, and according to Ralph Ehrmann, who joined Airfix in 1950, the mould was a lovely one, which produced very detailed and accurate miniatures.

The problem was that the models had to be assembled by the Airfix workforce, which was both time-consuming and costly. Models were often returned because small parts had broken and needed replacing, and this was becoming an expensive headache for Airfix. By this time Airfix had gained Ferguson's approval to sell the tractor to the general public, so

it was decided to sell the model as a kit of parts in a box, to be assembled by the purchaser. This appears to have happened in around 1952 or 1953. Later, probably in around 1955, it would be sold in the standard Airfix kit package of a polythene bag with a header attached.

It is sometimes thought of as the first Airfix kit, although it was not designed as a kit but as a model assembled from parts. The credit for being the first true Airfix kit goes to the little replica of the *Golden Hind*. However, the kit that will always be associated with Airfix, more than any other, is the Supermarine Spitfire. A somewhat crude and inaccurate model was released in 1955, coded BT-K, but it led the way to hundreds of other kits of aircraft, and indeed today the main output of Airfix is still aircraft. Today, Airfix has released around thirty different models of the Spitfire in three scales, more than any other manufacturer, and is set to produce more Spitfires in the years ahead with an accuracy and detailed finish that was undreamt-of in 1955.

My own involvement with Airfix dates back to the late 1950s. I remember going into the little newsagent next to my primary school, which was selling a boxed kit of the Spitfire, probably the Aurora 1:48 kit. I never managed to buy it, but I did later make an Airfix Spitfire, which was almost certainly BT-K. Since I did not have any proper paint, I used the oil paint from a 'Painting by Numbers' set. It took a week to dry, but it did get rid of all the unsightly rivets and trench-deep panel lines! Then I remember my father coming back from a conference and bringing my elder brother and me two Airfix kits: one of us got the Beaufighter and the other the Bristol Fighter. In those days fitting the top wing on to a biplane was a nightmare, as all the struts were separate and you had to get them all lined up and get the wing on before they moved and the glue dried. More often than not the whole thing would not sit right, or it moved out of place and you had to start again. When it did finally sit right it was remarkably strong, but it helped develop in me a liking for monoplanes!

It was in August 1963 that I decided to buy *Airfix Magazine* each month, and I also bought my first catalogue to add to the various leaflets I had picked up and fortunately not discarded. I was in the habit of carefully opening any kit and always saving the box, header and instructions. Soon I had several old kit boxes filled with bits

ABOVE: *Nicholas and Clothilde Kove.*

LEFT: *Airfix model tractor from 1949.*
JOHN DOLAN

and pieces from earlier kits. I also cut out any news items in the daily papers about Airfix, and squirrelled them away for future reference. This collecting habit would stand me in good stead when I came to run the Airfix Collectors' Club, for I had quite an archive of all things relating to Airfix, most of it collected at the time.

In the 1950s and 1960s the main source of supply for Airfix kits was the F. W. Woolworth chain of stores. In those days every town had a 'Woolies' and many suburbs of cities had small branches. One could always see the Airfix kits because high above the maroon-coloured counters were huge sheets of white pegboard, to which were affixed numerous made-up Airfix kits, so one could automatically make a bee-line for the Airfix counter.

Originally, Airfix kits were only sold in Woolworth's, which ensured that they had an excellent distribution system. The growing range of Airfix kits was extremely popular, and in the mid-1950s Woolworth's tried to capitalize on this success by selling kits from other small kit companies. This rather upset Airfix, which then arranged to sell its kits through other retailers. None of the other ranges of kits were as successful for Woolworth's as the Airfix range, and their exclusivity was lost. However, Woolworth's did retain its priority regarding new releases.

In those days Woolworth's had an agreement with Airfix whereby they received the first run of any new kit, about three or four weeks before the other shops got theirs. Effectively, the Woolworth's order paid the development cost of the early Airfix kits. By the late 1970s, Woolworth's was no longer the Mecca for Airfix kits and one could buy them in most newsagents, department stores, ironmongers and many other shops. Many young boys would take their Saturday 'pocket money' into their village shop, or go to their nearest town, and buy the latest Airfix aeroplane or tank, which they would make as soon as they got home and play with in the afternoon. Ah, happy days!

In the next four chapters I shall look at the way the range developed over the four distinct periods in the life of Airfix, and how it lived up to its claim to have 'the largest range of plastic kits in the world'!

For each year I shall list the kits or models announced in that year. Some may have taken a couple of years to appear, and some arrived in the shops unannounced, but generally most made it into the shops in the year of their announcement. I shall

ABOVE: *Airfix toys of the late 1940s.*

RIGHT: *'Zoobrix', an Airfix toy of the 1940s.*
JOHN DOLAN

give a very brief history of each kit, and a little more space to important or innovative kits.

Each model will have the Airfix number first applied to it. Initially the kits used pattern numbers taken from those used by all the other Airfix products in the 1950s, but in around 1959 the kits started to use catalogue numbers, which were more specific to series and type of kit and helped

the purchaser to know where to find it in the catalogues or leaflets. These replaced the original pattern numbers. In the early 1970s, with computerization appearing, the kit range had 'computerized' catalogue numbers applied by which they are still identified today. In the Palitoy era most kits issued had a prefix '9' added to their catalogue number, while Hornby prefixes its releases with an 'A'.

Some kits, like the venerable Gloster Gladiator from 1956 and the Tiger Moth from 1957, have been in almost continuous production for nearly sixty years, and have used the same excellent Roy Cross paintings to sell them for most of that time. Others, like the Showjumper and Boy Scout, were only available for a short period and then withdrawn. Whether they will ever return is doubtful, but the barely-used moulds still exist. Perversely, these are among the most sought-after kits by collectors, who wouldn't give a week's pocket money in the early days to buy them, but will now contemplate spending a week's wages to acquire one!

The four periods referred to earlier begin with the first kit in the early 1950s up to the closure of the parent company, Airfix Industries, in January 1981. This is often considered to be the 'Golden Age' of Airfix kits. Then from 1981 until 1986, the Airfix construction kit division was owned by the American General Mills Company, operated through its Palitoy subsidiary in Leicester. Production of Airfix kits was moved to General Mills' factories in France.

In 1986, General Mills withdrew from toy-making in Europe and sold Airfix to Humbrol, which was based in Kingston-upon-Hull. Humbrol had previously bought the French kit company Heller, and production of Airfix kits was moved to Heller's factory at Trun in France.

Finally in mid-2006, Heller got into difficulties and Humbrol found it could not gain access to its moulds or completed kits. Consequently the banks withdrew their support for Humbrol and so the administrator was called in for the second time. Fortunately, the famous British brand of Hornby came to the rescue and bought Humbrol along with Airfix, and returned the brands to Britain. Today, both brands are based at Hornby's headquarters in Margate, Kent, and the famous and valuable Airfix mould tools are therefore once again back in Britain.

The majority of Humbrol paints are now being made in Britain, but the Airfix kits are presently being made in China and India. The new Airfix 'Quick Build' kits, though, are being made in this country. The good news for modellers is that after twenty-five years or so of a lack of investment in the range, Hornby is now investing large sums in new tools, and it seems Airfix is entering a second 'Golden Age'.

If the last kit you made over thirty years ago was the Gloster Gladiator, then you can still get it today, but you now have the option of buying the new Gladiator, which is an infinitely superior kit and every bit as good as the much more expensive Japanese kits such as Tamiya. The new Tiger Moth kit is superb.

The big news in the plastic modelling world in 2014 was the release of an exquisitely detailed 1:24 model of the Hawker Typhoon. In 2006 it was felt that Airfix was finally going to disappear, but instead it is now back at the very top and is doing more than any other company to get children back into the old ways of building and creating something with their hands. Also in 2014, Airfix released a small model of the *Mary Rose* similar in size to the first *Golden Hind* kit.

So things seemed to have turned full circle, with Airfix once again leading the world in new models and introducing innovative details to the kits. As we have come to the end of the first six decades of Airfix kit production, we can look forward with excitement to what the next sixty years will hold.

CHAPTER TWO

The Golden Age, 1952–1981

In the early 1950s, Airfix was selling huge numbers of its ready-assembled ice cream tricycles in the UK branches of Woolworth's, as well as other toys it was producing. Comb production, a market in which Airfix had been the main player for several years, was winding down, and Airfix was looking for new products to replace the combs. In late 1951 or early 1952, Ralph Ehrmann, who had joined Airfix in March 1950, went on a trade visit to the United States where he saw a range of sailing ship kits being produced by an American company, Gowland and Gowland.

Later in 1952, Jim Russon, chief buyer for the UK Woolworth's stores, approached Airfix because it was one of the largest suppliers of toys to their stores. He suggested Airfix might like to manufacture UK-produced versions of a series of 'ships-in-a-bottle' kits being produced in the United States by Gowland and Gowland, the very ones Ralph had seen earlier. The first one suggested was the *Golden Hind*, which it was proposed would be sold exclusively in the UK Woolworth's branches.

Despite the mould already existing, Airfix concluded that it could not be produced cheaply enough, so they looked at the idea of producing just the ship without the bottle. It still looked too expensive. Since Airfix was probably the most experienced plastic injection-moulding company in Britain at the time, Ralph Ehrmann and John Gray considered the feasibility of Airfix making their own mould of the *Golden Hind*, without a bottle, to sell instead of someone else's. Once the mould was paid for there would be no licence fees to eat into the profitability of the kit, and they could produce as many as they liked, whenever they liked. At this point I do not think they were contemplating designing a huge range of kits.

Airfix first suggested a retail price of 5s (25p), with the model being sold in a box. This was too high for Woolworth's, so Airfix looked at ways to reduce the cost. At that time new clear polythene bags were beginning to appear, and so it was proposed to put the kit parts into a plastic bag with a simple folded colour header stapled to the bag. The assembly instructions, history and so on, would be printed on the header. Woolworth's accepted the idea and gave Airfix an order for 30,000 *Golden Hind* kits to retail at 2s (10p) each – and so the first of the famous 'two-bob' kits was born.

The *Golden Hind* first appeared in late 1952, or more likely early 1953, though the date of release cannot at present be confirmed, and it was so popular that the moulding machines were in continuous production and sales easily exceeded the original 30,000! It seems that almost by accident Airfix had stumbled on the formula that would result in them becoming one of the most famous names in the toy-making world, and more than sixty years later it would still be moulding new kits.

Ralph Ehrmann and John Gray concluded that they had a winner, so decided to mould more ship kits. Again they looked to the States to see what other ships were being sold in bottles, and decided to mould the *Santa Maria* as number two.

Ralph told me that when it came to number three, he seems to remember that the Americans were producing a kit of the USS *Chesapeake*, which had had some success against Royal Navy vessels during the war of 1812, and so he thought, 'Why not produce a kit of HMS *Shannon*, which had eventually captured the *Chesapeake*'? This would explain why the *Shannon* was produced before the likes of the *Victory*, *Cutty Sark*, *Revenge* and so on. I have often thought that the *Shannon* was the odd one out because it was not very well known: had it not been for the fact that every year it appeared in the Airfix catalogue and I was reminded that the *Shannon* had captured the *Chesapeake*, I would probably never have heard of the *Shannon*. It also added a British-inspired element to the new range of ships.

The huge success of the *Golden Hind*, which was not, I am sure, originally seen as the first of a huge range of kits, meant that the next few kits would take a year or so to plan and produce, which is why there were no other new kits in 1953. By

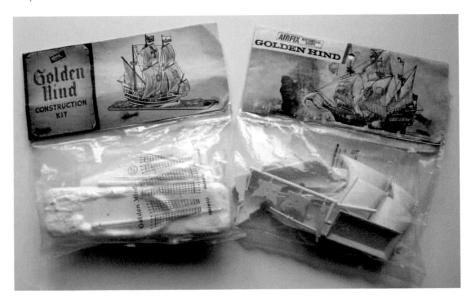

The original Golden Hind *kit (left) with the later full-hull version (right).*

1954, when the two new ship kits were entering the market place, numbers four to twelve were already being planned and tooled.

Nicholas Kove was apparently reluctant to move away from ships, as this was proving to be a very successful range, but Ehrmann and Gray, who had been promoted to buyer at Airfix in 1949 and later general manager, were already looking at other manufacturers' ranges for inspiration. Gowland and Gowland also produced a range of 1:32 vintage cars, two of which were kits of a 1911 Rolls-Royce and a 1930 Bentley. These were obvious choices for the British market. Clearly Airfix got their inspiration from the other kits, but the moulds were new and tooled by Airfix. John Gray told Arthur Ward that he remembered chasing a Bentley owner to his home, where he persuaded him to let Airfix measure his car. The Bentley owner did not want his paintwork scratched, so the Airfix designer had to cut off the metal end to his measuring tape and then add half an inch to all his measurements!

1:32 was a popular scale in the United States, and 1:32 figures roughly equated to the scale of 54mm, which was used for many toy soldiers.

Both Ehrmann and Gray had been in the RAF in the war, so they felt the third range should be aircraft. The obvious choice for the first aircraft kit would be the Spitfire, arguably the most iconic aircraft of World War II and, rightly or wrongly, seen as the one that had saved Britain; so there was really no better choice to launch the aircraft range.

Once again Airfix looked to other manufacturers and found that an American kit company, Aurora, had just released a 1:48 Spitfire of indeterminate mark. Almost from the beginning Airfix researched, designed and moulded each kit, and still does, but it is fair to say that for the first few kits, Airfix looked to see how their competitors had designed a kit they were proposing to mould before actually starting work. There are still some kit companies in the Far East that will take an existing kit from another company to use as the basis for a new kit they want to mould.

Since aircraft were seen as a bit of a gamble and Nicholas Kove had insisted that the mould be underwritten by Messers Ehrmann and Gray, it appears that the decision was taken to use the Aurora model as a 'pattern' for the new

Three typical kits of the 1952–55 era.

kit. The 1:48 kit could be pantographed down to 1:72 scale, but apart from the size difference the two kits were virtually identical, seeming to confirm that the Aurora kit was copied. Furthermore the Aurora markings of BT-K did not come from a Spitfire but from a different aircraft altogether, and Airfix even used those! This first Spitfire is now referred to by Airfix collectors as 'BT-K'. The Airfix kit is clearly a direct copy of the Aurora kit, albeit scaled down to 1:72 scale, unlike the ships and cars which owed only their inspiration to the other manufacturers. Whether Aurora gave their blessing to Airfix to scale it down still cannot be stated categorically, and is probably best left alone! All subsequent kits, with a very few exceptions, would be Airfix-designed.

The scale they chose was to be 1:72: 1in to 72in, or 1in to 6ft. This was important, because at the time many of the kit manufacturers were scaling their aircraft kits to fit into standard box sizes. Thus it was not uncommon to find kits that were to 1:69, 1:75, and so on. Of course, once the modeller began to build up a collection of aircraft, these size differences began to be noticeable and could spoil a collection of scale models. The decision by Airfix to adopt a 'constant scale' for each series meant that they could continue to sell their early kits well into the next century, and the rapidly growing ranges meant that other manufacturers had to fall in step or lose out. In fact the 1956 Gloster Gladiator, the second Airfix

aircraft, would not leave the catalogue until 2013, to be replaced by an excellent new-tool Gladiator. Since the initial tooling costs were effectively paid for by Woolworth's, this means that Airfix has enjoyed fifty-six years of profitable production out of that one mould! The only work on the mould, apart from necessary maintenance, has been the provision of an alternative propeller. No production figures are known to exist for the Gladiator, but they must run into seven figures.

Since large numbers of kits were never actually built, one's chances of picking up an early Airfix kit on eBay or from a dealer are good. There are lofts all over the country where in the 1950s and 1960s, Airfix kits became the preferred choice of loft insulation. With the arrival of eBay many people have taken to going into their lofts to remove the kits to sell. So beware when a seller describes his 1950s issue of an Airfix kit as 'rare', as the likelihood is that the newer issues are rarer. Nowadays, annual production runs are a fraction of the size of the early days, which means that, with a few exceptions, there are likely to be more unmade kits from the 1950s lying around than from the 1990s and later.

So 1954 would see only the two ships released, but in 1955 another sailing ship, the first two vintage cars and the Spitfire were all introduced. Another kit also appeared and was to prove a bit of an oddity, being a replica of the then new cruise liner SS *Southern Cross*. It was moulded to the scale of 1:500, several years before Airfix settled on 1:600 (1in equals 50ft) as the 'constant scale' for its modern warships and liners series, initiated by HMS *Cossack* in 1959. It was also joined by the bagged kit version of the Ferguson tractor.

Both the *Southern Cross* and the Ferguson tractor were sponsored by the owners. The tractor was, as stated earlier, delivered to Ferguson's as an assembled model, but after Airfix was allowed to sell it to the general public they sold it as a kit in a box in the early 1950s. It went into the popular polythene bag in about 1955, and was retailed at 3s 9d (roughly 19p).

In 1955, four further kits were produced to make three ranges of kits. The *Southern Cross* was to be a one-off, produced as a promotional kit for the Shaw Savill Line, so does not constitute the beginnings of a new range. Of these four kits the Spitfire was the most important, as it was to be aircraft that would make Airfix's name, but it was easily the worst kit moulded so far by Airfix – in fact it was so poor that it prompted a young ex-RAF national serviceman to write into Airfix and complain. He even went so far as to say he could do better! So he was summoned to Airfix and offered the job of designer of the new kits. His name was John Edwards, and he would go on to become the chief designer of Airfix kits. His replacement for the poor Spitfire would arrive in 1960 as a Mark IX kit, and would remain in the catalogue for fifty years until replaced by a new Mark IX in 2010.

So by the end of 1955, Airfix had a range that consisted of nine kits, including the tractor and *Southern Cross*, which like the first Spitfire did not last too long, but only seven if these two are not counted. The Spitfire would only last for five years until replaced by John Edwards' much superior Mark IX. The *Southern Cross* disappeared from the leaflets in 1959, and the moulds for both models are no longer with Airfix. All the other kits would still be in production, or capable of being produced fifty or more years later, although the *Shannon* has not been seen now for many years. The *Cutty Sark* is currently in the 2014 catalogue.

Below is a list of the early years' releases, which includes the Ferguson Tractor kit:

1952/3

1264	*Golden Hind*	N/A

1954

1265	*Santa Maria*	N/A
1266	HMS *Shannon*	N/A

1955

1216	Spitfire – BT-K	1:72
1315	1911 Rolls-Royce	1:32
1344	1930 Bentley	1:32
1268	*Cutty Sark*	1:130
1298	SS *Southern Cross*	1:500
480K	Ferguson Tractor (bagged kit)	1:20

It is interesting to look at these first kits. Some, like the Spitfire, were not very good, but others such as the 1930 Bentley were surprisingly good and would be re-released as recently as 2004. The *Cutty Sark* is still in the 2014 range!

The first five ship kits were all released as 'waterline' models set on a rectangular sea base. To this could be glued two right-angled pieces of plastic which had angled holes in them so they could be 'tacked' to the wall for display purposes. The waterline design was clearly based on the 'ship-in-a-bottle' design of the original kits. However, after the later ships were designed as full hull models on little display stands, the early ones would also be redesigned to become full hull.

Interestingly, sixty years later Airfix would revisit the small sailing ship market with a delightful model of the *Mary Rose* to 1:400 scale.

Making a kit can be a long process, anything from eighteen months to several years, particularly as before the onset of

ABOVE: *Ferguson tractor kit of 1955.*

LEFT: *Spitfire BT+K from 1955, the very first Airfix Spitfire kit.*

CAD design, everything was done by hand. Firstly, research material was collected: Airfix once had a huge library of books, magazines and papers referring to its hundreds of different models. Once studied, the Airfix designer would decide upon the breakdown of parts and then complete a series of technical drawings of each component. Some, like the 1:12 Rolls-Royce, ran to more than eighty drawings. Once the kit had been drawn, the plans were passed to the pattern maker, who produced wooden or resin patterns of each part. These patterns were usually several times life-size.

The toolmaker would then use a pantograph to scale down the patterns to the required size, and cut the reduced pattern into a block of steel. This was the most expensive and time-consuming part of the process and explains why several kits made it to the pattern-making stage only to be stopped before the tool-making process began.

Once the tool was basically finished, the tool maker could add detail by hand. This was when the raised panel lines and rivets, so beloved of early Airfix models, were added. Inscribed detail or panel lines had to be built into the pantographing stage, and this was more difficult and expensive. The toolmaker also had to plan the layout of the ejection pins to ensure a satisfactory removal from the machines. Water-cooling holes also had to be built in.

When the mould was ready, it was test-run to check for fit, ejection and other details. Adjustments usually had to be made before it was passed as finished. In the meantime, the decals had been designed and the instruction sheets readied. The artwork was completed, and a proof of the box top or header was produced. Once everything was in place, production could begin.

The first run of a new kit was typically about 70,000 units, all of which went to Woolworth's stores. Once Woolworth's lost its exclusivity it still got the first run, but a second run of 50–60,000 kits was made a few weeks later, which went to model and toy shops. Such was the popularity of Airfix kits in those early days that a new kit could be run several times in its first year. Thereafter they would be run regularly to restock the shops. The initial Woolworth's order virtually guaranteed the payback on the mould, and so on.

In the early to mid-1950s the plastic construction kit market in the US and Europe was in its infancy, and the choice of what kits to make was consequently wide. Airfix's choice of subjects, their easy availability and 'pocket money' prices, must have been a godsend to aspiring modellers. This, and the knowledge that many more new kits were planned, would catapult Airfix into the front ranks of model-making companies.

1956

By 1956, Airfix was well into its programme of new kits covering the three ranges they had established the previous year. Nine new kits were scheduled for release that year; in order of their pattern numbers these were as follows:

1306	HMS *Victory*	N/A
1335	Gloster Gladiator Mark I	1:72
1336	1905 Rolls-Royce	1:32
1337	1910 Model 'T' Ford	1:32
1338	1904 Darracq	1:32?
1355	Westland S-55 Helicopter	1:72
1384	Messerschmitt Bf 109F	1:72
1385	Westland Lysander	1:72
1386	Bristol F2B Fighter	1:72

For the first few years all the kits used pattern numbers, which were also used by other toys and games made by Airfix. In 1959, around the time that the packaging changed to 'Type 2', the kits were allocated catalogue numbers, which indicated more clearly the series number and type of kit. For example, the DH Heron released in 1959 was issued as 381, the first Series 3 aircraft, number 81. All the 1:72 aircraft in each series started at 81. At this stage, however, all the kits were still in Series 1 at 2s each.

In 1956 the new range of Airfix construction kits was only available from Woolworth's, so it is hard to find any mention of them in the trade press because they were not yet available to trade outlets, as were the other Airfix toys and games. It is believed they were all released in 1956, but there are no surviving records to confirm this.

It was this valuable contract with Woolworth's that effectively made Airfix the most famous construction kit company in the world. In the 1950s and 1960s, the UK branch of F. W. Woolworth Ltd had shops in virtually every town, large and small, and in many suburbs of large towns. I remember being able to go into any Woolworth's store in the late 1950s and 1960s, and gazing over the purple counters and seeing, high up above a counter, a large pegboard sheet: attached to these sheets, by nylon strips with a peg on each end, was a selection of made-up Airfix kits. Airfix employed workers whose task was to make and paint the latest Airfix kits so they could be fitted to these display boards. I searched for years,

*Gloster Gladiator
kit of 1956.*
AIRFIX

but was unable to find any of the nylon clips to make my own mini Woolworth's display!

Even when Woolworth's lost its exclusive deal with Airfix, it still received the new kits about four weeks before the other shops. This tie with Woolworth's was to make Airfix the brand leader, certainly in the UK, and it also made 'Airfix' a household name, as well as the generic name for any kind of self-assembly item. Even today all such kits are usually referred to as 'Airfix kits', and any item that is assembled from parts is likened to an Airfix kit.

The choice of kits is very interesting and shows the way the range was to develop. The *Victory* was the last of the small sailing ships to feature a 'waterline' hull, and in fact would later be altered to a full hull. It also shows that the production of new small sailing ships was slowing down. However, along with the *Cutty Sark*, it still features in the 2014 catalogue – not bad for a kit that is nearly sixty years old!

The remaining nine kits featured three cars and six aircraft! Two of the cars were moulded to 1:32 scale, but the Darracq was not, I think, 1:32 and is only one of a handful of Airfix kits that were not moulded to the 'constant scale' of the main ranges. It was chosen, I suspect, because a 1904 Darracq had featured in the hugely successful 1953/4 film *Genevieve*. It was possibly moulded to a larger scale because the original was smaller than the other kits and might have looked out of place alongside them. The early vintage cars did not have driver figures, but these would be added in the 1960s. Of the other two kits, the 1910 Model 'T' would be replaced in the 1960s by a two-seater version from 1912.

The aircraft are really interesting because Airfix chose aircraft from all eras rather than concentrating on World War II. Thus we had three fighters and a 'spy' plane from World War II, the first one of several World War I aircraft, and a modern post-war machine. The latter was also the first helicopter model produced by Airfix. The initial kit was of a civilian model operated by BEA, but later it would be modified twice to represent a Royal Navy machine; extra parts would be added to the kit to suit it for its Royal Navy role. Airfix soon realized that military aircraft were more popular than civil ones, and later tended to mould the military version of a civil aircraft.

Airfix was noted for its range of excellent helicopter models over the years, and in 2012 and 2013 released superb 1:48 models of the Lynx and Merlin helicopters currently being used by the British armed forces.

The Gladiator was modified shortly after release to have a different propeller, but otherwise was not altered in any way for the next fifty-six years and has been available for most of that time, despite being a very rudimentary model. In 2013 it was finally retired, but it was replaced by an all-new model featuring optional skis. The new Gladiator is a superb model and a worthy successor to the venerable 1956 kit.

The Messerschmitt Bf 109F was altered later into a 'G' model and, like the Spitfire, was replaced in 1965 by a new kit, a Bf 109G-6. This kit would remain in the range until replaced by Hornby in 2009. The Lysander was replaced in 1972 by a new tool, which featured a 'secret agent' figure climbing up the ladder attached to the side.

The Bristol Fighter was the first of a comparatively small range of World War I aircraft. As mentioned earlier, I can remember my father returning from a conference in the late 1950s and bringing my brother and me kits of the Beaufighter and Bristol Fighter as presents. I can't remember which one I had to make, but I do know that with those early biplane kits it was very difficult to fit the top wings: you had to stick up to eight interplane struts into the bottom wing, add the two mid-wing struts, and then hope you could push all the struts into the top wing before the whole thing moved out of place and you had to start again! Later kits had better ways of fixing the wing struts, and a small jig was provided to keep things in place until the glue dried. Like the real thing, once dry it was surprisingly robust. Hornby has introduced a new method of fitting the struts in place, and even includes tiny holes for rigging wires! Hopefully the 100th anniversary of World War I will see many new early biplane kits released that should be easier to construct than their predecessors!

Starting in 1965, six of the early World War I aircraft were released as 'Dogfight Doubles' in Series 2. At this time the Bristol Fighter, along with several of the early World War I fighters, had extra fabric detail added to the mould, bringing it more in line with the detail of the

newer aircraft such as the Sopwith Pup. It was deleted from the 2013 catalogue along with other World War I aircraft.

Some of the very early aircraft kits did not feature a separate pilot figure. The pilot or 'blob' was either moulded into each fuselage half, or in the case of open cockpit aircraft such as the Bristol Fighter, a separate head and shoulders was cemented to a projecting tab just below the rim. Shortly after, the cockpits on new kits were opened up and a somewhat spindly figure was moulded, which sat on the moulded tab. This would be a definite improvement, as better-quality pilot figures could be added later on.

Also that year three sets of kits were released – probably Airfix had its eye on the mail-order market, where several kits in one box were more likely to be sold than single kits. Thus the Armada gift set had five sailing ships, the vintage car rally set had five vintage cars, and the historical air fleet had five aircraft. All the kits were from those models released so far; paint and brushes were included. Surviving examples are rare.

So 1956 saw twice as many kits introduced as 1955, and the following year that number was to be doubled again. More importantly it showed the direction in which the range was to develop in the years ahead, with an emphasis on aircraft models.

1957

1957 was an important year for Airfix: not only were twenty-one new kits announced, but Airfix became a public company and was quoted on the stock market. Also a new range of kits was added, to cater to a new market. The kits were as follows:

1388	*Mayflower*	N/A
1397	PS *Great Western*	N/A
1394	1907 Lanchester Landaulette	1:32
1387	Fokker Dr.1 tri-plane	1:72
1391	Supermarine S.6B	1:72
1392	Sopwith Camel	1:72
1393	Albatros D.V	1:72
1395	Junkers Ju 87B *Stuka*	1:72
1396	Hawker Hurricane IVRP	1:72
1398	Hawker Hart	1:72
1399	DH88 Comet Racer	1:72
1400	De Havilland Tiger Moth	1:72
1401	RE8	1:72
1402	De Havilland Mosquito FB.VI	1:72
1404	Supermarine Walrus	1:72
4001	Country Inn	OO/HO

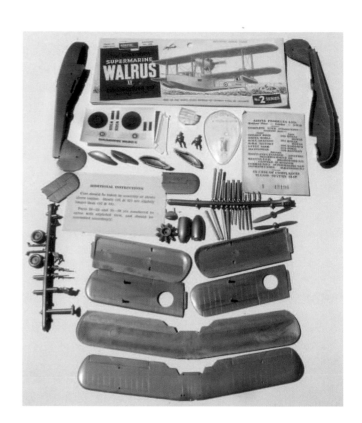

LEFT: *1957's Mosquito and Walrus kits.*

RIGHT: *The 1957 Walrus kit ready to construct...*

BELOW: *...and in finished form.* AIRFIX

4002	Detached House	OO/HO
4003	Service Station	OO/HO
4004	General Store	OO/HO
4005	Signal Box	OO/HO
4006	Bungalow	OO/HO

Two more ships were added to the range, along with just one vintage car. Eleven aircraft were tooled, and two were produced in the new Series 2 at 3s (15p): the Mosquito and Walrus.

The *Mayflower* and *Great Western* were both designed with full hulls and a display stand, and the earlier kits were shortly to have their hulls modified to this standard. The Lanchester was in the range until the mid-1970s, but when the cars were put into boxes and moved to Series 2, it does not appear to have made the transition and has not been seen since.

Four more World War I aircraft were included: they each appeared in the 'Dogfight Doubles' series in the mid-1960s and in the 'Aircraft of the Aces' series from 1989 onwards. The RE8 was memorable for its very large top wing, which was always difficult to stick in place. Again they had extra detail added in the mid-1960s, and some received improved pilot figures.

The infamous *Stuka* joined the ranks of World War II fighting aircraft. It was replaced by two *Stuka* kits in the late 1970s: a Ju 87B/R in Series 3, and a simplified Ju 87B-2 in Series 2.

The Hurricane was upgraded slightly in the 1960s by the addition of improved surface detail to the mould. In 1972 a new Hurricane was released, which was supposed to cover the Mk IIB and IVRP versions, but it suffered from outline inaccuracies and was shortly after sold only as the IIB version. The original kit then made a comeback to cover the IVRP version. In 1979 a superior Mk I version was produced, and the old kit faded out. Recently Hornby has started to replace the old Hurricane kits.

Four inter-war kits appeared. One was the Hawker Hart, which in the 1960s was modified to represent a Hawker Demon. The legendary Tiger Moth training aircraft was tooled and has remained in the catalogue ever since, finally leaving in 2013. It had fabric detail added in the 1960s, and despite its simplicity and inaccuracy, seems to have been a very popular kit. At 'Scale Modelworld', Telford, in November 2013, a brand new tool of the Tiger Moth was announced for release in 2014.

The other two were models of famous race-winning aircraft. Both had very smooth finishes and don't appear to have received any detail improvements. The Supermarine S.6B was made available in a tin along with the Spitfire I in 2006 to celebrate the seventieth anniversary of the Spitfire. The Comet Racer is in the 2014 catalogue, and has recently been sold in red, green and black variants of the race-winning aircraft.

The important news was the release of two larger aircraft that introduced Series 2, retailing at 3s (15p). The Mosquito FB.VI was the first, and was a nice little model with underwing rockets; the wheels were too thin, but otherwise it looked the part. In 1972, Airfix released a multi-variant kit in Series 3, but the old kit seems to have soldiered on into the 1980s. The Walrus has been available for most of the last half century, but was recently deleted from the 2013 range.

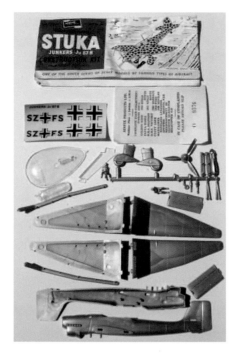

The 1957 Stuka kit.

Many of the moulds of the early aircraft would receive the attention of Airfix's 'superdetailer', who in the 1960s added fabric detail and rivets to the otherwise clean mouldings. Some companies, such as Frog and later Matchbox, seemed to prefer a smoother finish to their aircraft kits. Airfix, however, after the first few years, decided to add rivets to the models. At first these were small and very restrained, but even so, they often made it difficult for the transfers, or 'decals' as

they later came to be known, to adhere satisfactorily to the surface of the kit. Advanced modellers usually resorted to sanding off the offending rivets to create a smooth surface for better decal adhesion. In the later years, the Airfix 'riveter' applied oversize rivets that often marred the finish of the kit – some rivets when scaled up became the size of saucers!

A totally new range of kits was introduced, which was known as the 'Trackside' range. Modelled to the common model railway scale used by Hornby and Tri-ang of HO/OO scale (1:76/1:87), the buildings were made to 1:76 scale, which made them, as far as the eye could tell, more or less compatible with Airfix's 1:72 kits. Later rolling stock would be added, and the tiny figures and AFVs would be moulded to 1:76 scale, rather than 1:72 – and this small discrepancy in scale has been a bone of contention amongst the AFV, soldier and aircraft modellers ever since. Airfix was the market leader and chief innovator in these fields, so other manufacturers tended to follow its lead when it came to producing tanks and soldiers. Nowadays, Airfix tends to make its new AFV and small soldier figures to 1:72 scale, so as to be compatible with aircraft rather than trains.

The Trackside buildings were often based on actual houses or buildings; the signal box, for example, was based on the one at Oakham in Rutland. This building has recently received 'listed building'

The World War I Albatros fighter kit of 1957.
AIRFIX

status, but seems to owe its fame mainly to having been selected by Airfix! These 'Trackside' kits were a very cheap way of adding buildings to a rail layout, and were eagerly snapped up by the many railway modellers. Following the bankruptcy of Airfix in 1981, the entire range of trains and Trackside kits, with the exception of the RAF control tower, was sold to Dapol. They are still in production today, fifty years after they were first produced, a testament to the enduring popularity of model railways, particularly OO/HO scale.

1958

1958 was a sad year for Airfix, for on 17 March the founder of Airfix, Nicolas Kove, died. The rest of his family divested themselves of any interest in the company, and Ralph Ehrmann and John Grey were put fully in charge. Some twenty-five new tools were announced, including Airfix's first large kits:

1403	MiG-15	1:72
1405	North American	
	P-51D Mustang	1:72
1406	Westland Whirlwind Mk1	1:72
1407	Saunders-Roe SR 53	1:72
1408	Focke-Wulf Fw 190D	1:72
1409	Douglas A4D-1 Skyhawk	1:72
1416	Auster Antarctic	1:72
1421	Grumman Gosling	1:72
1413	Bristol Beaufighter TFX	1:72
1415	Lockheed P-38J Lightning	1:72
1417	Fairey Swordfish II	1:72
1418	Avro Lancaster BI	1:72
1419	Vickers Wellington BIII	1:72
1411	The *Revenge*	N/A
4007	Station Platform	OO/HO
4008	Shop and Flat	OO/HO
4009	Booking Hall	OO/HO
4010	Thatched Cottage	OO/HO
4012	Platform Fittings	OO/HO
4013	Station Accessories	OO/HO
4018	Kiosk and Platform Steps	OO/HO
4014	Footbridge	OO/HO
4015	Village Church	OO/HO
4019	Windmill	OO/HO
03265	Platform Figures	OO/HO

For its first large kits it chose the two most famous RAF aircraft of World War II, and effectively jumped straight from Series 2 to Series 5. The Lancaster was the first large aircraft released by Airfix, and required larger moulding machines than those previously in use in the 1950s for the Series 1 and 2 kits. It was released as the first kit in Series 5, at 7s 6d (37.5p). It featured rotating turrets with guns that could be made to elevate. The level of detail was high, and there was a crew seated inside the cockpit, which had a floor, seats and control panel. It bore the marking 'G for George' throughout its life.

In 1980, a new Lancaster kit was released in Series 8, replacing the original 1958 kit. The new kit would later be modified to represent 'Dambuster' and 'Grand Slam' variants. In April 2013, in time for the seventieth anniversary of the Dambuster raids, the first of several new Lancaster kits was released.

The Wellington was released early in 1959 as the first kit in Series 4, at 6s (30p). Like the Lancaster, it had crew members and a limited amount of cockpit detail – although at the time, the level of detail was considered to be very good; it also had revolving propellers and wheels, as well as movable control surfaces. Unlike the Lancaster, it was not replaced or upgraded,

and was finally deleted in 2001 after over forty years of continuous production. Given the current Hornby policy to re-tool popular old kits, we may well see a new Wellington in the near future.

Movable control surfaces and spinning propellers were fine and appealed to younger modellers, but to the older modeller they could lead to large gaps where they did not exist on the real thing. Also the use of too much glue by young modellers often put paid to spinning props!

The polystyrene cement that was sold initially in small soft metal tubes was, in fact, a solvent which 'welded' the parts together. It was very easy to apply too much, and if it got on to the outside surface it could easily obliterate any detail – and clear cockpit canopies could be quickly clouded over. Later, liquid 'poly' cement was sold, which was applied with a brush, and this did help to control the youngster's urge to squeeze too hard. I learned the hard way when I applied too much glue to an Aurora musketeer's ankles to glue them to his boots, only to find in the morning that he had gently fallen forward till he was resting on his sword tip!

The MiG, Mustang, Skyhawk and Swordfish were all re-tooled by Hornby recently. The Mustang was first replaced in 1974 by a Series 2 kit, which relied heavily on work done for the 1:24 Mustang kit. The Whirlwind fighter and Fw 190D were replaced with new tools in 1978. A P-38E/F kit was moulded in 1972 to supplement the original P-38J kit.

It is interesting to compare these 1970s re-moulds with the 1950s originals, as the level of detail and accuracy is considerably greater. However, when one compares the new Mustang, released in 2012, and the 1974 kit there is another quantum leap in quality and accuracy.

The SR 53 has not, to my knowledge, been released in over thirty years and is a basic, though highly sought-after, model of an important research aircraft. It is one of several kits that Airfix moulded of research and prototype aircraft, many of which did not go into production. Airfix liked to get in first when a new aircraft was announced, though this often meant that the kit was a reproduction of the prototype, and it was many years before the production version was actually modelled. The SR 53 never evolved into a production aircraft, so it remains the only 'mainstream' kit of this important research aircraft.

1958's North American P-51D Mustang kit.

The Antarctic was based on the float-plane version used in the Antarctic, and in 1979 it was reissued as an army AOP.6 variant. It was released as the Antarctic along with the Gosling in recent years.

The *Revenge* was the last of the original small sailing ships made by Airfix. By 1958 several kit manufacturers were modelling larger-scale sailing ships, and it was inevitable that Airfix would cease making new small ships, but we would have to wait until 1962 to see the first Airfix large-scale sailing ship. The small ships sailed on until the late 1970s, when they started to be released as 'SNAPnglue' kits. The more popular ones have been released on and off over the last thirty years, and even today two are still in the 2014 catalogue, and were joined by a new tool kit of the *Mary Rose* at 1:400 scale!

The Trackside range was considerably enlarged to include the first models in Series 2. Several were based on actual buildings: like the earlier signal box, the village church can be found on the Isle of Wight. Their continuing low price and easy availability ensured their ongoing popularity amongst model rail enthusiasts.

According to the computerized Mould Register produced by Airfix, a set of platform figures was moulded in 1958, although no one has actually seen a set. The number 03265 was allocated to them in the late 1970s in the Mould Register,

but there is no record of an earlier pattern number (possibly 1411).

The following year would see the first major change in packaging for the growing Airfix range, which would bring uniformity and a more striking artwork to the kits.

1959

In 1959 twenty-nine new kits were announced and three new series. Airfix was clearly in its stride now, and devoting much of its efforts towards the highly successful kit range. The development of new toys and games would continue, but the kit division was clearly the most important and profitable, and was rapidly becoming the brand leader. Its annual addition of two dozen or more new kits meant that Airfix was rapidly pulling ahead of its rivals, and keen modellers would look forward to the near-monthly release of new models in the UK. I well remember that in the mid-1960s, if I went into Woolworth's towards the end of the month, I would invariably find two or more new kits lying on the counter tops awaiting the expenditure of my pocket money. Kits such as the Sunderland and Superfreighter might have to wait until Christmas or my birthday, but the two- and three-'bob' kits were there for instant purchase. The new releases were as follows:

1423/105	Hawker Seahawk	1:72
106	Fiat G.91	1:72
107	Hawker Typhoon	1:72
108	Mitsubishi Zero	1:72
109	Jet Provost T.3	1:72
1422	Messerschmitt Bf 110D	1:72
381	De Havilland Heron	1:72
382	Bristol Belvedere	1:72
482	Fairey Rotodyne	1:72
1420	Bristol Superfreighter	1:72
681	Short Sunderland	1:72
4020	Trackside Presentation Set	OO/HO
4021	Trackside Accessories	OO/HO
4022	Level Crossing	OO/HO
4023	Signal Gantry	OO/HO
17	Fencing and Gates	OO/HO
18	Telegraph Poles	OO/HO
19	Platform Canopy	OO/HO
4017	Control Tower	OO/HO
205	Travelling Crane	OO/HO
207	Girder Bridge	OO/HO
1410	1923 Morris Cowley	1:32
M1F	Coldstream Guardsman	1:12
M2F	Lifeguard Trumpeter	1:12
M3F	Yeoman of the Guard	1:12
M4F	Napoleon	1:12
F2S	HMS *Cossack*	1:600
F401S	HMS *Victorious*	1:600
S1	Guards Band	1:76
S2	Guards Colour Party	1:76

The year 1959 also saw the introduction of what is now known as Type 2 packaging to the range, believed to have been

Showing signs of their age, three early aircraft kits from 1959. Left to right: Zero, Hurricane and Bf 109.

designed by Charles Oates, and most kits were released in this new style, most noticeable by the vertical stripe separating text from painting. Also the old logo on a scroll with the legend 'Products in Plastics' appended was simplified into a stylized scroll with simply 'AIRFIX' on it. One or two kits were issued in the old packaging style, but most came in Type 2. The old styling was distinctly uncoordinated, and the illustrations were not very eye-catching.

The main illustrator at Airfix until 1964 was Charles Oates, and he was responsible for most of the early kit boxes. Very little, if any, of the pre-1963 artwork survives, so it is not easy to attribute him to any particular box tops or headers. The Type 2 paintings he is believed to have executed were much better than the early ones and now had several colours in them, but were not full paintings as such. We would have to wait for Type 3 in 1963 for that.

To coincide with Type 2, the old pattern numbers were replaced by new series-specific numbers. The change can best be seen in the Trackside kits, where half the new releases used the new numbering system. The three new ranges had specific numbers to start with. For example, the aircraft kits all started at 81, preceded by the series number, thus 381 Heron. The Series 1 kits started at 81 for the Spitfire, leading up to the Gosling at 104, though these numbers were not really applied until 1964 when these kits went into Type 3 packaging. The Seahawk was first released in Type 1 packaging as 1423, but almost immediately went into Type 2 as 105, and only appeared in leaflets as 105.

Again, aircraft kits took the lion's share of new moulds, and two further large aircraft were added, the Superfreighter and Sunderland: this was the first Series 6 kit. Both featured various movable parts, a feature of early Airfix kits; they were not necessarily accurate, but increased the 'play value' for younger modellers. On the Superfreighter the 'clamshell' nose doors could be opened to permit the loading of toy cars. On the Sunderland, if the side panels under the wings were taken out, then it was possible to slide out the bombs on the racks inside, ready for dropping. Again, it was important to keep glue away from the moving parts!

The Sunderland is remembered as being one of the few kits that was found to be almost perfect following the first test shot! Usually various modifications

Autumn 1959 leaflet with the new Wellington.

have to be made to a mould to prepare it for mass production. It is still in the catalogue in 2014, albeit with new 'digital' artwork.

The Typhoon, Zero and Bf 110 have all been the subject of new tools from Hornby in the last couple of years. These three old kits were reasonably accurate for their time, and would remain in the catalogue for about fifty years. The new models have a level of detail that was unheard of in the 1950s and 1960s.

The other aircraft have all appeared in the catalogue in the last few years. The Jet Provost has not been seen for many years, having been superseded by a T.5/Strikemaster kit in the 1970s.

The Belvedere and Rotodyne were based on prototype/pre-production aircraft. The former went into service with the RAF and was a forerunner of other twin-boom helicopters such as the Vertol 107 and Chinook. The Rotodyne was a large autogyro that it was hoped would revolutionize city-centre travel, but unfortunately it was cancelled after the Airfix kit was produced. Having been dropped from the range in the late 1970s, the Superfreighter and Rotodyne both made a brief but welcome return under the Humbrol ownership.

The control tower was a bit of an oddity in the Trackside range, but when Airfield kits were added to the AFV ranges,

it migrated to join them. It remains the only Trackside kit not sold to Dapol and is still in the latest catalogue. It was updated slightly in the 1970s to include figures and some internal detail.

By this time vintage cars were being released at roughly one a year. The 1923 Morris Cowley was a four-seater variant that was replaced in 1966 by a two-seater kit. The 1:12 figure kits were launched with three London 'ceremonial figures', which were re-released in 2012 in one set called 'London Icons' in time for the 2012 Olympics. Napoleon was the first 'historical' figure but did not join the range until 1960. He was last released in the late 1970s but, like most of the historical figures, has not been seen since.

The first two sets of OO/HO (1:76) figures were also of London ceremonial figures, though oddly they did not feature in Airfix's Olympic line-up. They represented a brand new range of small 'fighting' figures, and when they were released they were snapped up by wargamers and small boys everywhere. Most toy soldiers at the time were manufactured by the likes of Britains, Herald and Timpo and to 1:32 scale, and were sold separately or in boxes of four or so. Now, the soldier enthusiast could buy boxes of up to forty-eight soldiers for only 2s! The fact that they were moulded to the same size as the standard railway sets, and that Airfix was also introducing a new range of army vehicles, was very important, because together they opened up a whole new market, and although other companies might well now produce more figures and tanks than Airfix, it was Airfix that created the market. Since 2007, Airfix has again been producing new models of tanks and support vehicles to add to its old range, and has moulded a new set of British infantry.

Airfix chose 1:600 scale, or 1in to 50ft, for its new range of warships and later liners. The World War II destroyer *Cossack*, famous for capturing the *Altmark*, the supply ship for the *Graf Spee*, in a Norwegian fjord, was selected to launch the range, with the recently modernized World War II aircraft carrier *Victorious* being the first large ship kit. The latter did not arrive until mid-1960, when she could be seen playing herself in the movie *Sink the Bismarck*. Over the next twenty years Airfix would add many famous ships to its range, culminating in 1981 with models of HMS *Repulse* and HMS *King George V*. Apart from the *Queen Mary 2*, there have been no new 1:600 kits from Airfix, but instead they have been introducing 1:350 modern warships in recent years.

The range of Trackside kits was added to, but the emphasis from 1960 onwards was to be on rolling stock and locomotive kits. Whilst not overly exciting, these Trackside kits are still very popular with railway modellers today. Airfix revisited the idea of the gift set with the release of the Trackside Presentation Set, which included five Trackside kits with brushes and paint.

During the late 1950s and early 1960s, one or two other sets of kits were released, but there is very little information about them.

1960

1960 was the year that the best-selling modelling magazine, *Airfix Magazine*, was launched, and a 'checklist' of the Airfix range in the August issue of *Airfix Magazine* reveals that the range of kits had reached 103! That year would see twenty-three new announcements:

1316	Supermarine Spitfire IX	1:72
110	Messerschmitt Me 262A	1:72
111	Boulton-Paul Defiant NF.1	1:72
287	SRN-1 Hovercraft	1:72
288	Hawker Hunter F.6	1:72
383	Dornier Do 217E-2	1:72
384	Blackburn NA.39 Buccaneer	1:72
483	Douglas DC-3 Dakota	1:72
583	Fokker F27 Friendship	1:72
F301S	HMS *Tiger*	1:600
F402S	HMS *Hood*	1:600
M5F	Joan of Arc	1:12
M201F	Henry VIII	1:12
M202F	Black Prince	1:12
206	Water Tower	OO/HO
208	Engine Shed	OO/HO
R1	Tank Wagon	OO/HO
R2	Cement Wagon	OO/HO
R201S	Railbus	OO/HO
A1V	Bristol Bloodhound	1:76
S3	Infantry Combat Group	1:76
S4	World War II German Infantry	1:76
S5	Civilians	1:76
S6	Farm Stock	1:76

The Spitfire IX was Airfix's chief designer John Edward's replacement for the original Spitfire kit of 1955. It used the same pattern number and would later become catalogue number 81. It was a very attractive-looking model and overall reasonably accurate, although in the early sixties it received the attentions of Airfix's 'riveter', which did somewhat spoil the smooth surface of the original. It was finally replaced by a new Mk IX in 2010, after several million kits had been produced. The Spitfire has always been a good money-earner for Airfix, and currently Airfix is producing new Spitfire kits at a rate not previously seen.

The SRN-1 was not really an 'aircraft' and was the prototype for all future hovercraft. It was sold until the late 1970s. A few years later Airfix would model the large cross-Channel SRN-4 hovercraft. The NA39 was also a proto-

HMS Hood *kit from 1960.*

Two advertisements from 1960, one of them showing the famous railway signal box kit and the other the Spitfire of famed World War II ace 'Johnnie' Johnson.

type, in this case of the future Buccaneer bomber. It remained in the range, but the original mould was largely altered in 1988 by Humbrol to make the S.2B version. In 2010, Hornby added extra parts to enable all versions to be modelled. So whilst 90 per cent or so of the kit is made up of 'new' mouldings, a few parts from the original 1960 release can still be seen.

The Me 262 and Defiant have both finally been withdrawn by Hornby, and I suspect we shall see new tools in the next few years. Lovely kit that it was, with its revolving turret and movable guns, the Defiant has been heavily criticized over the years for an inaccurate nose shape. Despite that, it continued to sell well, and is still the only mainstream Defiant easy to find.

The remaining aircraft have either been modified or had additional parts moulded to make different versions. The Dornier, which received the first Roy Cross illustration, had parts added in 1978 to make an optional night fighter variant, and in 2001 was sold as a 'Mistel' combination carrying an Me 328 rocket on its fuselage.

The Dakota was sold as a civil airliner with 'Silver City Airways' markings or as a C-47 transport. The latter option included a paratroop figure standing in the open doorway. It was criticized for having insufficient dihedral on the outer wings, but still sold well. In 1973, the mould was altered to make a Vietnam-era AC-47 gunship. It has not appeared for over twenty years, and the recent Dakota was a 'polybagged' Italeri kit. In 2014, a new tool C-47/DC-3 kit was released.

HMS *Tiger* was one of three 'new' cruisers entering service with the Royal Navy and was re-released in 2003. The 'mighty' and ultimately 'unlucky' *Hood* was the second large warship to be modelled, and was still in the Airfix range in 2013.

Three new 1:12 scale figures were released, but two would leave the catalogue in the late 1970s and only Henry VIII would later return, accompanied by one of his wives, Anne Boleyn.

The output of new Trackside kits had slowed, but we saw the first of the new rolling stock kits announced. The main competitor for rolling stock kits at the time was 'Kitmaster', and in 1962 Airfix bought the Kitmaster brand and its tools

both to add to its own range and also to eliminate a competitor.

Four more sets of OO/HO figures were released, including sets of civilians and farm stock to populate the railway models. The other two were the first of the military figures, which largely predominate in this range. The Infantry Combat Group was unusual in that it seemed to represent the 1950s British Army, and was therefore an unlikely opponent to the Germans. We would have to wait until 1973 for a true set of World War II British infantry to be moulded. This later mould appears to have been lost, so in 2011 Hornby moulded a new set to replace them.

With the introduction of military figures to the range, Airfix also announced the release of the first in a new range of OO/HO armoured fighting vehicles. The Bristol Bloodhound set included a Land Rover, RAF personnel and a dog! Maybe this was why the Infantry Combat Group was based on soldiers from a similar period?

Those wargaming modellers who had been seeking inexpensive figures and vehicles to use now found a whole new range to satisfy them. Other companies may later have produced more tanks and soldiers than Airfix, but it was Airfix who first exploited this segment of the market, and in 2014 the tanks and soldiers still form an important part of the Airfix range. New AFVs are again being moulded by Hornby.

1961

In the early 1960s, Airfix adverts used the slogan 'Just Like the Real Thing' and showed an Airfix kit in front of a photo of the 'real thing'. The range was increased by twenty-six new kits:

584	HP Halifax BIII	1:72
SK400	Sud-Aviation SE.210	
	Caravelle	1:144
SK500	De Havilland Comet 4B	1:144
F3S	HMS *Daring*	1:600
F4S	HMS *Campbeltown*	1:600
F403S	HMS *Nelson*	1:600
F501S	SS *Canberra*	1:600
A2V	Panther Tank	1:76
A3V	Sherman Tank	1:76
A4V	Churchill Tank	1:76
M1C	Sunbeam Rapier	1:32
M2C	Austin-Healey Sprite Mk 1	1:32
M3C	Renault Dauphine	1:32
M6F	Oliver Cromwell	1:12
M7F	Charles I	1:12
R3	Mineral Wagon	OO/HO
R4	Brake Van	OO/HO
R5	Cattle Wagon	OO/HO
R6	Rail Couplings	OO/HO
R7	Diesel Shunter	OO/HO
R202	Diesel Crane	OO/HO
302	Turntable	OO/HO
S7	Cowboys	1:76
S8	Indians	1:76
S9	8th Army	1:76
S10	Foreign Legion	1:76

Only one 1:72 aircraft was announced, and that was the excellent Halifax kit that has appeared regularly in the catalogue and returned again in 2014. The first two civil airliners to the new scale of 1:144 were released. At half the size of 1:72 kits, this was a gamble for Airfix as it meant moving away from 1:72 scale, but it seems to have paid off. The reasoning was that at 1:72 scale, large modern airliners would be far too big for most modellers to display easily, and when one sees the Nimrod kit that was released in 2008 and is basically a modified Comet, one can understand this viewpoint.

Three more current and World War II warships were added, along with the new

liner the *Canberra*. The two destroyers were recently released in sets with other ships rather than singly.

The first three tanks were moulded, and along with the small figure sets, were to become enormously popular and opened up a huge new market to Airfix. Nowadays they are criticized on the grounds of accuracy and detail, but at the time, modellers, and in particular wargamers, couldn't get enough of them. As well as producing new and very detailed AFV kits, Hornby continues to market these old kits successfully.

The production of new vintage cars had slowed a lot, but Airfix introduced a new range of 'modern' cars, starting with the Sunbeam Rapier, 'Frogeye' Sprite and Renault Dauphine. Unfortunately 'new' cars go out of fashion quite quickly, but some of them have made a comeback in recent years as they are now considered to be 'classic' cars.

The two main characters of the English Civil War were added to the 1:12 figure range, but neither has been seen since the late 1970s.

The Turntable was the only Trackside addition, but the range of Airfix locomotives and rolling stock was increased, to the delight of model railway enthusiasts, who could now add stationary models to their layouts for a fraction of the cost of Hornby or Tri-ang rolling stock. The only competition was from Kitmaster, and their kits would soon join the Airfix fold.

Four more sets of OO/HO figures were produced, and the emphasis was now clearly on militaristic subjects. The Cowboys and Indians were the first in a small range of Wild West figures, to which were later added a Wagon Train and US Cavalry sets. In 1970 the Cowboys was re-released with additional figures as the 'High Chaparral', to cash in on the successful television series.

The Foreign Legion and 8th Army were both released without foes to fight, but the Afrika Korps arrived the following year. The 8th Army set included two figures firing separately moulded Vickers machine guns, which served to show the level of detail incorporated in these sets. In the early 1970s, these three sets were re-tooled with better quality mouldings.

1962

Airfix diversified somewhat when it launched its new Airfix motor-racing sets, a rival to Scalextric. Some of the modern

car kits would later be offered as 'motorization kits' to run on the new racing track. These kits included the standard car kit plus a new 'chassis', which included the motor, axles and wheels, pick-up braids for the motor and a single-piece window transparency. The standard kit body then fitted over the completed chassis. Later racing-car kits were designed from the outset to better fit this modification. Airfix also purchased Model Road Racing Cars (MRRC), which company largely produced the racing sets for Airfix. A range of kits of racing buildings, such as pits and grandstands, was also moulded.

Twenty new kits were announced that year, and included the following:

112	North American Harvard II	1:72
289	Avro Anson I	1:72
484	Heinkel He 111H-20	1:72
585	Boeing B-17G Flying Fortress	1:72
SK501	Vickers Vanguard	1:144
F404S	*Bismarck*	1:600
F601S	RMS *Queen Elizabeth*	1:600
701	*Endeavour* 'Bark'	1:120
78	1904 Mercedes	1:32
471	1910 'B'-type Bus	1:32
M4C	Austin Mini-Minor	1:32
R8	Meat Van	OO/HO
R203	Refrigerator Van	HO/1:87
20	Scammell Scarab	OO/HO
M203F	Richard I	1:12
S11	Afrika Korps	1:76
S12	ACW Union Infantry	1:76
S13	ACW Confederate	
	Infantry	1:76
S14	ACW Artillery	1:76
S15	Wagon train	1:76

The first edition Airfix kit catalogue was released and sold for 9d (about 3.5p), and the Airfix catalogue would become a regular annual event for most of the next fifty years. Previously Airfix had issued a regular series of kit leaflets, which listed the entire range but included the latest releases. They were issued three or four times a year. Some were also released with the legend 'See the Airfix Range at your local F. W. Woolworth Store' on the front, and were given away in Woolworth's stores. They were generally identical to the others. The leaflets continued to be produced until 1980, and showed the current prices, which were not shown in the catalogues.

The four 1:72 aircraft included a Heinkel bomber, though oddly not a Battle of Britain variant; it is in the 2014 catalogue, but a new model is proposed

Two 1962 kits in the 'Skykings' series: the de Havilland Comet 4B and Vickers Vanguard, both in British European Airways livery.

An advertisement from April 1962.

into the Orion ASW aircraft; this arguably would have provided greater sales for Airfix in the years ahead. However, it is unlikely that any mainstream manufacturer will ever mould a Vanguard, so fans of this superb British turbo-prop liner will always have to turn to Airfix to satisfy their modelling needs.

The 1:600 ships would see another liner, the *Queen Elizabeth*, and also the famous German battleship *Bismarck* moulded. The *Bismarck* had a few extra parts moulded so that it could be released later as *Tirpitz*. *Bismarck*, unlike *Hood*, is currently in the 2014 catalogue.

The most interesting kit, however, was Airfix's first large-scale sailing ship, Captain Cook's *Endeavour*. As we have seen, Airfix started its kit range with small models of famous sailing ships, but in 1958 moulded its last, the *Revenge*. Other companies had been making large sailing ships, but it was a 'first' for Airfix. The kit featured 'furled' sails moulded to the yard arms, a tiny set of crew figures and a sheet of plastic 'ratlines' that had to be cut out and stuck on. Later the yard arms were re-moulded so that vacuum-formed sails could be cut out and stuck to them.

This was my first large sailing ship and I still like it the most. It may be somewhat dusty today and one or two bits are falling off, but as a twelve-year-old I was immensely proud of my efforts, particularly with the rigging. The slightly larger scale used compared to later ships meant that the figures and guns were better moulded. The final model in the range was HMS *Bounty* in 1980. A planned model of the *Santa Maria* was cancelled shortly before Airfix went under in early 1981.

Another 1:32 vintage car was added, along with the first large model of a 1910 'B'-type bus. It was a lovely model moulded in red plastic, and had figures of passengers and a driver and conductor. It would later be sold as a 1914 'Ole Bill' bus complete with a set of British infantry and printed cardboard sheets to cover the windows. Throughout much of the 1970s it was sold as a 'two-in-one' kit, but since 1981 it has appeared only as the 'B'-type bus. It was released in 2014 as part of Airfix's Great War celebrations in both versions.

The iconic 'Mini' was moulded and would go on to serve in its motorized form in Airfix's racing sets. Following the 1981 bankruptcy, the Mini is the only car

for 2015. The B-17G was immensely popular, even more so after Roy Cross painted a stirring picture of it flying at high altitude, dropping bombs. It was finally retired in 1999, when we are told about four million had been moulded! It was replaced briefly by an ex-Academy kit. It was such an important aircraft for Airfix that I am sure we will see a new Airfix tool in the next few years.

The Anson was 'superdetailed' in the 1960s, and has appeared on and off in the

catalogue for the last fifty years. The Harvard was replaced in 2005 by the superior Heller 'Texan' kit but that has now been withdrawn. That mould is believed to have been sold to the Mexican firm Lodela.

The Vickers Vanguard was a good replica of this large turboprop airliner, which unfortunately would only be sold to two airlines, BEA and Trans-Canada Airlines. The rival Lockheed Electra went on to much greater sales and was developed kit not to have been sold to General Mills, but instead stayed with MRRC, which is now based in Jersey.

A fine model of Richard I, complete with detachable helmet and axe, joined the 1:12 historical figures. The Black Prince from the previous year had featured a removable helmet and lance.

The three railway kits included the last Trackside kit, a fine model of a Scammell Scarab lorry which was only available for two or three years. It was intended to be re-released in 1981 along with all the railway kits, but the demise of Airfix prevented that from happening. The Refrigerator Van was produced to the European HO scale of 1:87 and was not, certainly in the UK, a good seller! The Meat Van, like most of the railway kits, stayed in production until the bankruptcy in early 1981. In 1962 Airfix also bought Kitmaster, and in the following year began the integration of the Kitmaster range into its own.

Five more figure sets were moulded. The Afrika Korps, complete with a Rommel-like figure, joined the range to fight the new 8th Army set. Both sets would later be replaced by new figure sets moulded to a higher standard.

The three American Civil War sets were to be Airfix's only ones made for that war. The Artillery set was designed so the figures could be painted blue or grey to represent either side in the Civil War. The nicely moulded cannons and their limbers showed what could be achieved in this scale. The set included a mounted officer, a limber with four horses and riders, two cannons and two firing crews, so the modeller could quickly field a battery of guns, with several more being brought up at very little cost. Airfix, of course, would sell several sets!

The Wagon Train set had a good reproduction of a 'prairie schooner', complete with walking, riding and camping figures and various fireside accoutrements. Again, by purchasing several sets, one could arrange them into a wagon train or a circular camp site, as was done every week on the popular television show *Wagon Train*.

1963

1963 was an important year for me. Like the vast majority of boys, I was obsessed by various 'interests'. For most boys it was subjects such as football or cars, and still is today. As a thirteen-year-old, mine were British civil aircraft, the Zulu wars

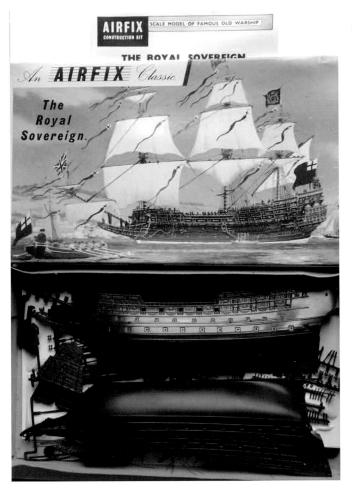

1963's Royal Sovereign *kit.*

and, of course, Airfix. In the summer of 1963 I decided to buy *Airfix Magazine*, *Flight* and various other aircraft magazines on a regular basis. I also started to keep detailed records and lists of my three main interests. Over the years since the early 1960s I accumulated a large collection of kits and associated paraphernalia (I never threw anything away), which has helped me enormously when it comes to writing articles in *Constant Scale* and for this book.

The second edition of the Airfix catalogue was released, and was the first catalogue I bought. I wish now I had bought a dozen because of the prices they fetch on eBay, but 9d in 1963 was a lot of money to a schoolboy, who could have bought two Mars Bars for that sum. Like the first edition it retailed at 9d and was very similar in layout to that issue. New releases were usually shown by a photograph of the real thing.

Twenty-five new models were announced in 1963, including the first two ex-Kitmaster tools, the Aerial Arrow motorcycle and the Prairie Tank Loco, which also has the honour of being the first kit released in the new Type 3 packaging style introduced in August 1963.

The new models were as follows:

113	Hawker P.1127	1:72
114	Yak-9D	1:72
290	EE Lightning F.1a	1:72
291	Lockheed F-104G Starfighter	1:72
385	Douglas Boston III	1:72
386	Lockheed Hudson III	1:72
586	Consolidated B-24J Liberator	1:72
SK600	Boeing 707-420	1:144
F302S	HMS *Devonshire*	1:600
F405S	HMS *Warspite*	1:600
F602S	SS *France*	1:600
901	*Royal Sovereign*	N/A
M204F	Julius Caesar	1:12
A301N	Human Skeleton	1:6
M5C	Jaguar 'E' Type	1:32
M201C	Ford Zodiac	1:32
1635	Aerial Arrow	1:16
R204	Lowmac & JCB	OO/HO
R205	0-6-0 Saddle Tank Loco	OO/HO
R301	Prairie Tank Loco	OO/HO
A5V	25-Pdr Field Gun and Tractor	1:76
A6V	Stug III 75mm Assault Gun	1:76
A7V	Stalin 3 Tank	1:76
A201V	Scammell Tank Transporter	1:76
S16	US Marines	1:76

It was a good year for aircraft models, led by the impressive Liberator kit which was

Douglas Boston bomber kit from 1963.

still in the catalogue in 2014. The Boston and Hudson have only recently been dropped. The Lightning and Starfighter both showed the Western approach to interceptors. The Starfighter has not been around for some years. The Lightning was upgraded slightly to an F.3 version, but was replaced by a brand new F.2A version in 2013, with an F.6 following in 2014. The Yak-9D was recently issued in a starter set. The Hawker P.1127 was the forerunner of the Harrier jet and disappeared in the late 1970s; it was, however, released briefly in 2000. Airfix has produced more Harrier kits than any other manufacturer, and in 2013 replaced its old Harrier GR.1/3 kits with two new kits.

The Boeing 707 was the Rolls-Royce Conway-powered version and was released in BOAC markings; over the years it would have the latest BOAC and BA markings added. It had not been available for some time but was re-released in 2014.

Ship modellers were rewarded with models of the venerable battleship HMS *Warspite* and the Royal Navy's new guided missile destroyer, HMS *Devonshire*. *Warspite* left the catalogue in 2014, and *Devonshire* was later modified to have Exocet missiles added for various Falkland anniversary releases.

The SS *France* was a model of the world's latest super liner. In the late 1970s it was planned to re-release it as SS *Norway*, which name it took when it was sold, but it is doubtful if it was released. Shortly after, when Airfix was sold, the mould appears to have been lost and consequently unmade examples are highly sought after.

The *Royal Sovereign* was the second of Airfix's large sailing ships and the first in Series 9. It was an impressive kit: moulded in dark brown plastic, it came with the new vacuum-formed sails.

Julius Caesar joined the 1:12 figures, but has not been issued since the mid-1970s. The Skeleton was moulded to 1:6 scale and was 12in (30cm) high. He was released a few years ago with 'Day-Glo' paint added to make him 'glow in the dark'!

The Jaguar E-Type captured the beauty and grace of the original; it was released in Type 2 packaging. The Ford Zodiac was the first car in Series 2, and was released in a hybrid Type 2/3 packaging, in which it stayed throughout its short life. Both kits were later sold as 'motorized' car kits for use with Airfix Motor Racing. The Jaguar was in the 2014 catalogue as a starter set, with paints and brushes included.

The Aerial Arrow motorcycle was one of the last kits produced by Kitmaster before Airfix bought the company, and was one of the first to be released by Airfix. In 1966, it was released with a humorous figure on it and was called 'Ton-up Tony'. It was to be the first of a new range of 'wacky' kits, but it didn't sell well so no further conversions were made.

The railway locomotives and rolling stock were added to, and by this time

Catalogue shot of the Trackside range, showing the new Prairie Tank Loco of 1963.
AIRFIX

Airfix had completed its range of Trackside buildings. From 1964 onwards virtually all the train kits were ex-Kitmaster as Airfix sought to integrate them into its own range. Only a few Kitmaster tools were actually used by Airfix, and the rest went to Dapol later. The Saddle Tank loco was one of the last Airfix-designed rolling-stock kits; the mould was destroyed in a fire at Dapol's factory in the 1980s.

A good selection of World War II armoured fighting vehicles was moulded, all of which are still in the catalogue today. The Scammell Tank Transporter was the first AFV kit in Series 2, and was an adventurous example with its rotating wheels and other moving parts. Both the Transporter and the Field Gun Tractor were the subject of numerous articles in *Airfix Magazine*, as models to convert to other variants.

The US Marines was the only addition to the small figure sets, and came complete with inflatable dinghies and the soldiers paddling them. The Marines were re-tooled in the 1970s, and it is that tool which is in use today.

1964

1964 saw a record, so far, of thirty-one new models announced and some thirty actually released; these included:

115	F4U-1D Corsair	1:72
116	Folland Gnat T.1	1:72
117	Grumman Wildcat	1:72
118	Curtiss P-40E Kittyhawk	1:72

RIGHT: *1963 25-pounder field gun set.*
AIRFIX

BELOW: *Historical figures set from 1963.*
AIRFIX

LEFT: *BAC One-Eleven kit from 1964.*

BELOW: *First release of Dennis fire engine in Type 3B boxing – 1964.*

292	Dassault Mirage IIIC	1:72
293	IL-2M3 Sturmovik	1:72
387	Junkers Ju 88A-4	1:72
587	Consolidated PBY-5A Catalina	1:72
SK401	BAC One-Eleven	1:144
SK601	Vickers VC10	1:144
F5S	HMS *Hotspur*	1:600
F303S	HMS *Suffolk*	1:600
F406S	*Scharnhorst*	1:600
F407S	RMS *Mauretania*	1:600
801	*Revenge*	1:126?
M6C	Volkswagen 1200	1:32
M7C	M.G. 1100	1:32
572	1914, Dennis Fire Engine	1:32
R9	0-4-0 Saddle Tank Locomotive	OO/HO
R10	Prestwin Silo Wagon	OO/HO
R11	The 'Rocket' Locomotive	OO/HO
R401	*Evening Star* Locomotive	OO/HO
A8V	Tiger Tank	1:76
A9V	Bren Gun Carrier & 6-Pdr Gun	1:76
A10V	Centurion Tank	1:76
A11V	Sd Kfz 234 Armoured Car	1:76
S17	World War II Russian Infantry	OO/HO
S18	World War II Japanese Infantry	OO/HO
S19	Arabs (Bedouin)	OO/HO
S20	Robin Hood	OO/HO
S21	Sheriff of Nottingham	OO/HO

Three of the Series 1 aircraft kits were of World War II American aircraft. They were typical of Airfix kits of the time, being fairly accurate in outline but possessing somewhat overdone rivet details, which tended to produce problems in getting the decals to adhere properly. In 2011, Airfix released a new tool of the Curtiss Hawk in time for the seventieth anniversary of Pearl Harbor. The Wildcat and Corsair have recently been withdrawn, but a new Wildcat is due to be launched in 2015.

The Folland Gnat T.1 represented the RAF's new advanced trainer/attack aircraft, and came equipped with under-wing tanks and rockets. After a few years it was dropped from the range and replaced by a tool modification sold as a 'Red Arrows' Gnat. This was enormously popular, and despite the release of a 'Red Arrows' Hawk kit, it has remained in the catalogue ever since. In 2011, Airfix announced a new tool of the Gnat trainer, and in 2012 this replaced the venerable Gnat kit as the 'Red Arrows' Gnat in the catalogue.

The Mirage IIIC was in the range for many years, but has not been seen recently. The Sturmovik was Airfix's second and only other World War II Russian aircraft. There have been complaints about the shape of the kit, and also Airfix's spelling of 'Sturmovik', but it has been regularly issued over the years and was only withdrawn in 2013.

The Junkers Ju 88 was a much requested subject and today is one of the few old aircraft kits still in the range. It was well served by an excellent Roy Cross painting showing the aircraft dive-bombing a Royal Navy destroyer, and is a classic example of what sold an Airfix kit: guns blazing, bombs exploding and plenty of action. How could a schoolboy resist buying one: I couldn't! It was released at around the same time as the Frog Ju 88, and it is interesting to compare the two manufacturers' approach to aircraft kits: Frog kits tended to have smoother surfaces, whereas the Airfix ones were festooned with rivets.

The Christmas big kit for 1964 was the Catalina. It was an impressive kit with its retractable wing-tip floats and opening side blisters with pivoting machine guns. It was still in the catalogue in 2014.

Airliner enthusiasts were rewarded with models of the new VC10 and BAC One-Eleven. The One-Eleven was based on the prototypes, so requires a small amount of work to make a production version. The British United decals were later replaced with British Caledonian ones. It has not been issued for a few years. The VC10 mould was altered in the early 1980s to represent the tanker version used by the RAF; it was last issued a few years ago.

Warship modellers had three World War II ships to model; the *Suffolk* left the range in 2014, and the other two were recently in the catalogue. RMS *Mauretania* was added to the small liners' range and has appeared on and off over the years, making a return in the 2014 catalogue. The first *Revenge* was the last of the original small-scale sailing ships, and this kit was modelled at approximately 1:126. By this time Airfix was releasing one large sailing ship a year, and *Revenge* has not been issued for a few years.

Two modern cars were released, along with a very nice kit of a 1914 Dennis Fire Engine. Unlike modern cars the Fire Engine does not date, and consequently is regularly reissued. The detachable ladder could be made to extend by means of cotton thread, but I wonder how many modellers actually managed to make it work! It came with a crew of seated firemen, but none to actually fight the fire.

Airfix had finished producing new Trackside kits, but was still making rolling stock. However, the acquisition of Kitmaster meant that the bulk of new releases would come from its tool bank: the Evening Star and the Rocket were ex-Kitmaster, and they all currently reside with Dapol.

Wargamers and military enthusiasts were treated to four more World War II armoured fighting vehicles. With the exception of the Centurion Tank, all are in the current catalogue. The Tiger Tank has always been criticized for its shape, and at times, somewhat unfairly, voted as the 'worst Airfix kit'. However, it remains incredibly popular and has never been unavailable. To a fourteen-year-old it looked like a Tiger, and that's what counted.

The Bren Gun Carrier was small, but spawned a host of articles in *Airfix Magazine* about how to convert it into any of the many versions of the full-size vehicle that were produced. The German Armoured Car was criticized for having the wrong mudguards! It should have had single-piece ones on either side as the twin ones were used on the earlier Sd Kfz 232. This error has never been corrected.

The OO/HO (1:76) figure range was expanded to include medieval figures. Sets of Robin Hood and Sheriff of Nottingham figures were made, and included several men-at-arms and other period figures. Both sets were deleted by the 2014 catalogue. The Arabs, complete with camels and horses, were made to fight the earlier French Foreign Legion set.

The Russians and Japanese were very well moulded sets and are both in the current catalogue. In the 1970s, when Airfix was considering scaling down the figures in the 1:32 sets, a prone figure of a Japanese soldier firing a machine gun replaced one of the figures in this set. Whereas several of the early sets were re-tooled to include new figures and those used at 1:32 scale, the Japanese were not re-tooled, although this figure remains in the set.

Also in 1964 Airfix released several kits for its motor-racing sets; these included a Press Box, Racing Pit and Grandstand. They were technically not part of the kit range but are kits. The first of the motorization kits of the modern cars were also released.

1965

1965 was the tenth anniversary of the release of Airfix's first aircraft kit, the Spitfire BT-K. That aircraft had been replaced by the superior Mk IX kit in 1960, and in 1965 Airfix was to replace the equally poor Bf 109F/G of 1956 with a new tool Bf 109G-6 model. The new kit was much more accurate, and came with a choice of markings, rockets or cannons and a tropical filter. It would remain in the range until 2009, when it was replaced by a new tool Bf 109G-6. Thirty new kits were planned, over half of which were aircraft; they included:

1384	Messerschmitt Bf 109G-6	1:72
119	Bell P-39Q Airacobra	1:72
120	Roland CII	1:72
121	CA-13 Boomerang	1:72
294	Aichi D3A1 Val	1:72
295	Mitsubishi Dinah	1:72
296	Boeing-Vertol 107-11	1:72
388	McDonnell F-4B Phantom	1:72
485	NA B-25 Mitchell	1:72
588	Junkers Ju 52/3M	1:72
781	Boeing B-29 Superfortress	1:72
SK502	Handley Page HP42 Heracles	1:144

1965 models of the B-29 Superfortress bomber, and Me 163 Komet rocket-propelled interceptor from 1977.

SK503	Boeing 727-100	1:144
D260F	Camel v. Albatros	1:72
D261F	Bristol F2B v. Fokker Dr.1	1:72
D262F	Roland CII and R.E.8	1:72
F304S	HMS *Ajax*	1:600
902	HMS *Victory*	1:180
M8C	Ford Lotus Cortina	1:32
M9C	Vauxhall Viva	1:32
721	1965, Corvette Stingray	1:25
821	1928, Lincoln 'Gangbuster'	1:25
?	1965, Dodge 2+2	1:25
M212F	Boy Scout	1:12
R302	*City of Truro* Locomotive	OO/HO
A12V	DUKW	1:76
A202V	Buffalo and Jeep	1:76
A301V	LCM111 and Sherman Tank	1:76
S22	US Cavalry	OO/HO
S23	World War II British Paratroops	OO/HO

The other small aircraft were all slightly unusual choices. The P-39Q was a strange fighter, with its engine behind the cockpit! It has appeared in the catalogue fairly regularly, but was deleted from the 2013 one. The Roland was a lesser known World War I fighter, but was a step up in terms of detail for Airfix. It included two dedicated crew figures, complete with billowing scarves. It has appeared on and off over the years and was included in the 'Aircraft of the Aces' series in the 1990s.

The Boomerang was, not surprisingly, an Australian-designed aircraft which was brought to the attention of young aircraft modellers by virtue of appearing in the Airfix catalogue. It has been frequently reissued but is not currently in the range.

The Val and Dinah were Airfix's only two other Japanese aircraft. Both have appeared frequently in the Airfix catalogue and both were in the 2013 one, where they were joined by the new-tool Zero.

The Vertol 107 was an early twin-rotor helicopter and appeared in Swedish colours. Sweden has always been a very good market for Airfix kits, and this probably accounts for the large number of Airfix aircraft which have appeared, and which continue to appear, with Swedish decals. In 1979 it was modified slightly and released as a Boeing 'Sea Knight'; shortly after it was released as a SNAPnglue kit.

The Phantom was probably the most famous fighter of the 1960s and 1970s, and it went on to enter service with the Royal Navy and the RAF. Airfix chose to model the US Navy variant, but it only lasted for six years in this guise because in 1971, extra parts were moulded to enable several versions to be modelled. It moved up to Series 4 and received a fine Roy Cross painting showing an Israeli Phantom flying over the Suez Canal. It has not been issued recently.

The B-25 was a multi-version kit and three versions could be made: two with solid noses and one with the standard Perspex one. Decals were provided for three aircraft, and all three were shown flying over a huge fireball: very dramatic. It was a lovely model, but to my way of thinking was spoilt somewhat by the host of oversized rivets. Had Airfix employed the smooth finish which they did on the B-29, it would have been a better model. It is currently in the 2014 catalogue.

The Junkers Ju 52 was Germany's equivalent of the Dakota and came in wheeled and floatplane versions with decals for both. It involved a more complicated construction to make the fuselage, but did produce a very good replica. It is currently in the 2014 range.

The B-29 was Airfix's largest 1:72 aircraft to date. It was shown on the box flying over Japan and dropping bombs whilst being attacked by Japanese fighters, an impressive painting by Roy Cross which has rarely been bettered. Unlike the B-25, it had a very smooth surface finish with a few raised panel lines. It is not currently available.

The final two new aircraft were both in 1:144 scale. The HP42 Heracles was one of eight aircraft built for Imperial Airways in the 1930s, and they were regarded as the epitome of luxurious and safe travel. It would have been a very large kit in 1:72 scale, but it was later reported that the decision makers at Airfix wished they had made it to 1:72 scale. One hopes that Hornby may one day correct that decision! It has appeared over the years, and in 1985 it was included in a set with the Kamov Ka-25 and Arthur Ward's first Airfix book, *The Model World of Airfix*.

The Boeing 727 was Boeing's answer to the Trident airliner, and ultimately it would go on to outsell the Trident many times over. Airfix chose to model the initial Series 100 version, but Boeing soon replaced it with the larger Series 200 version. In the late 1970s Airfix considered re-tooling it into the 200, but it was not until 1983 that the longer fuselage replaced the short one in the mould. Consequently, early 100-series kits are now sought-after. It was re-released in 2014 with new decals and illustration.

The final three aircraft kits were not strictly new kits but were a new range. Airfix decided to put two Series 1 aircraft kits in a box with a new two-armed stand and sell them as Series 2. This was good

1965 advertisement.

Three 'dogfight doubles from 1965. AIRFIX

available. Currently it can be bought as a single kit or in a 'gift set' with paints and brushes.

Two modern cars were moulded, both of which were released as 'motorization kits' for use with Airfix Motor Racing sets. Both cars disappeared in the early 1980s, but the Viva returned briefly around 2006, when it was sold in a set of 'Classic Cars of the 1960s', which included the Herald and Escort. The Cortina was one of four cars selected to be converted into 'street cars' for the 1980s. These did not last long, and it is believed that the mould modifications make them difficult to release as standard cars at that time.

Airfix's relationship with MPC (Model Products Corporation) in the USA resulted in an initial three American car kits being sold in Airfix-labelled boxes; they were to 1:25 scale. However, the Dodge 2+2, despite being reviewed in *Airfix Magazine*, never appeared in a catalogue and I don't think has ever been seen.

The Boy Scout was the last of the early range of 1:12 figures. Despite coming with a choice of beret or hat, he proved to be very unpopular, and as far as we can tell, only one run of kits was produced. Consequently he has become, arguably, the most sought-after Airfix kit and fetches very high prices every time he ventures on to eBay! With the benefit of hindsight, I should have bought ten or so, for 30s, put them in a drawer and waited until eBay arrived; I would have made a fortune and my pension would have been assured!

value to younger modellers. They were called 'Dogfight Doubles' and all six aircraft were from World War I. Five of the aircraft were old kits from the 1950s, but they received the attentions of Airfix's moulders who added extra fabric and other details to the moulds. The sixth kit was of the newly released Roland CII.

The concept of the 'Dogfight Doubles' was extended the following year, and currently Airfix is releasing its new moulds in similar pairings.

Warship modellers received a neat model of HMS *Ajax*, famous for her part in the Battle of the River Plate. It would be a few years before the *Graf Spee* was added. Neither kit is currently available.

The big sailing ship for 1965 was a 1:180 replica of Nelson's *Victory*. It is a very impressive model and has always been

LCMIII and Sherman tank kit from 1965. AIRFIX

1965 British Paratroops Set.

The only railway kit was the ex-Kitmaster 'City of Truro' locomotive, which today is sold by Dapol.

Two landing craft were added to the AFV range: the Buffalo included a nice little Jeep model that was very useful, and I suspect has resulted in many wargamers having lots of unmade Buffalos lying around. The LCM III had a standard Sherman Tank kit included as well as some nice figures.

The US Cavalry completed the Wild West range of figures; the Paratroops are still in the range today, and the patterns were used for the 1:32 figures later.

1966

Thirty-two new kits were planned and released in 1966, which made an average of three new models every month! The new models were as follows:

122	Westland Scout	1:72
123	Northrop F-5A	1:72
124	Westland HAR.1 Helicopter	1:72
125	Republic P-47D Thunderbolt	1:72
297	Grumman TBM-3 Avenger	1:72
298	Fairey Firefly 5	1:72
299	Arado Ar 196 Floatplane	1:72
682	Short Stirling	1:72
D360F	Beaufighter and Bf 109G-6	1:72
D361F	Spitfire Mk IX and Bf 110D	1:72
SK504	HS Trident 1C	1:144
F408S	HMS *Ark Royal*	1:600
802	PS *Great Western*	N/A
79	1902 De Dietrich	1:32
80	1926 Morris Cowley	1:32
571	1914 'Ole Bill' Bus	1:32
M202C	Triumph TR4A	1:32
M203C	MGB	1:32
722	1929 Ford 'Woodie'	1:24
823	James Bond Aston Martin DB5	1:24
824	1932 Chrysler 'Gangbuster'	1:24
825	1927 Lincoln 'Roadster'	1:24
621	Beam Engine	N/A
A13V	M3 Half-Track	1:76
A14V	Matador and 5.5 Inch Gun	1:76
S24	Zoo Animals – Set 1	OO/HO
S25	Zoo Animals – Set 2	OO/HO
S26	World War I German Infantry	OO/HO
S27	World War I British Infantry	OO/HO
S28	World War I French Infantry	OO/HO
M401F	James Bond and Odd Job	1:12
331	'Ton-up Tony'	N/A

1966 was also the year when the unthinkable actually occurred: Airfix kit prices rose for the first time after thirteen years! On 1 August a 2s kit became 2s 3d, a rise of around 10 per cent. The most expensive kits, the sailing ships in Series 9, went from 17s 6d to 19s 6d, an increase of 2s, the cost of an old Series 1 kit. As a schoolboy, I had received my first lesson in 'inflation' – unfortunately not my last!

The 1:72 aircraft were a mixture of helicopters and World War II and modern aircraft. The Westland Scout was the new Army Air Corps new machine, and it has appeared regularly ever since. The Westland HAR.1 was a modified mould of the original S.55 helicopter of 1956, number 1355.

The Northrop F-5A 'Freedom Fighter' has been a popular model and was available recently in a 'starter set' with paint and glue. The Avenger and Firefly represented the US and UK's use of carrier-borne aircraft in World War II. They were not in the 2013 catalogue. The Arado Ar 196 was a German floatplane carried on board German warships such as *Bismarck*. It featured in the 2014 range.

The Short Stirling was the first of the RAF's trio of World War II heavy bombers; it was released in Series 6 and included parts to make a tractor and bomb trolleys to arm the aircraft. Unfortunately the parts were spread out in the mould and it has not been possible to extract them to make a separate mould. However, in mid-2013 Airfix released a new Bomber Re-Supply Set, which included a tractor and bomb trolleys, so modellers will no longer have to purchase a Stirling to get the bomb trolleys! The Stirling is still available.

Having completed its range of World War I 'Dogfight Doubles', Airfix embarked on a range of World War II and beyond pairings. These kits used one aircraft from Series 2 and one from Series 1, retailing in Series 3. Both were sold until recently, but the Bf 110 and Spitfire has been replaced by a set containing the new tools.

The Trident was based on the initial Series 1C aircraft bought by BEA. It was a very accurate model and captured the lines of the original; it was regularly updated with new BEA and BA decals over the years. It is currently withdrawn from the range.

HMS *Ark Royal* was the ill-fated World War II ship that was sunk by a U-Boat. It can be bought today in a gift set with paints, glue, paints and a display board with the history on.

The paddle steamer *Great Western* is the only large sailing ship to have a Roy Cross painting. In 2007 it was released as a gift set to celebrate the 200th anniversary of Brunel's birth.

The two vintage cars were both in Series 1, and the Morris Cowley replaced the earlier 1923 model. They are not currently available. The 1914 'Ole Bill' Bus was the earlier 'B'-Type Bus but with a set of soldier figures and cardboard planking added to make a model of the early buses that were used in World War

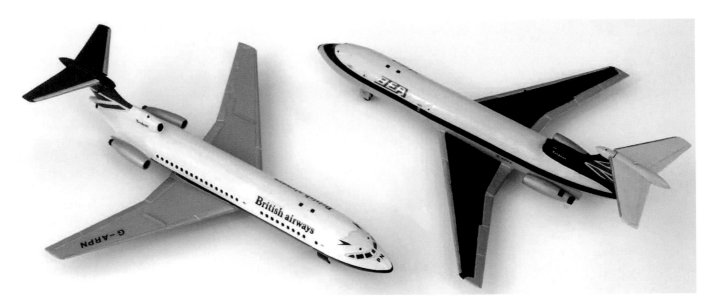

The 1966 Trident 1C kit, in British Airways and BEA livery.

I. It was later sold as an option in the 'B'-Type kit. It is returning for the anniversary in 2014 of World War I.

The two sports cars returned to the range in recent years, and the TR4A was in the 2014 catalogue. Sports cars have always lasted longer than saloon cars, which seem to go out of fashion more quickly and then have to wait thirty or forty years to become 'classics'! Both cars, along with the 'E'-type and Ford Escort, are currently being sold in boxes for Haynes, the motor manual company, in their 'Workshop' series.

The three American cars were MPC kits that were sold briefly in the late 1960s. The Aston Martin DB5 was one of several kits designed for a James Bond licence, which Airfix held. It was later believed to be converted into a DB6. Unstarted examples can fetch a very high price. James Bond and Odd Job was another licensed kit that was made available again a few years ago. 'Ton-up Tony' was the first of a short-lived range of 'weird' kits. It utilized the Arial Arrow motorcycle with a newly tooled figure riding it. It was not very successful and has only ever been seen in one packaging style. Consequently it is a sought-after kit.

The Beam Engine was the first in a small range of kits representing developments of commercial engines. All four 'engines' were in the 2013 catalogue, but the Beam Engine was dropped from the 2014 one. A fifth, a Mill Engine, was advertised on box sides but was never actually tooled.

Both of the 1:76 AFVs were popular conversion subjects in *Airfix Magazine* and are still available.

OO/HO figure collectors were rewarded with two sets of zoo animals that would also be sold in a 'Zoo Set' with zoo enclosures and so on.

The first three World War I sets appeared. They were modelled on early war uniforms, which made them incompatible with the later Americans. They are all still available, and some of the sets are included in a current 'Western Front' set. The World War I anniversary in 2014 has ensured their place in the catalogue, and they feature in several of the sets for that anniversary. In 1980 it was planned to release a 1:32 scale set of British infantry, but this was not proceeded with.

1967

A phenomenal forty-two new releases were listed for 1967; clearly Airfix was at the top of its game!

126	Fiat G50 Bis	1:72
127	Fieseler Fi 56 *Storch*	1:72
128	Avro 504K	1:72
129	Spad VII	1:72
131	De Havilland DH.4	1:72
251	Vought OS2U Kingfisher	1:72
252	Douglas SBD-3/5 Dauntless	1:72
254	MiG-21	1:72
486	Northrop P-61 Black Widow	1:72
487	SM SM79 Sparviero	1:72

The 1966 Beam Engine kit. AIRFIX

488	General Dynamics F-111A	1:72
589	Heinkel He 177A-5	1:72
D362F	Mosquito v. Me 262	1:72
SK602	Boeing 314 Clipper	1:144
SK700	BAC/Sud Concorde	1:144
350	James Bond Wallis WA-116	1:24
F201S	MV *Free Enterprise IV*	1:600
903	*Cutty Sark*	1:130
M204C	Triumph Herald	1:32
M205C	Ferrari 250LM	1:32
M206C	Aston Martin DB5	1:32
M207C	Porsche Carrera 6	1:32
826	Dodge Charger (Ex-MPC)	1:24
827	GTO Pontiac (Ex-MPC)	1:24
828	Ford Mustang FB (Ex-MPC)	1:24
829	Ford GT (Ex-MPC)	1:24
830	Mako Shark (Ex-MPC)	1:24
831	Monkeemobile (Ex-MPC)	1:24
622	1804 Steam Locomotive	N/A
531	Toilway Daddy (Ex-Hawk)	N/A
532	Freddie Flameout (Ex-Hawk)	N/A
A14V	World War I 'Male' Tank	1:76
A203V	88mm Gun and Tractor	1:76
S29	World War I US Infantry	1:76
S30	Romans	1:76
1663	Centurion Tank	1:76
1664	Field Gun and Tractor	1:76
1684	Fort Sahara Set	1:76
1685	Sherwood Castle Set	1:76
1686	Zoo Set	1:76
1700	D-Day Set	1:76
1701	Beachhead Set	1:76

This is an impressive list, although six kits were actually MPC kits and the two 'Weird-Ohs' were Hawk kits. The Hawk kits represented an inexpensive way of developing the new 'weird' range of kits, started by 'Ton-up Tony' the previous year. The range was not successful, and plans to add further kits were scrapped, but in

The 1967 Triumph Herald kit.

1976 two more American-designed kits were tried, but again were unsuccessful. Toilway Daddy has the distinction of being the only Airfix kit that Woolworths would not sell because it was considered to be too macabre! Once again, unsuccessful kits have become highly sought after by collectors and often command high prices.

The six MPC cars were all current 'sporty' cars, and the 'Monkeemobile' was launched following the successful television series, *The Monkees*. Airfix boxings of them are now highly sought after.

The twelve new 1:72 aircraft covered a wide spectrum of types. The three-engined SM79 and the Fiat G50 were the only World War II Italian aircraft produced by Airfix, and both have appeared, on and off, over the years. The *Storch* was the German equivalent of the Lysander. The three biplanes showed how Airfix had improved its design of early aircraft. For the fortieth anniversary of the Australian airline Qantas, the Avro 504K was briefly repackaged with Qantas colours and decals for a promotional gift for the airline. Surviving kits are very collectable! None of the above kits is in the 2013 range.

The Kingfisher and Dauntless were neat models of two US Navy aircraft and both were in the 2014 catalogue. The MiG-21 was a reasonable copy of the original famous Russian fighter, but has not been in the range for some time.

The Black Widow was a large American night fighter which has made regular appearances in the Airfix catalogue; however, it is not currently available. The F-111A was the new American swing-wing bomber, which had just been selected by the UK government to replace the

cancelled TSR2. Later it would be converted into the newer F-111E variant.

The Heinkel He 177A-5 was modelled on the large and not wholly successful German bomber, which could carry underwing anti-shipping missiles. It was to be the big aircraft kit for Christmas 1967. It enjoyed over forty years of sales without a rival, but a recent new tool from Revell has relegated it, for the time being, to the mould store.

The Mosquito and Me 262 pairing was the third in the larger Dogfight Double sets. They made regular appearances in the catalogue but have not been seen recently.

The two additions to the 1:144 'Skyking' range were a fine model of the Boeing 314 Clipper, which had decals for a pre-war Pan-Am Clipper and a wartime one, and a superb model of the original prototype Concorde. When a model of it was fitted into the BAC wind tunnel, it was found to produce the same flow patterns as the BAC models! It was replaced in 1976 by a new tool of the production Concorde.

The Wallis autogyro was produced with firing rockets to represent 'Little Nellie' from the James Bond film *You Only Live Twice*. It was re-released in 1997 for a short run.

The only 1:600 ship was an attractive little model of the cross-Channel car ferry, the *Free Enterprise IV*. It was sold in Series 2, and enabled modellers to make a model of a 'liner' relatively cheaply. However, it has not been available for over thirty years, largely because following the capsizing of *The Herald of Free Enterprise* in Zeebrugge harbour in 1987, it was not released because the similarity of the name (it was part of the same fleet) might be considered unfortunate. As a result surviving examples fetch high prices when they become available.

The *Cutty Sark* was a large kit of the famous tea clipper. Along with the original 'little' kit it is in the current range.

The Triumph Herald was a particularly fine model of the 1960s Triumph two-door car. Such a Triumph was my mother's first car, and I learnt to drive on it and used to drive it after I passed my test in September 1967. I bought a kit of it and painted it in my mother's car's colour scheme of light yellow. It is now sold as a starter set.

The three racing cars were designed to be sold as 'motorization' kits and 'ready-to-run' kits for Airfix Motor Racing. They were also sold as standard kits. The Aston Martin is still available as a starter set.

A selection from Airfix's 1967 modern car range.
AIRFIX

Castles, forts and associated figures from 1967. AIRFIX

The 1804 Steam Locomotive was modelled on Richard Trevithick's engine. It was the second in a small range of 'working' engine kits, and like the Beam Engine, came with a battery-powered motor. All four were in the 2013 catalogue, but the Steam Loco, like the Beam Engine, was deleted in 2014. Like the earlier Beam Engine, I am not sure many of them actually worked. They needed judicious use of the glue and liberal amounts of graphite, from pencils, to lubricate the plastic.

The remaining models were all to OO/HO, or 1:76 scale. The American Infantry completed the quartet of World War I infantry sets. Unfortunately, the other three sets were of early war figures so the uniforms were incompatible with the Americans. The five World War I sets

are in the catalogue today, along with the two tanks and a large playset. The tank was based on a 'Male' tank from 1916, and in 2010 extra parts was moulded to make a 'Female' tank.

World War II modellers received a fine model of an 88mm gun and an Sd Kfz7 tractor, still in the range today. The gun could be traversed, raised and lowered and the gun trails moved, and the whole thing could be put on to wheels to tow it. Pretty impressive!

The Romans included a chariot, though they would have to wait until 1969 for the Ancient Britons to be released. The Romans were withdrawn in 2012.

The range of tanks and buildings to support the OO/HO figures was expanded to include assembled polythene

models ('polyprop') of a Centurion tank and field gun and tractor. These models disappeared following the bankruptcy of 1981, but may one day return.

Three clip-together buildings were produced, which were initially sold in sets which included two sets of opposing OO/HO figures. The Sherwood and Sahara buildings would shortly after be available separately. A Wild West Fort Set was probably introduced a year earlier, and the three sets, including figures, were re-released in 1993. The Zoo Set was composed of various zoo enclosures and both sets of Zoo Animals. The buildings for the Zoo Set were not available separately.

The final releases, which included the 'polyprop' assembled vehicles, were the D-Day Set, Beachhead Invasion Set and

The 1967 Zoo Set. AIRFIX

an Attack Force Set. These early sets did not last as long as the 'building' sets and were the forerunners of the later, more successful sets.

1968

Thirty-six new models were announced, not as many as the previous year, but they were all Airfix-owned moulds. It is difficult to say accurately when some models were actually announced. Most were revealed in the annual catalogue, but because of the large number of new models in the late 1960s and early 1970s, some appeared in the leaflets given away late in the previous year, on the side of kit boxes or sometimes in modelling magazines. Occasionally, kits would appear when there had not been an announcement. The models expected in 1968 were as follows:

130	Hannover CLIII	1:72
132	Hawker Demon	1:72
253	Grumman F6F Hellcat	1:72
255	Beagle B.206 Bassett	1:72
256	Angel Interceptor	1:72
257	Bristol Blenheim IV	1:72
258	Petlyakov Pe-2	1:72
259	Fairey Battle	1:72
260	Douglas A-J1 Skyraider	1:72
261	Curtiss SB2-C Helldiver	1:72
262	Henschel Hs 129B	1:72

263	Grumman J2F-6 Duck	1:72
389	HS Dominie T.1	1:72
489	Ford 5-AT Trimotor	1:72
490	Ilyushin Il-28 Beagle	1:72
491	Handley Page Hampden	1:72
590	Handley Page 0/400	1:72
D363F	Mirage v. MiG-15	1:72
D364F	Sturmovik v. Fw 190D	1:72
F305S	HMS *Fearless*	1:600
F409S	*Tirpitz*	1:600
F603S	RMS *Queen Elizabeth 2*	1:600
60	1912 Ford Model 'T'	1:32
M205C	Ferrari 250LM	1:32
M208C	Mercedes 280SL	1:32
M301C	Jaguar 420G	1:32
M210C	Honda CB450	1:16
732	James Bond Toyota	1:24
R402	'Harrow' Locomotive	OO/HO
R501	'Biggin Hill' Locomotive	OO/HO
A16V	T-34 Tank	1:76
A204V	RAF Emergency Set	1:76
S31	1914 Royal Horse Artillery	1:76
S32	World War II Commandos	1:76
S33	Tarzan Set	1:76
1712	British Paratroops	1:32

Aircraft enthusiasts were treated to seventeen new kits and two more Dogfight Doubles, over half the new releases!

World War 1 was covered by an excellent replica of a not-so-well-known German fighter, the Hannover CLIII, and in Series 5 by a beautiful replica of the Handley Page 0/400 bomber, or 'Bloody Paralyser' as it was often called. It required the rectangular fuselage to be constructed in four parts, and there was internal detail with a fine crew to fit in it. There were tiny holes in the wings so that rigging wires could be fitted by keen modellers. It has made regular appearances over the years and is in the 2014 catalogue.

The Hawker Demon was a mould alteration to the old Hawker Hart kit of 1957, and featured improved fabric detail and small modifications to the fuselage to make the Demon. Consequently, the Hart no longer exists as a separate kit. The Demon has appeared frequently over the years but is not in the current range.

The Series 2 kits covered a range from World War II through to the 1960s. The Hellcat and Helldiver both featured for many years in the range, with the Hellcat being released as a 'Fighter of the Aces' aircraft in the 1990s. The Helldiver left the range in 2013. The Duck was the US equivalent of the Walrus; it was re-released in 1995 by Humbrol and was in the 2013 catalogue, but deleted in 2014.

The Blenheim and Battle were models of two important RAF aircraft. The Battle came in for much criticism because it was based on drawings supplied by Fairey's, who unfortunately sent the plans for the prototype! Hopefully we shall see a new Battle soon, as the old one was withdrawn in 2013. The Blenheim IV was released around the same time as the Frog Blenheim I kit, and again it is interesting to see the differences in both manufacturers' approach to kit design. The Frog featured smooth surfaces, whereas the Airfix was festooned in rivets. The Blenheim was last produced a few years ago. In 2014, new models of both variants of the Blenheim were announced.

The Henschel and Pe-2 were both 'rivet free' and very nice replicas, though the Henschel has not been released for several years, and the Pe-2 was deleted in 2013. As we have seen, Airfix was always an innovator when it came to kit design, and the Pe-2 was one of the first Airfix kits to receive an improved method of fixing the undercarriage in the down position. Previously, the doors were cemented separately to the open nacelles and the legs fitted into the wing. The Pe-2 featured a one-piece moulding with both doors fitted to it, and the legs were then stuck to it, and it was fitted up into the opening. This led to a much sturdier method of fitting the undercarriage, and the open space was blanked off. The 'closed' doors were supplied as one part, which simply fitted over the space. Gone, therefore, were the days of 'wonky' doors and ones that fell off easily.

The Skyraider was a post-war US Navy fighter. It has not been available for some time. The Bassett was the RAF's transport for its V-Bomber crews, and was a nice replica of the Beagle B.206-based aircraft. Unfortunately it was marred by the unsightly rivets so loved by Airfix at that time. It was released in the late 1970s as the 'Regal Beagle', as flown by Prince Charles, but has not been released since.

The Angel Interceptor was the 'odd one out' as it was modelled on the fictitious aircraft flown in the television series *Captain Scarlet*. In 1981 it was released as a SNAPnglue kit, but then disappeared. In 2011 it was re-released, and can be found again in the shops.

The Dominie was the RAF's new trainer aircraft based on the DH.125 executive jet. It was a lovely model which expertly caught the shape of the original. Unfortunately the RAF only bought twenty, so the modelling options were somewhat limited. Over a thousand of the civil variants were produced, but it would have required major surgery to produce any of those. It disappeared in the early 1980s for many years, although it did make a brief comeback in 2005.

The three Series 3 planes came from three different eras. The Ford Trimotor was a contemporary of the Ju 52 and was built in much the same way. It was released in the 1990s by Humbrol, but has not been on sale for some years. The Il-28 was a Russian bomber used during the early 'Cold War'. It was typical of Airfix's jet aircraft in having a smooth surface with fine raised panel lines. It has been released for short periods since 1981, but is not currently available. The Hampden, often referred to as the 'Flying Panhandle', has made regular appearances over the years and is in the current range.

The two 'Dogfight Doubles' again used existing Series 2 and Series 1 kits. They have not been issued since 1981.

HMS *Fearless* was one of two assault ships used by the Royal Navy. *Tirpitz* was actually the *Bismarck* mould, which had been tooled to contain a couple of extra parts so it could be released as *Tirpitz*. The original illustration is one of only half-a-dozen Roy Cross originals whose whereabouts are known today. In 2013 it was displayed at RAF Hendon as part of a gallery of original Airfix artwork. The

Aircraft from the 1968 range. Clockwise from top right: Storch, Hanover CL.III, DH.4, Spad, Fiat G.50, Gnat, T-6, P-47, S-55. AIRFIX

QE2 was the new Cunard flagship and was the last liner tooled by Airfix before the *Queen Mary 2* in 2004. All three are currently unavailable.

The Ferrari 250LM was announced last year, when it appeared as a Motor Racing car; it did not appear as a kit until late 1968. The Mercedes was designed as a kit only; it has not been issued for some time. The Jaguar 420C was listed in the leaflets as M209C and M301C, but was released in 1969 as M301C. It has not been sold since 1981, so unmade examples fetch high prices.

The Honda CB450 was Airfix's second motorcycle kit following the Arial Arrow. It was also moulded to 1:16 scale. It has not been issued in over thirty years. It was numbered in the Modern Cars series, but soon received its own number to match the Arrow.

The James Bond Toyota was a licensed model for the James Bond series. Two years later it was converted into a standard Toyota 2000GT so it could continue to be sold.

The two railway locomotives were both from the Kitmaster tool bank that Airfix had acquired earlier. They bene-

fited from new Roy Cross illustrations and were sold up to 1981. They are today available from Dapol.

The only AFV released was a model of the Russian T-34 tank. It included two turrets so that a 76mm- or 85mm-gunned version of the tank could be built. Like the rest of the 1:76 AFVs, it remains in production. The AFV range did see, however, the first of a new range of RAF Airfield sets. Two more would follow, but this set included an ambulance and fire engine plus a variety of figures. They have been available for most of the last forty years, and in 2013 received new digital artwork and were joined by a brand-new Bomber Re-Arming Set.

The Royal Horse Artillery completed Airfix's small range of World War I figures. All five are in the catalogue today.

The World War II Commandos Set was a popular addition to the range and included figures climbing ladders and a canoe. It was replaced by a second revised set in 1977, but this later mould appears to have been lost because the current issues are all from the first mould.

The Tarzan Set contained figures from the then popular television series of *Tarzan*, though military and historic modellers did not think much of it. On the plus side it provided several more wild animals and a few native figures, who could, at a pinch, be painted as Zulus. However, one would have to buy hundreds of sets to mount a successful attack at Rorke's Drift! It has not been released for over thirty years, although HaT in France recently released it as 'Jungle Adventure', which I suppose got round any license issues.

The final new release was the first in a new range of 1:32 scale figures. It included twenty-nine figures that were moulded from the 'patterns' used for the 1:76 figures. They were initially sold in a flat open-top box, but soon moved into brown boxes with an illustration on the front. In 1972 they were replaced by an excellent set of new figures, which used totally new patterns. In the late 1970s they were also sold in smaller boxes containing fourteen figures, but from the mid-1980s onwards the 1:32 soldiers disappeared. In 1995 seven sets, including the Paratroops, reappeared in bags of six figures, but since most sets had a mini-mum of seven different poses, this did not seem a good idea. From 2009, Airfix has been reintroducing the 1:32 sets in boxes

of fourteen figures. These are made of a new compound which overcomes many of the problems brought on by the soft plastic used on the originals, where the paint did not easily adhere and flaked off when the plastic flexed.

Thus once again Airfix had introduced a cheap source of soldiers to the market place. The sculpting of the figures was usually superior to the later competitors produced by rival manufacturers.

1969

In 1969 there was an increase of forty-one new models to the ranges, although not all would appear that year; these included the following:

133	Cessna 0-2	1:72
134	DHC Chipmunk	1:72
264	Douglas TBD-1 Devastator	1:72
265	NA OV-10A Bronco	1:72
266	HS Harrier GR.1	1:72
267	Focke-Wulf Fw 189	1:72
390	Sikorsky SH-3D Sea King	1:72
393	Lunar Module	1:72
881	Lockheed C-130K Hercules	1:72
SK505	Boeing 737-200	1:144
SK811	Boeing 747-100	1:144
SK701	Pan-Am Orion Spacecraft	1:144
SK911	Apollo Saturn V Rocket	1:144
904	HMS *Prince*	N/A
905	HMS *Discovery*	N/A
201	1933 Alfa-Romeo	1:32
M209C	Ford 3-Litre GT	1:32
M210C	Ford Escort	1:32
M302C	Vauxhall Victor 2000 Estate	1:32
832	Aston Martin DB6	1:24
4635	BSA C15 Motorcycle	N/A
4636	BMW R69 Motorcycle	N/A
623	Paddle Engine	N/A
A17V	Lee/Grant Tank	1:76
S34	Ancient Britons	1:76
S35	Waterloo Highland Infantry	1:76
S36	Waterloo French Cavalry	1:76
1718	World War II German Infantry	1:32
1729	World War II American Infantry	1:32
1692	DUKW (Polyprop)	1:76
1706	Roman Fort	1:76
1707	Gun Emplacement	1:76
1720	Caesar's Gate Set	1:76
1734	Beachhead Invasion Set	1:76

The bulk of the aircraft releases were of modern aircraft; the only two World War II aircraft were a US Navy Devastator and a Luftwaffe Fw 189, both of which were

A selection from Airfix's 1969 classic car range, with the Alfa-Romeo top right. AIRFIX

World War II 'polyprop' armour from 1969. AIRFIX

relatively little known aircraft but made decent replicas. Both made appearances after 1981 and were in the 2012 catalogue, but were deleted in 2013.

The 'push-pull' Cessna 0-2 and the Bronco were two rather unusual Vietnam-era aircraft. The Bronco was modified to make the OV-10D variant in 1983. They have not been released for some time.

The Chipmunk was a very nice little model that came with two canopies to make RAF and RCAF models, though it was marred somewhat by large rivets. It is in the 2014 catalogue.

Back in 1963, Airfix produced a model of the Hawker P.1127 prototype aircraft; in 1969 a new Harrier GR.1 model was produced. It came with a wide selection of underwing weapons, and the exhaust nozzles were linked so they could be rotated together. However, I never succeeded with this, and I doubt if many others did! Airfix was keen on gimmicks, but they appealed more to younger modellers. In 1983, the tool was modified to create the later laser nose-equipped GR.3 version. In 2013, Airfix released two new models of the GR.1 and GR.3.

The Hercules was based on the C-130K as bought by the RAF. It was rivet-free, and was moulded in an ochre-coloured plastic similar to that worn by RAF Hercules transports at the time. A novelty was the inclusion of the Bloodhound Missile Set, which could be loaded through the opening rear ramps. In 1977 it was modified into the C-130E variant as used by the USAF. In 1984 the mould was altered to make the AC-130H Gunship version. In 2001 it was replaced by a 'polybag' standard C-130 version, as the mould could not be converted back.

1969 saw the release of several models connected with the moon landing of that year. The Sea King was released as the machine used in the first moon pick-up.

The decals were altered slightly to show a later moon rescue helicopter. In 1985, the tool was modified to represent a Westland-built machine used by RAF rescue teams. In 2008 it was sold as the HAR.5 rescue version, and in 2010 was modified into AEW versions. The old kit was clearly showing its age with fit and detail problems. The AEW version was dropped in 2013, and the original rescue version returned for a year. However, Airfix is producing a new Sea King for 2015, initially sold as the Commando variant.

The Lunar Module and Saturn V rocket represented the first moon landing. Several other models were produced, but when interest in the moon landings began to wane, and we are told more Americans watched re-runs of *I Love Lucy* than the later landings, Airfix stopped making new models. Fortunately a 1:12 model of 'Lucy' was not made! A 'SNAPnglue'

variant of the Saturn V was made in 1981, but in 2009, the Saturn V was released with new parts to correct faults in the original kit. The Lunar Module was released as 'One Small Step for Man' and included a vac-form base and a set of astronauts. It was deleted in 2012.

The Pan-Am Orion appeared in the film *2001, a Space Odyssey*. It was released as a 'SNAPnglue' kit in 1981. It is not currently available.

The Boeing 747 and smaller 737 were both produced. The 737 was based on the 200 series, which quickly replaced the original short-body 100 series. It is in the 2014 catalogue. The 747 was the initial version and was a large kit. It was later sold with alternative decals and updated to a production version.

The two sailing ships were good replicas and sold over the years, but neither has been seen for some time.

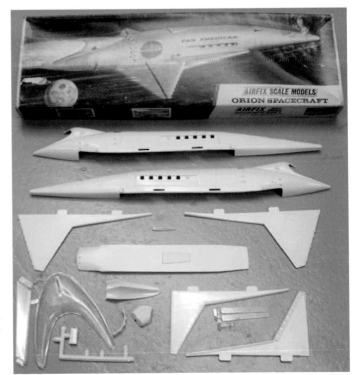

The 'Pan Am Orion' spacecraft kit from 1969 – coincidentally, the same year that Man first walked on the Moon.

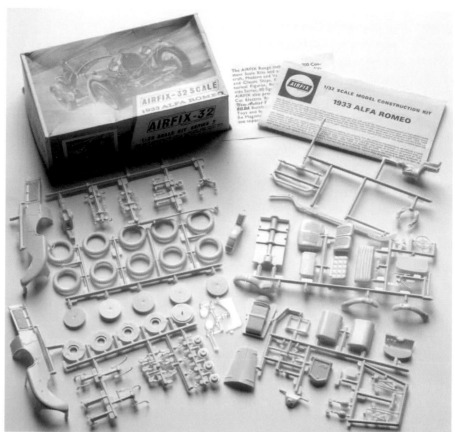

ABOVE LEFT: *An 'Airfix-32' kit, the Jaguar 420 from 1968.*

ABOVE RIGHT: *1969 kit of the 1933 Alfa, in 1:32 scale.*

LEFT: *The DUKW HO-OO kit from 1969.*

Airfix seemed to be moving towards vintage cars of the 1930s with the release of the 1933 Alfa-Romeo. It was released as a 'Special Edition' in 1988 and made frequent appearances thereafter; however, it is not currently available.

The Ford 3-Litre GT took the catalogue number previously allocated to the Jaguar 420, and the Ford Escort represented a current small car. In the 1990s and around 2007 it appeared in two sets of cars of the 1960s. It is currently available as a starter set and as a Haynes 'workshop' kit. The Victor 2000 was not very successful and soon disappeared from the range.

However, it was one of four kits selected in the late 1970s to be converted into 'Street Cars' in an effort to get further sales from the moulds. Three were issued, but 'Rebel Rouser', as it was to be named, does not appear to have been issued.

The Aston Martin DB6 seems to have had a fairly haphazard release and has not been seen for many years.

The two motorcycles were sold as 'scale models', which suggests they were larger than the 1:16 scale of the first two. They used a new number range for motorcycles, and were the last Airfix-designed ones. They have not been released since 1981.

The 1827 Maudslay Paddle Engine was the third in this small series. Like the others, it did not survive the events of 1981, but all four were in the 2013 catalogue, and it was still in the 2014 one.

The only tank this year was a replica of the Lee and Grant tanks of World War II. One kit had two separate turrets to make either version. It is still in production today.

The Ancient Britons, complete with chariots and knives, were released to fight the earlier Romans. To facilitate this, a set called 'Caesar's Gate' was released, which included the Romans and new Britons. The

fort would be available as a Roman Fort. The set was one of four released in 1993.

The exciting news for 1969 was the release of the first Napoleonic figure sets in OO/HO scale. The stunning Brian Knight box tops showed the Waterloo Highlanders preparing to do battle with French cavalry. Napoleonic figures were in short supply in most scales and in OO/HO there appeared to be none, so when Airfix announced another 'first', the world of wargaming and figure modelling became very excited. Nowadays some companies produce dozens of sets of Napoleonic figures, but the impact these Airfix figures made cannot be underestimated.

1:32 figure enthusiasts were to get a similar treat when Airfix released sets of World War II German and US infantry. These figures were beautifully sculptured and still to this day beat most of the competition for shape and accuracy. They feature in the 2014 range. The Waterloo figures were recently sold in a large Waterloo Assault Set, which contained all the figures.

A Gun Emplacement was released along with a DUKW polyprop model. The Beachhead Invasion Set used these models. The Gun Emplacement formed part of Airfix's seventieth anniversary of D-Day range in 2014.

1970

A total of twenty-six new models was proposed for 1970, including the magnificent 1:24 Spitfire; these comprised:

135	Bristol Bulldog	1:72
136	Henschel Hs 123	1:72
268	Gloster Meteor III	1:72
391	BAC Jaguar	1:72
392	HP Jetstream 3M	1:72
394	Blohm und Voss Bv 141B	1:72
SK912	BHC SRN-4 Hovercraft	1:144
1201	Supermarine Spitfire Mk Ia	1:24
SK702	Vostok Rocket	1:144
803	*Mayflower*	N/A
F6S	HMS *Leander*	1:600
F410S	HMS *Iron Duke*	1:600
M303C	Ford Capri	1:32
641	Toyota GT2000	1:24
A18V	Leopard Tank	1:76
A205V	Chieftain Tank	1:76
A302V	RAF Refuelling Set	1:76
S37	Waterloo French Artillery	1:76
S38	High Chaparral	1:76
1708	Pontoon Bridge	1:76
1735	World War II Russian Infantry	1:32
1736	World War II British Commandos	1:32
1737	World War II Japanese Infantry	1:32
1762	Abbot Self-Propelled Gun	1:32
1763	Bedford RL Truck	1:32
1764	105mm Gun	1:32

The 1970 Focke-Wulf Fw 189 kit.

The big aircraft kit for 1970 was the first in a new range of 1:24 'superkits', the Supermarine Spitfire Mk Ia. Previously the largest kits were to 1:32 scale, and produced by the likes of Revell. Airfix chose to go larger with 1:24 scale, and this first model revealed an unprecedented level of internal and external detail. There was full cockpit detail, and the wing-mounted guns could be seen through the detachable covers. Perhaps the most important feature was the design of the one-piece lower wing. A distinctive feature of all Spitfires is the 'gull wing' effect, where the wings join the circular fuselage. This neat design enabled this feature to appear on a model for the first time, and has featured in all Airfix Spitfires since then. Most manufacturers have adopted this design, though some have missed it.

Apart from the first two or three, Airfix has always designed its kits from scratch, which means that it has always been at the forefront of kit design, and arguably its most important innovator. Some Far Eastern manufacturers still base their new kits on a competitor's existing kit.

The range of 1:24 aircraft would be developed over the following ten years, culminating in the Focke-Wulf Fw190A, released just before Airfix was closed.

Apart from a few modified kits produced by Humbrol, the days of the 1:24 superkit looked as if they were over. However, shortly after Hornby took over in 2006, a magnificent new Mosquito was announced, and in 2014, an exquisitely detailed Hawker Typhoon was released – and it looks likely that we shall see more new 1:24 kits coming out of Margate.

1:72 modellers received a beautiful replica of the Bristol Bulldog inter-war biplane fighter. The quality of detail was superb, and it would be difficult to better

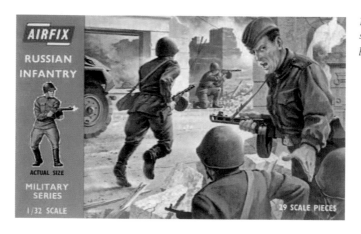

Russian Infantry set in 'Brown Box' packaging, 1970.

it today. It was last available in Swedish Air Force markings. Sweden has always been an important market for Airfix kits, and Airfix has responded by releasing many kits in Swedish colours over the years.

The Henschel was a 1930s Luftwaffe bomber used in the Spanish Civil War. It was one of several Series 1 kits that moved to Series 2 later because they would not fit the new 'blister' packs introduced in 1974.

The Meteor was introduced at about the same time as the Frog model. Fortunately both were of different marks, and again the Airfix version featured many rivets to the Frog's smooth finish. It would later be sold in a 'Dogfight Double' with a V-1 flying bomb.

The Jaguar was a smooth rendition of the RAF's new ground-attack aircraft. Later it would be converted to a production GR.1 version and later still to a GR.3.

I remember the Jetstream arriving unannounced in Woolworth's. It was based on the military 3M version, of which 175 were to be sold to the USAF as trainers. Unfortunately the order was cancelled and, shortly after, Handley Page went out of business. The Jetstream went on to healthy sales as an eighteen-seater airliner,

using the same engines as the 3M, but it has not been possible to convert the kit. None of the above are currently available.

The final kit was a model of an unusual experimental German aircraft, the Bv 141. It recently returned to the range and was in the 2013 catalogue.

'Space race' fans were treated to a nice 1:144 replica of a Vostok/Soyuz spacecraft. It was re-released in the 1990s, and in 2011, when many of these space kits were reissued by Hornby, the correct colour scheme was applied.

In this year the *Mayflower* was released in Series 8; it was also the subject of the second of Airfix's books, *Classic Ships, Their History and How to Model Them*. The first book, on HMS *Victory*, was also released that year. These were the first in what was to become a large range of books, printed in company with PSL books, that were concerned with modelling Airfix kits. However, all the Airfix/PSL books have been out of print since 1981.

HMS *Leander* was a good replica of the wide range of 'Leander' class frigates produced for the Royal Navy and others. In the mid-1970s it was sold with stickers proclaiming 'HMS *Hero*' after the popular television series of the time. At the time

Two 1969 de Havilland Chipmunks, showing the alternative cockpit canopies.

of the Falklands War, guided missiles were added to the kit. In 2004 it was briefly sold in a set as 'Falklands Warships'. The *Iron Duke* was a beautiful replica of the famous World War I battleship, illustrated by an exquisite painting by Roy Cross. It was still in the range in 2013, with a new painting by Mike Trim.

The Ford Capri was an iconic sports/saloon car and was produced in 1:32 scale. In an effort to revitalize the range of 'modern' cars, which had become slightly passé by the late 1970s, in 1981 four of them were selected to be altered into 'custom' cars to try and reinvigorate the range. Three were actually produced, including the Capri, now called 'Krackle Kat'. This small range was very short-lived, however, and none of the four has been seen since.

When the licence for the 1968 release of the 'James Bond Toyota' expired, the kit was modified to represent a standard Toyota GT2000; it has not been issued for many years.

Two of the Rhine Army's main battle tanks, the German Leopard and British Chieftain, were modelled in 1:76 scale. The Leopard was released as A206V in Series 2. Both were very detailed models, but the Chieftain has made more appearances in the catalogue. Neither is currently available.

The RAF Refuelling Set was the second of Airfix's small range of wartime Airfield Sets. It included AEC and Bedford QL tankers and ground crew. It was very popular with modellers, and the two tankers were the subject of numerous conversions in *Airfix Magazine*. It features in the 2014 range, with a new illustration by Adam Tooby.

The Waterloo French Artillery was the third in the new range of Waterloo-era figures. They have not been released recently, but did appear in the 2008 Waterloo Battle Set, along with all the other sets. The 'High Chaparral' was simply the Cowboys (S7), to which were added five figures representing characters from the then popular television series of the same name. On the occasions they have been released since that time they are sold simply as 'Cowboys', and do not mention the earlier television connection.

A 'clip-together' Pontoon Bridge was released, which has appeared in several sets and is still in the range today.

Three new sets of beautifully sculptured 1:32 World War II figures were produced, and they are all in the range in 2014. Three

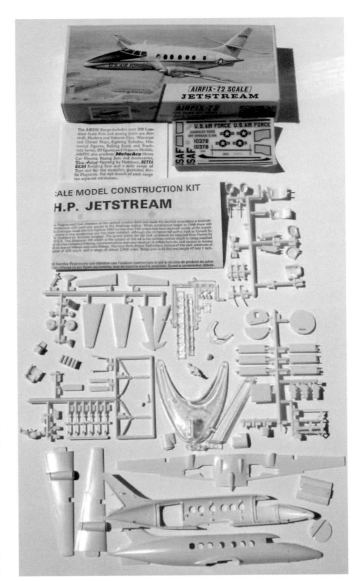

The Handley Page Jetstream model from 1970.

post-war 'polyprop' vehicles were added in 1:32 scale, though none of them could be used with the earlier figures, and it would not be until 1977 that the sets Modern British and German Infantry were added to the range. The models have not been sold for many years, but maybe could make a comeback?

1971

Having released the first 'superkit' in 1970, modellers were expecting great things for 1971 – and they were not disappointed, because in addition to forty-one new tools, Airfix released the second 'superkit' as well as launching two new series.

269	SAAB Draken	1:72
271	Britten-Norman BN-2 Islander	1:72
395	SAAB Viggen	1:72
396	Vought Corsair II	1:72

RIGHT: *1:32 scale Abbot self-propelled gun from 1970.*

BELOW: *Two 1970s, snap-together kits showing World War II scenes: an assault on a gun emplacement and a pontoon bridge.*

397	DHC-2 Beaver	1:72	642	Aston Martin DB6	1:24	1805	8th Army	1:32
492	NA RA-5C Vigilante	1:72	2001	1930 4.5-litre Bentley	1:12	1806	Afrika Korps	1:32
493	Phantom II (B, C, D, E and J)	1:72	R403	BR Mogul Locomotive	OO/HO	1807	Alvis Stalwart	1:32
591	Douglas A-26 Invader	1:72	A208V	Panzer IV Tank	1:76	1808	Strongpoint	1:32
D365F	Cessna 0-2 and MiG-21	1:72	A210V	Crusader Tank	1:76	C101S	British Guardsman, 1815	54mm
1202	Messerschmitt Bf 109E	1:24	S39	Washington's Army	1:76	C201S	British Hussar, 1815	54mm
SK621	Lockheed L-1011 TriStar	1:144	S40	British Grenadiers	1:76			
SK622	Saturn 1B	1:144	S41	Astronauts	1:76			
F202S	*Rommel*	1:600	S42	Station Accessories	1:76			
F203S	HMS *Manxman*	1:600	S43	Waterloo British Cavalry	1:76			
F411S	*Graf Spee*	1:600	S44	Waterloo French Infantry	1:76			
906	*Wasa*	1:144	1693	Coastal Defence Assault Set	1:76			
M10C	Bond Bug 700E	1:32	1694	Coastal Defence Fort	1:76			
M211C	Porsche 917	1:32	1709	Waterloo Farm House	1:76			
M304C	Austin Maxi	1:32	1712	British Paratroops (new mould)	1:32			
0301	1911 Vauxhall Prince Henry	1:32						

Airfix followed up its magnificent 1:24 Spitfire kit with a model of its main enemy, the Messerschmitt Bf 109E, both from the Battle of Britain. The new kit showed one or two improvements over the Spitfire, and was beautifully illustrated by Roy Cross. The second painting was later the subject of the first of a new series of 'Datacharts', and was used on the cover of the second book in the *Classic Aircraft and How to Model Them* series. The kit is still in the Airfix range today.

The 1:72 aircraft were all post-war. The two SAABs comprised the current Draken fighter and the new Viggen or 'Thunderbolt'. Both were very smooth kits with fine raised panel lines. They have appeared regularly over the years, but the Viggen has never been updated to production standard, which has made it less attractive for re-releases.

The Islander and Beaver were two workhorses of remote territories. Both were excellent models, but were marred by heavy rivet detail. The Islander was later modified to make the Defender variant, and the Beaver was promoted with optional floats.

The Corsair II and Vigilante were both modelled with smooth surfaces and fine panel lines. The Invader was a particularly good model, but like the Mitchell bomber was, in my opinion, spoilt by heavy rivet detail. If the decals were to adhere satisfactorily, the rivets had to be sanded off. It is interesting to note that the models made for the Hornby Display Rooms tend to have all the rivets removed by the modeller.

The final 'Dogfight Double' pairing featured the small Cessna 0-2 spotter plane with the MiG-21. None of the above is currently in the catalogue.

Coincidental with the collapse of Rolls-Royce in early 1971, brought about by costs involved with the new RB.211 aero-engine, Airfix released a lovely model of the Lockheed TriStar, for which the RB.211 was designed. It appeared in Air Canada colours, and was included regularly over the years, often with different decals. But with the TriStar leaving service with the RAF, and there being only a handful left in service, the kit has not been issued for a few years.

The Saturn 1B was a forerunner of the Apollo Saturn V, and a model was released in 1971. Forty years after its first release it was back in the catalogue with the other 'Space Race' rockets, but was withdrawn in 2014. The space kits all received new illustrations by Mike Trim.

Naval modellers received a model of the new West German destroyer, the *Rommel*, which was one of several supplied by the Americans, based on their 'Charles F. Adams' class of destroyers. It was a very attractive model with a stunning Roy Cross painting, but like other post-war German military models, they were not used in anger and the kit has not been issued for many years.

HMS *Manxman* was one of a class of fast mine-laying destroyers that was last released in a set with HMS *Suffolk* in 2005. The *Graf Spee* joined HMS *Ajax*, which was part of the task force sent out to sink the 'pocket battleship'. It has appeared regularly over the years but is absent from the current catalogue.

54mm Hussar and Coldstream Guardsmen from 1971.

Coldstream Guardsman with first issue Type 4 Packaging, 1971.

RIGHT: *1971 Bachmann 'Mini Army' soldiers. From left to right, Japanese, American, British and German.*

BOTTOM: *First edition of the 1971 sales leaflet.*

With all the excitement concerning the salvage of the Swedish sailing ship the *Wasa*, it was inevitable that Airfix would model it. In 2014 she was available as a gift set with paints and brushes.

The three 1:32 modern cars included models of the Austin Maxi 'hatchback', a Porsche 917 racing car, which would also feature in the Motor Ace range, and a model of the Bond Bug 700E. The latter has achieved something of a 'cult' status, but has not been seen for many years.

The Aston Martin DB6 was produced to 1:24 scale but was not in the catalogue for long. The Vauxhall Prince Henry does not seem to have survived the events of 1981, but might make a comeback to go with the World War I celebrations, as it was used as a staff car in World War I. However, back in the 1970s, Airfix was not able to discover any firm details about its use as a staff car other than one or two cases in the UK. It would make a nice companion to the 'Ole Bill Bus'.

The second of the big announcements for 1971 was the release of a 1:12 scale

model of a 1930 4.5-litre Bentley 'Blower'. It was a magnificent kit and came with chromed parts as well as black and green runners. The mould for it cost a whopping £80,000 and it has been a consistent seller. It appears in the 2014 range. Modellers were hoping for further additions to the range, and a Rolls-Royce 'Silver Ghost' was long rumoured. But the cost of this second kit continued to spiral upwards, and by the late 1970s it was going to cost around £260,000 to tool. Despite favourable sales forecasts and an early return on the investment the money was not available and so it was reluctantly cancelled. Nevertheless, with the advent of computer-aided design methods which are cheaper than the old system, it may one day be modelled, like the Mosquito; we will have to wait and see.

The British Rail 'Mogul' was to be the last ex-Kitmaster mould to be introduced by Airfix. In 1986 it was sold to Dapol.

Two tanks from the desert war were introduced, the Crusader and rival Panzer IV. The Panzer IV is part of the 2014 range.

Six sets of OO/HO figures were announced, covering a wide range of periods. Washington's Army and the British Grenadiers were Airfix's only small-scale incursion into the American War of Independence. They were produced for many years, but are not currently in the range. The Astronauts were designed to be used with the Lunar Module and were recently sold in a set with the Lunar Module, called 'One Small Step for Man', by Hornby.

The Station Accessories was the old 1958 set, but is now moulded in the soft plastic used for the figures. They are believed to be with Dapol.

Two more sets of Waterloo figures were added, along with a clip-together model of a Waterloo farmhouse. The farmhouse was included in a Waterloo Assault Set, which was updated recently. Until it was withdrawn in 2011, it was the only way to acquire the range of Waterloo figures.

British Paratroops were the first figures to be released in 1:32 scale; they were based on the patterns for the OO/HO figures. They were replaced by these using brand new patterns and covered seven new positions. The 8th Army and Afrika Korps sets were likewise modelled on new patterns, and were scaled down to help make the second sets of these figures in 1:76 scale. They are all in the range today. At least four of these sets were later issued by Bachmann as single painted soldiers in its 'Mini Army' range.

A model of a modern Alvis Stalwart vehicle was added to the range of 1:32 polythene vehicles, but there was no sign of any modern British infantry to fight with them. The first of a small range of clip-together buildings was announced for use with the 1:32 figures. Strongpoint was based on a typical ruined European-theatre house. It was re-released in 2013 after many years of being withdrawn.

Finally, the third big announcement was the release of the first two 54mm figure kits. For some years the French firm Historex had been producing kits of Napoleonic figures, mainly French, to 54mm or 1:32 scale. They were very finely detailed kits with many separate parts. They were quite expensive, so when Airfix announced its new range at about a quarter of the price, modellers made a bee-line for the model shops. The first two were models of British soldiers and were very neatly executed. The mounted figures each had a different horse so they could be interchanged once more horses became available. The foot soldiers usually had alternative parts so that two poses could be made. The level of detail was very fine, whilst the Historex ones were just a little bit finer; but the Airfix ones with their much lower price and easy availability were more popular, and many were used in conversions.

RIGHT: *Another snap-together set, this time from 1971 and of a coastal defence assault scene.*

BELOW: *De Havilland Beaver kit from 1971.*

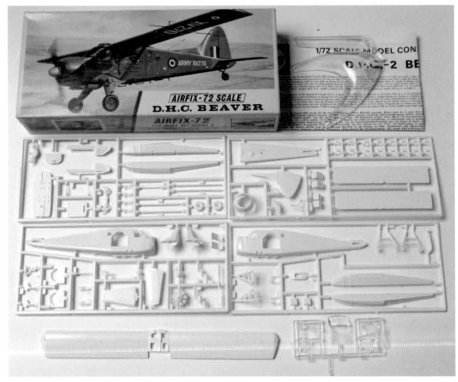

1972

Fans of large-scale aircraft and of soldiers were looking forward to 1972, and they were not to be disappointed. Airfix also announced two new series. Thirty-two kits were scheduled for release that year; these included:

84	Westland Lysander II	1:72
137	Brewster Buffalo	1:72
272	Hawker Hurricane Mk I/IIB	1:72
361	Dassault Mystère B2	1:72
398	Lockheed P-38E/F Lightning	1:72
399	Mosquito NF.II/FB.VI/ Mk.XVIII	1:72
494	Dornier Do 17E & F	1:72
1401	NA P-51D Mustang	1:24
F204S	HMS *Amazon*	1:600
D5213	Vosper MTB	1:72
M212C	Beach Buggy 'Bugle'	1:32
M305C	Morris Marina TC	1:32
M306C	Maserati Indy	1:32
M401C	Monty's Humber	1:32
A211V	Sheridan Tank	1:76
A303V	SAM-2 Guideline Missile	1:76
C102S	42nd Highlander, 1815	54mm
C202S	2nd Dragoon 'Scots Grey' 1815	54mm
S45	Waterloo British Infantry	1:76
S46	Waterloo British Artillery	1:76
S47	RAF Personnel	1:76
1830	Panther Tank	1:76
1831	Tiger Tank	1:76
1804	British Infantry Support Set	1:32
1809	Australian Infantry	1:32
1835	Footballers	1:32
1836	German Half-Track	1:32
1837	Cromwell Tank	1:32
1838	Bamboo House	1:32
C701S	4-Stroke Engine	N/A
R301	Prairie Tank Locomotive	1:76
R302	City of Truro Locomotive	1:76

Seven more 1:72 aircraft were added, although most were replacements for early kits. The Lysander was a direct replacement for the 1956 model, 1384. It bore the same catalogue number, 84, as the original adopted. When the kits moved into blister packs it was elevated to Series 2. It was produced regularly over the years, but was not in the 2013 catalogue.

The Brewster Buffalo was a nice model of this rather lack-lustre aeroplane used mainly against the Japanese. It has been reissued several times with different markings, and has only recently been withdrawn. It, too, moved to Series 2 as it was too big to fit into the new 'blister' pack.

The Hurricane was the much-vaunted replacement for the 1956 Hurricane IV, 1396. It was released in Series 2 and contained parts to make Mk I/IIB/IVRP variants; it came with a stunning Roy Cross painting. But almost immediately things went wrong! It was not possible to make a Mk IV, so soon afterwards the Mk IV option was dropped and the old Hurricane IVRP made a return. Whilst the kit was very well detailed, there was a major outline flaw, in that the 'hump' behind the cockpit was too low and it did not look

right. A new Mk 1 was released in 1979, and recently Hornby made a new Mk II. It has now been retired.

The Dassault Mystère B2 was a fine model of an ageing French jet, and the Dornier Do 17 was a very nice replica of this early World War II bomber. Both are currently unavailable.

The Lightning and Mosquito were replacements for the earlier kits, although both early models did carry on for some time. The Mosquito was a particularly fine model and could be made into several versions, and in 1995 further parts were added to make even more versions. It is still in the range today.

The third 1:24 superkit was a replica of the P-51D Mustang. It featured a retracting undercarriage and more detail than the earlier two. Airfix's insistence on retracting undercarriages for many of its superkits meant that the oleos on the main undercarriage legs were extended to allow for the retraction. When the kits were placed on the ground they tended to sit 'high' as the oleos were not depressed. It should be possible to mould separate legs in the depressed position for those who wish to portray their models on the ground. In 2005, extra parts were moulded to enable the 'K' version to be modelled. Both kits are still available.

Warship modellers received a model of one of the Royal Navy's latest frigates, HMS *Amazon*. She would later appear in the Falkland's ship sets.

The first of a new series of fast motor launches to 1:72 scale was a very fine model of a Vosper MTB. It had nicely sculptured crew figures, and could be used alongside the aircraft and tanks that Airfix was producing. Three launches were produced, and all three were reintroduced

in 2013. Plans to mould a replica of the Fairmile 'D' patrol boat were well advanced and tooling had started, but it was cancelled just before 1981.

Three more modern 1:32 cars were introduced, representing a 'fun' car, saloon car and 'supercar'. None has been seen since the early 1980s.

The first in a new series of 1:32 military staff cars was produced. Advertised as a 'Humber Staff Car' it was actually sold as 'Monty's Humber'. Although the Japanese were flooding the market with AFV kits to 1:35 scale, Airfix bravely carried on with 1:32 suiting its figures and buildings. After 'Rommel's Half-Track' in 1975, the range changed to tanks and guns. Both kits were reintroduced in 2013.

The two AFVs in 1:76 scale were of modern vehicles. The Sheridan tank is one of the few tanks not to be currently available. The SAM-2 Guideline Missile Set was a contemporary of the Bloodhound Set. Unfortunately it is one of a very few kits that for reasons unknown was not delivered to Humbrol's Trun factory when Airfix was bought from General Mills in 1986. It is presumed lost, and like the SS *France* mould, which was also missing, it fetches high prices on eBay.

The two new 54mm kits both had a Scottish flavour and made very fine replicas of these two British regiments at Waterloo. I remember spending a long time painting the tartan on the Highlander's kilt! They have been released over the years but have not been seen for some time.

Continuing the Waterloo theme, Airfix released two more sets of British infantry and artillery in 1:76 scale. They were last seen in the recently withdrawn Battle of Waterloo Set. A set of RAF Personnel was produced, and later three other sets of

airfield figures would be moulded. All four were in the 2013 catalogue.

Four new 'polyprop' AFVs were produced, two in 1:76, the Tiger and Panther tanks, and two in 1:32, the German Half-Track and Cromwell tank. All four left the catalogue in 1981 and have not been issued since. However, they were run by Humbrol for CTS in the USA. The 1:32 vehicles could be used by the World War II figures Airfix had produced and would appear in the combat packs produced later.

In 1:32 scale, Airfix produced a fascinating set of British Infantry Support figures, although we would have to wait until 1980 for a set of British Infantry for them to support. The support set included several figures as well as a couple of Vickers heavy machine guns and mortars. Sets of support troops and equipment for the Germans and Americans were sadly not forthcoming. A set of Australian Infantry wearing 'bush' hats was also released. Both sets are currently available. The third set was a set of footballers! Airfix was planning sets of figures of different sportsmen, but these plans were curtailed following the lack-lustre sales of the footballers. They have not been issued for over thirty years.

A clip-together Bamboo House was produced for use with the new Australians and Japanese to fight over. It was later scaled down to 1:76 scale. Along with the later Checkpoint Set, it joined the other buildings and was re-released in 2014.

The 4-Stroke Engine completed the small collectors' series of museum models. It is currently available. A fifth, the Mill Engine, advertised on the box sides, was never released.

The Prairie Tank and *City of Truro* Locomotives were the ex-Kitmaster kits that were re-released as 'limited production' kits.

With all the new ranges being added, modellers couldn't wait to see what 1973 would produce.

1973

In 1973 thirty-three new models were announced and a new series of Waterline Warships was launched. Also the old pattern numbers and catalogue numbers were replaced by a new computerized system, and these numbers are still in use today. The 1973 models include the following:

01058-2	Cessna 0-1 Bird Dog	1:72
01059-5	Westland SA341 Gazelle	1:72
03021-6	Westland SA330 Puma	1:72
04015-4	Martin B-26 Marauder	1:72
04016-7	Douglas AC-47 Gunship	1:72
05012-8	BAC (EE) Canberra B(I).6	1:72
09502-8	Hawker Hurricane Mk I	1:24
09601-4	HS Harrier GR.1	1:24

04212-3	HMS *Belfast*	1:600
05202-9	*Moskva*	1:600
01801-8	2 x Tribal Class Destroyers	1:1200
02701-2	HMS *Hood*	1:1200
02702-5	*Bismarck*	1:1200
09257-1	*St Louis*	N/A
09300-4	Honda 750 Four	1:8
01318-1	Matilda Tank	1:76
03304-8	RAF Recovery Set	1:76
01553-2	French Imperial Guardsman	54mm
02553-5	Polish Lancer	54mm
09651-9	D-Day Allied Attack Set	1:76
09652-2	D-Day German Defence Set	1:76
09653-5	El Alamein Allied Attack Set	1:76
09654-8	El Alamein German Defence	1:76
01703-5	World War II British Infantry	1:76
01711-6	Afrika Korps	1:76
01749-1	Waterloo French Imperial Guard	1:76
09781-9	T-34 Tank (Polyprop)	1:76
09782-2	Elephant Tank (Polyprop)	1:76
09783-5	Sherman Tank (Polyprop)	1:76
09784-8	Half-Track and Gun (Polyprop)	1:76
51460-6	Waterloo French Grenadiers	1:32
51461-9	Waterloo British Infantry	1:32
51508-7	Desert Outpost	1:32

The Bird Dog was a fine little model of a 'spotter' plane used in the Vietnam war. It has not been released for several years. In the early 1970s Westland and Aerospatiale collaborated to produce three helicopters for the UK and French armed forces. The two Westland helicopters were French

designs and made very detailed models. Thirty years later, in 2004, the Puma kit was upgraded to make the latest version. Both kits were recently withdrawn.

The Martin Marauder was the favourite aircraft of the late John Edwards, Airfix's chief designer. It is an extremely fine replica with much detail and a very smooth surface, lacking the rivets that marred so many other aircraft. Oddly, I seem to remember the FROG model being festooned with rivets! It has made regular appearances in the catalogue but is not currently available.

One of the earliest Series 4 kits was the DC-3 Dakota, which was a good kit but suffered from a lack of dihedral on the outer wings. It was not possible to correct that fault, but in 1973, Airfix rejuvenated sales of the kit by converting the mould to make the AC-47 gunship version as used in Vietnam. In recent years, Airfix has used a mould from another company when it wished to sell a standard DC-3 kit, although in 2014 a brand new tool Dakota was released. It should be feasible to mould a new AC-47 from the new kit.

The BAC, formerly English Electric, Canberra was one of the most requested models and was a very good, well detailed model. The nose, however, was not quite right, but it still sold very well. In the early 1980s Palitoy drastically altered the mould to make a Martin B-57 Canberra model. This solved the problem of the suspect nose, but the B-57 was never as

Desert Campaign tanks from 1973:
Panzer IV (left), Crusader (top) and Matilda.

Desert tanks from 1973:
left to right, Panzer IV, Crusader, Lee and Matilda.

popular as the BAC Canberra. Hornby has now produced new Canberra kits to fill the gap in the range.

Two new 'superkits' were announced. The Hurricane had full internal detail in the wheel wells and wings because the undercarriage was not retractable. The aircraft had the correct 'sit'. The Harrier was an excellent representation of the first VSTOL aircraft; USMC variants could also be built. Later additional parts were added to make the GR.3 and Sea Harrier FRS.1 variants. Both later kits are still on sale.

Modellers of 1:600 scale ships received a model of the famous World War II cruiser, HMS *Belfast*, and the kit is still in production today. The other ship was a model of the then new Russian helicopter carrier, the *Moskva*. However, it has not been seen for many years.

In 1973 Airfix introduced a new series of ships, Waterline Warships, made to 1:1200 scale, or half the size of the standard warships. In the late 1950s and early 1960s, the British company Eaglewall had produced a large range of warships to this scale, which enabled wargamers to fight naval battles on a table top. Now Airfix took up the baton with a small range based on the hunt for the *Bismarck*. Six kits would be produced, but they disappeared after 1981. However, in 2011 Airfix released them all in a set entitled 'Sink the *Bismarck*'.

A fine model of the French warship the *St Louis* was released. It has not been modelled for several years.

Airfix signalled its intention to enter the large-scale motorcycle market with the release of a model of the Honda 750 Four. The large-scale kits, all at 1:8 scale, would all come from other manufacturers' tools. None of the motorbikes was released after the early 1980s.

A model of the Matilda tank was introduced, and in 2006 Humbrol added extra parts to make a rocket-firing 'Hedgehog' model. Both are still in production today. The third RAF Airfield set was released as the RAF Recovery Set, and includes a Coles crane and *Queen Mary* aircraft transporter. A much requested kit, it remains in production today.

The 54mm kits saw the addition of the French Imperial Guardsman and the Polish Lancer. Both have been produced on and off over the years, though are not currently available. The Guardsman would later be modelled at 1:12 scale. Airfix would capitalize on its investment on research and tooling for the Guardsman by producing 1:76 and 1:32 figures from the same patterns.

Airfix utilized the patterns for the 1:32 Afrika Korps to produce a new set of 1:76 figures, and the old Infantry Combat Group was replaced by a new set of World War II British infantry. The mould for the latter appears to have been lost around 1986, and Airfix has recently used a set modelled by Esci; however, lately it has produced a new set, its first in thirty years.

In 1:32 scale, the French Grenadiers were joined by a set of British Line Infantry. We can expect to see them in 2015, at the anniversary of the Battle of Waterloo.

The remaining kits were all of polythene vehicles and buildings to support both scales. The Desert Outpost in 1:32 scale returned in 2013, and in 1980 was scaled down to 1:76 scale. Four 'Polyprop' tanks were announced for the 1:76 range.

Airfix also started a small range of sets based on famous World War II battles. There were two sets for each, an Allied Attack Set and an Axis Defence Set, each containing a set of infantry, an aeroplane and a tank that could be posed on a Vacform base. By buying the opposing set the modeller could now fight the battle. These sets have long been out of production and are highly prized by collectors.

1974

In 1974, thirty-six new models were announced and thirty-one were actually released. Series 1 aircraft, tanks and 54mm kits were taken out of the plastic bags and put into the new 'blister' packs. The complaint with the bags was that parts got broken easily, whereas the new packs gave much greater protection and still allowed the buyer to view the contents. Cars moved into boxes. Some Series 1 kits would not fit into the blister so they were renumbered and moved to Series 2.

01060-5 Piper Cherokee Arrow II   1:72
01061-8 Scottish Aviation Bulldog   1:72

RIGHT: *1974's SAM-2 surface-to-air missile kit.* AIRFIX

LEFT: *BAC Strikemaster kit from 1974, in the markings of the Sultan of Oman's Air Force.*

09657-7	Guadalcanal US Attack Set	1:76
09658-0	Guadalcanal Japanese Defence	1:76
06501-6	Rommel's Half-Track	1:32
51462-2	Waterloo Highland Infantry	1:32
52463-5	Waterloo French Infantry	1:32

The three Series 1 aircraft were lovely little models with very fine detail and smooth finishes. The Pup was Airfix's best World War I fighter aircraft so far. The Cherokee Arrow was their only venture into light civil aircraft, and although the Bulldog was based on the similar Beagle Pup, Airfix chose to model the military trainer version that was entering service with the RAF and Swedish Air Force. All have been produced over the years, with the Sopwith being released in the 'Aircraft of the Aces' range. None is currently in the catalogue.

The Shooting Star was a good model of one of the USA's early jet fighters. The Strikemaster was the last variant of the Jet Provost trainer aircraft and could be modelled as a JP5 trainer or the Strikemaster attack variant. It was a beautiful little kit with very fine details and small parts. However, both kits are currently out of production.

The Mustang was a replacement for the original 1958 kit and was clearly based on the 1:24 Mustang. It was replaced in 2013 by a new kit. The Spitfire was supplemental to the old Spitfire IX kit. It was very accurate and well detailed, but the chord on the top surface of the ailerons was wrong. This error was corrected on the 1978 new Spitfire Mk Ia kit. The Vb is still in the range and has been released as a Vc.

01062-1	Sopwith Pup	1:72	01554-5	95th Rifleman, 1815	54mm
02043-3	Lockheed F-80C Shooting Star	1:72	01555-8	American Soldier, 1775	54mm
02044-6	BAC Strikemaster/JP5	1:72	02554-8	George Washington, 1775	54mm
02045-9	NA P-51D/K Mustang	1:72	02555-1	French Cuirassier, 1815	54mm
02046-2	Supermarine Spitfire Mk Vb	1:72	01319-4	Type 97 Chi-Ha Tank	1:76
02056-9	Westland SB HAR 22	1:72	01320-4	Scorpion Tank	1:76
03022-9	Republic F-84F Thunderstreak	1:72	02312-6	German Reconnaissance Set	1:76
03176-5	McDonnell-Douglas DC9-30	1:144	01705-1	World War II German Infantry	1:76
06173-5	Airbus A300B	1:144	01709-3	World War II 8th Army	1:76
03206-5	Narvik Class Destroyer	1:600	01748-8	USAF Personnel	1:76
06702-7	KM *Prinz Eugen*	1:600	01750-1	World War II Australian Infantry	1:76
09301-7	Suzuki TM-400J Cyclone	1:8	51653-6	Waterloo Assault Set	1:76
03452-8	Anne Boleyn	1:12	09655-1	Stalingrad German Attack Set	1:76
03453-1	Queen Elizabeth I	1:12	09656-4	Stalingrad Russian Defence	1:76
06301-8	Showjumper	1:12			

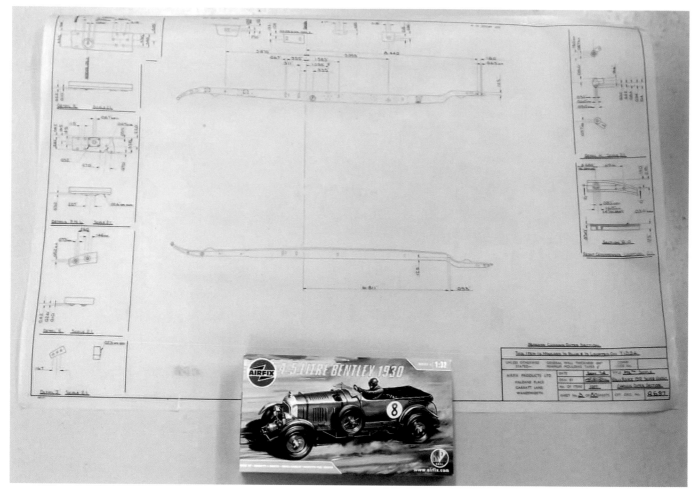

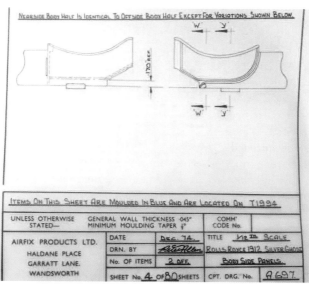

Plans for the proposed 1:12 Rolls-Royce kit, with a Bentley kit box to show the scale.

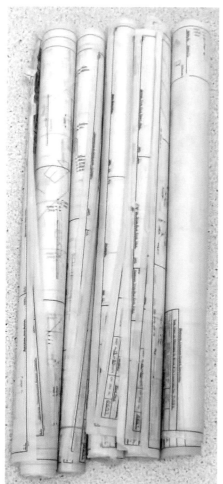

The Westland SB HAR 22 was a further refinement of the old S55 Whirlwind kit from 1956. It was released in Series 2 as it would not fit the 'blister'.

The Thunderstreak was very similar in design to the Shooting Star. It has been released fairly regularly over the years.

The DC9 complemented the BAC 1-11 and Boeing 737 kits. Like several of the airliners, it has received different liveries over the years. The Airbus A300B was the wide-body that started it all for Airbus. It was also the last box-top painting executed by Roy Cross before he left to pursue a career in marine painting.

Airfix chose two World War II German warships for its 1:600 range: the 'Narvik' class destroyer would match the several Royal Naval destroyers already offered by Airfix, and the *Prinz Eugen* accompanied *Bismarck* on her only operational voyage. The *Narvik* was last available in a set of four destroyers a few years ago, but *Prinz Eugen* was still available until 2014.

The Suzuki TM-400 Cyclone was the second in Airfix's range of large-scale motorcycles, and like the Honda 750 Four, used another manufacturer's mould.

After a break of several years, Airfix revisited its range of 1:12 figures by announcing two new figures of 'Famous Women of History' intended to appeal to girls. Two Tudor queens, Anne Boleyn and Elizabeth I, were announced. The kits were sold in Series 3, but they have not been available for many years.

The first horse and rider kit was also announced, the Showjumper. The female rider was clearly based on Princess Anne, although it was never officially confirmed. However, sales were so poor that, like the Boy Scout, it quickly disappeared and has not been re-released. In the late 1970s consideration was given to converting it into a mounted cowboy to try to improve sales, but this idea was not proceeded with.

Four new 54mm kits were revealed, two more from the Napoleonic wars and the first two of three figures for the forthcoming 200th anniversary of the American War of Independence. Only the Cuirassier has been released since 1981.

Three more 1:76 AFVs were added to the range. The Scorpion was one of the British Army's new light tanks recently introduced. As a 'modern' AFV it has tended to have a shorter production life as the original leaves service. The Chi-Ha was Airfix's only Japanese tank and along with the Reconnaissance Set, is still available. The Reconnaissance Set had two models of a Kubelwagen and a light armoured car with several nice figures included.

The range of 1:76 figures was expanded by four, although only two were new subjects, the German and 8th Army being replacements for the earlier sets. They featured new positions, plus those pantographed down from the later 1:32 figures. They utilized the catalogue numbers of their predecessors. The USAF Personnel joined the RAF Personnel, and the Australians were available to fight the new Chi-Ha tank. Like the other two sets of soldiers, they were based on the masters for the 1:32 figures.

A large Waterloo Assault Set was released, which included the eight sets previously released along with the Waterloo Farm House. Released only in the set was a 'farm' set, which included a couple of wagons, drivers and various loads. It was released again in 2008, in the Waterloo Battle Set, which this time included the later Prussian Infantry.

Four more 'Battlefront' sets were released, two for Stalingrad and two for Guadalcanal, which included the new Chi-Ha tank. The Stalingrad Set had the Germans as the attackers! All four sets are now highly collectable.

Rommel's Half-Track followed Monty's Humber and was re-released in 2013. It was a very detailed model and showed that Airfix could produce large-scale AFVs, which whilst perhaps not quite up to the standard of the Tamiya tanks, were a lot cheaper. Plans were drawn up to model Patton's Jeep, but this kit was not proceeded with.

Two more Waterloo sets were revealed in 1:32 scale; these were to be the last devoted to Waterloo in that scale. They could be released in time for the 200th anniversary of the Battle of Waterloo in 2015.

1975

In 1975 twenty-three new models and one modified model, the Control Tower, were announced:

02061	NA F-86D Sabre Dog	1:72
03026	Hawker Siddeley Hawk	1:72
04018	Short Skyvan	1:72
04019	Panavia MRCA 200	1:72
05013	Grumman F-14A Tomcat	1:72
18002	Junkers Ju 87B-2 *Stuka*	1:24
03380	RAF Control Tower	1:76
02073	HMS *Ark Royal*	1:1200
09281	German E-Boat	1:72
03442	Bugatti 35B	1:32
08401	1927 Lincoln Roadster	1:25
08301	Crusader II Tank	1:32
03580	8th Army – Multipose	1:32
03581	Afrika Korps – Multipose	1:32
51508	Desert Outpost	1:32

51509	Daimler Armoured Car	1:32
51510	Panzer IV Tank	1:32
51511	Combat Pack	1:32
51464	World War II US Paratroops	1:32
51465	Cowboys	1:32
51466	Indians	1:32
01751	World War II US Paratroops	1:76
01556	British Grenadier, 1776	54mm
01557	French Infantryman, 1815	54mm

Following the release of the Shooting Star, Airfix produced a decent model of another early US jet fighter, the Sabre. It chose the Sabre Dog, as the basic Sabre had been modelled by several other companies. It has not been released for many years. In 2003, Humbrol released the Heller Sabre in the range, and in 2010 Hornby produced two new Sabre kits.

The RAF's new advanced jet trainer, the Hawk, was modelled, based on the pre-production aircraft. It was a particularly fine model, and in 1980 it was released as a Red Arrows Hawk. It was a strong seller until it was replaced by the first of several new Hawk kits in 2008.

Short's rugged utility transport, the Skyvan, was moulded in Series 4. A cleverly designed kit, it was available as a civil model in Olympic Airways colours and a military version in the Sultan of Oman's colours. It has made sporadic appearances since 1981.

The MRCA, or Multi-Role Combat Aircraft prototype, produced by Panavia, was released in this year. In 1983 it was modified to produce the Tornado GR.1, and in 2004 was released as a GR.4/4A kit. Later it was also converted into the F.3 variant.

The new US Navy carrier-borne fighter, the Tomcat, was produced to the high standard Airfix was achieving with its jet aircraft. It remained in the catalogue for many years, but has now been withdrawn.

A magnificent model of the infamous *Stuka* joined the 1:24 range. It was beautifully detailed, and one modelling magazine at the time described it as the 'finest model aircraft kit of all time'! It is also memorable for John Grey's insistence that the box-top illustration show the aircraft in its famous role – dive-bombing. The excellent Ken McDonough painting required the box to be produced in 'portrait' mode, and many retailers were worried that it might topple off high shelves. A later Humbrol release showed the aircraft in 'landscape' mode. It is still in the range today, sporting a new Adam Tooby illustration, in 'landscape' mode.

In 2014 I managed to speak to the retired toolmaker responsible for the Stuka mould. Now aged ninety-one, Basil Wallis told me that it was one of the few tools that did not require much modification before going into production. He said the tool took over two years to complete, and he remembered having to put in all the rivet detail and some panel lines by hand. Three other moulds were required for the rubber tyres, clear cockpit glazing and the stand for the kit.

To go with its growing range of RAF airfield sets, Airfix added extra parts to its old 1959 Control Tower kit and re-released it. The kit is still in production today.

The 1:1200 range of Waterline Warships, themed around the 'Sink the

Bismarck' story, received a model of HMS *Ark Royal*. This range was dropped in 1981, but thirty years later they all returned in the 'Sink the *Bismarck*' set released by Hornby.

The only other ship model was a lovely replica of a German *Schnellboot* or 'E'-Boat to 1:72 scale. It returned to the range in 2013.

Vintage cars saw a 1:32 scale Bugatti 35B modelled and an ex-MPC 1927 Lincoln Roadster added to the 1:25 range. The Bugatti was released in the 'special edition' range in the late 1980s. In the 1990s, Humbrol proposed a 1:12 Bugatti 35 but did not go ahead with it.

Airfix decided not to pursue its range of 'celebrity' AFVs in 1:32 and so a proposed kit of Patton's jeep was stillborn. Instead, the first of a small range of World War II AFVs was announced, being a good model of a Crusader III tank. Although Airfix had a large range of buildings and figures to 1:32 scale, the huge number of Japanese kits being produced to 1:35 scale meant that Airfix was 'up against it', and the range was never really developed as it should have been. After a long time out of production, the kit did return in 2005 in a Desert Rat Set, which included the Multipose 8th Army and Afrika Korps kits.

The last two mentioned kits were the first of an exciting new range of kits to be produced to support the 1:32 AFVs. The multipose concept utilized separate bodies, arms, legs and heads for the soldiers; once assembled, separate packs, weapons and helmets could be added. It was similar in many respects to the 54mm collectors' kits. Some Japanese

Scottish Aviation Bulldog model released in 1975. AIRFIX

Basil Wallis and his Stuka *kit.*

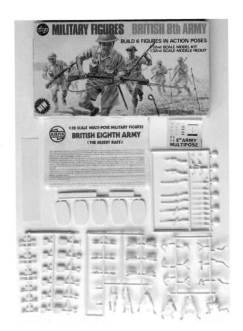

8th Army 'Multi Pose' set from 1975.

manufacturers had produced similar sets, but Airfix scored in that the faces were all individual. The parts to make six figures were included, but the instructions showed that twelve different poses could easily be made. In reality, by playing around with the parts, many more positions could be created. Seven sets would eventually be produced. In the 1990s, Humbrol released them with parts for twelve figures in a box, and in 2014, three sets were released as starter sets.

A 1:32 scale clip-together Desert Outpost kit was produced to go with the above. A 'polyprop' Panzer IV Tank and a Daimler Armoured Car were announced. I don't think they were ever available as separate models, but they were included in the Desert Combat Pack available in 1977. Later they were produced by Humbrol for CTS to sell in the USA.

The Combat Pack was the first of two combat packs to be announced. It included the Strongpoint, Cromwell Tank, German Half-Track and two sets of 1:32 figures. Also included were plastic pill boxes which fired discs, presumably to knock over enemy soldiers. Cardboard scenery completed the set. Both sets are highly sought after by collectors.

Three further sets of 1:32 figures were revealed. The US Paratroops were produced in 1:32 and 1:76 scales, being produced from the same patterns. The Cowboys and Indians were tooled together. A third tool with six horses and saddles was made, which could be added to each set. The horses could also be used with the forthcoming 7th Cavalry Set.

The final two kits were 54mm figure kits. The British Grenadier completed Airfix's figures for the 200th anniversary

1975's Desert Outpost kit.

The impressive combat pack from 1975.

ABOVE: *54mm Collectors' Series figures, 1975.*

LEFT: *1975's 'Datachart'.*

of the Declaration of Independence. The French Infantryman was the final Waterloo Infantry figure in the range. Neither is currently available.

Also released in 1975 was the first in a new series of Datacharts. This poster came in a triangular box and had details of World War II Luftwaffe fighters. The Roy Cross painting of the 1:24 Bf 109E was prominent. Sadly the range does not appear to have gone beyond number 1. A calendar for 1975 was sold, which featured Roy Cross artwork and the Bentley by Stephen Hipwell.

1976

Thirty-six new models were announced in 1976, although eight were from other manufacturers; nevertheless it was still an excellent year for modellers:

02047	Fouga Magister	1:72
02048	Messerschmitt Bf 109E	1:72
03011	SEPECAT Jaguar GR.1	1:72
03025	Westland Army Lynx AH.1	1:72
04008	General Dynamics F-111E	1:72
06175	Concorde (production version)	1:144
06174	*Space 1999* Eagle Transporter	N/A
03443	1933 MG Magnette	1:32
08364	M3 Lee Mk 1 Tank	1:32
08365	M3 Grant Tank	1:32

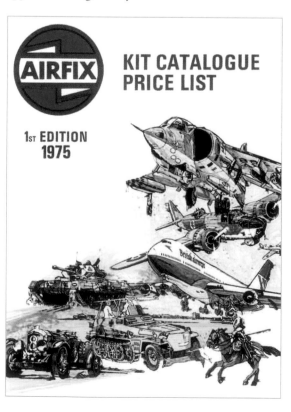

LEFT: *First edition of the 1975 leaflet.*

RIGHT: *Bengal Lancer in the 54mm Collector's Series, 1976.*

The Fouga Magister was a replica of the French 'butterfly-tailed' trainer that was in widespread use. It was heavily riveted, which tended to spoil the slim lines of the original. It was produced sporadically after 1981, though did return in 2014. The Bf 109E is famous as the Battle of Britain version of the famous German fighter. It was a very good model, but unfortunately again heavily riveted. In 2012, Hornby produced a new-mould kit to replace it.

The Jaguar and F-111E were both minor updatings of the original kits which made them current. In 2004, the Jaguar was again updated to the latest GR.3A – but neither it nor the F-111E are produced any longer.

The Lynx was one of three helicopters, the others being the Puma and Gazelle, which were produced jointly by the British and French for their armed forces. The Lynx kit was designed as one standard mould to produce the model with separate runners to make the specific Army and Navy versions. The Navy Lynx was announced the following year. The Army Lynx has never been updated, but was sold regularly for many years.

Airfix's original Concorde was released in 1967 and was based on the prototype. The new kit was to the final production standard. Following the withdrawal of Concorde from service it, too, has returned to the hangar.

ABOVE: *1976 Stuka diorama in 1:24 scale.* AIRFIX

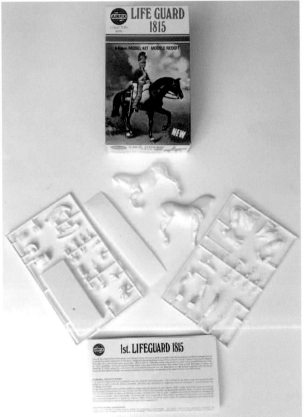

LEFT: *1815 Life Guard from 1976 in the 54mm Collectors' Series.*

BELOW: *First issue of the Fouga Magister kit, in a Type 4C box with artwork by Ken McDonough, 1976.*

ABOVE: *First edition of the 1976 leaflet.*

LEFT: *The September 1976 Marketing Review.*

BELOW: *1976 Scalecraft catalogue.*

The Eagle Transporter was one of several models produced to tie in with the television series *Space 1999* and was possibly tooled by Esci. Since 1981 it has not featured in the Airfix range, but is available from other manufacturers.

The MG Magnette was the last of Airfix's 1:32 vintage cars to be produced. Humbrol sold it as a 'special edition', but it has not been sold recently. It was also proposed by Humbrol as a 1:12 model but was never produced.

Airfix introduced two fine kits of the American Lee and Grant tanks to 1:32 scale. Basically they were one mould with separate runners so the two slightly differ-ent variants could be made. Along with the Lynx helicopters it showed a develop-ing trend by Airfix to produce 'two for the price of one' kits.

The Desert Combat Pack and Checkpoint were both designed for use with the 'polyprop' vehicles and the soldier sets. The Combat Pack combined the Desert Outpost and the two AFVs from the previous year with two sets of figures, some cardboard scenery and a pillbox that fired discs to knock the soldiers down! The two Combat Packs are now highly sought after, but oddly, the Panzer IV and Daimler AFVs do not appear to have been available separately.

However, Humbrol did supply them to CTS in America in the 1990s. Checkpoint was a kind of frontier outpost with a bridge, watch tower, sentry box and barrier. The bridge seems to be based on the Motor Ace 'Hump-Back' bridge, only smaller. The mould appears to have been damaged, and I understand CTS paid to have it repaired before selling it. It was released in 2014 by Hornby as 'Frontier Checkpoint'.

Popular though 1:32 scale was, the arrival of Tamiya and many Far-Eastern kit companies in the 1960s who all picked 1:35 scale for their military vehicles and figures meant that Airfix risked being side-lined for its use of 1:32 scale. The Japanese company MAX had produced a wide range of 1:35 AFVs, and the company that later acquired MAX granted Airfix a licence to sell these kits in the UK, Europe, South Africa and Australia. It was a cost-effective way of Airfix getting a foothold in the 1:35 market. They were sold in the late 1970s, but moved else-where when Airfix went under in 1981.

In 1:76 scale Airfix produced a lovely model of a Bofors Gun with a Tractor. It is still in production today. The Forward Command Post was a scaling down of the 1:32 Strongpoint clip-together kit, both of which are still in production.

Three more 54mm kits were announced: a Lifeguard to add to the Waterloo range, and a Bengal Lancer and French Foreign Legionnaire to cover different eras. The Lifeguard has been available more often than the other two.

In 1:12 scale, Airfix revealed the last of the range of 'Famous Women of History' kits, a young Queen Victoria. More excit-ing was the release of a kit of the 54mm French Imperial Guardsman. It looked as if we were going to see all the other kits produced to this size, and the Bengal Lancer was announced in 1979. Sadly they were the only two kits to be produced in 1:12 scale. They were based on the original 1:12 scale patterns, which no longer exist. The Bengal Lancer did receive a brief release by Humbrol.

Several 1:76 and 1:32 scale figures were announced. The World War II soldiers were all based on joint patterns to reduce cost. The German Mountain Troops was a particularly innovative set, while the Luftwaffe Personnel completed the sets of World War II airfield figures.

A set of US Cavalry, which shared the horses from the Cowboys and Indians, was introduced, along with a set of Modern British Infantry. The latter were very fine mouldings but unfortunately quickly dated and lacked suitable opponents. The addition of Modern German Infantry didn't really help! However, both sets could be used with the 'modern' 1:32 'polyprops'.

In an attempt to broaden the appeal of kit-making and attract a wider audience, the first of a new range of British birds was produced, a pair of bullfinches. They were very attractive models, and the range was expanded to six different birds – but ultimately they were unable to compete with Spitfires and Tiger Tanks for the modellers' pocket money.

Finally, Airfix produced a run of two ex-MPC 'horror' kits of giant-sized 'creepy-crawlies'! They were not particularly popular, but because they utilized the American packaging, they were relatively inexpensive to produce. Airfix-packaged versions are now much sought after by collectors.

Ex-MAX Dodge Command Car, 1976.

1977

1977 was another good year, with thirty-four kits announced and thirty-three actually released:

01063	Messerschmitt Me 163B *Komet*	1:72
02062	Britten-Norman BN2 Defender	1:72
02063	Focke-Wulf Fw 190A-8/F-8	1:72
02064	Westland Whirlwind Mk I	1:72
03024	Westland Navy Lynx HAS Mk 2	1:72
03027	Douglas F4D-1 Skyray	1:72
03028	Henschel Hs 126A1/B1	1:72
04020	Dornier Do 217E/J	1:72
05014	Lockheed S-3A Viking	1:72
04100	Supermarine Spitfire Mk Vb	1:48
04101	Messerschmitt Bf 109F	1:48
07100	DH Mosquito FB.VI	1:48
10201	USS *Forrestal*	1:600
01231	HMS *Suffolk*	1:1200
02233	KM *Prinz Eugen*	1:1200
09258	*Golden Hind*	1:72
11481	Honda Road Racer	1:8
08366	Bedford QL and Six-Pounder Gun	1:35
08367	Chevrolet 15cwt Truck and Gun	1:35
08368	British Field Gun Tractor	1:35
07501	Bengal Lancer, 1901	1:12
01559	English Civil War Pikeman	54mm
01560	English Civil War Musketeer	54mm
02558	Roundhead/Cavalier, 1642	54mm
04582	World War II German Infantry	1:32
04583	World War II US Marines	1:32
04584	World War II Japanese Infantry	1:32
03831	Blue Tits	1:1
03800	Tyrannosaurus Rex	N/A
03801	Triceratops	N/A
51471	World War II Gurkhas	1:32
51473	Modern German Infantry	1:32
04381	Jungle Headquarters	1:76
01732	World War II British Commandos	1:76

With the exception of the three ex-MAX 1:35 AFVs and the ex-MPC motorcycle, all the releases were Airfix moulds.

The Messerschmitt *Komet* was a neat little model of the late war German rocket-propelled interceptor. It has not featured in the range in the last few years, however, and the mould tool was on display in the Hornby Visitor's Centre until displayed at RAF Hendon in the Airfix Box Art Exhibition, in 2013.

The Defender and Do 217 were minor modifications of existing kits, and the Navy Lynx was the second of the new Lynx kits. All have featured recently in

1977's Me 163 Komet model. AIRFIX

ABOVE: *Box artwork and actual models for the 1977 German infantry multipurpose kit.* AIRFIX

LEFT: *French Grenadier models of 1973 (left) and 1977 compared.*

the catalogue and the Lynx has been upgraded to the latest HMA.8 standard.

The Focke-Wulf was Airfix's first attempt at the early Fw190 variants. A good model, it was finally replaced by a new tool in 2013. The Westland Whirlwind was the replacement for the old 1958 kit and was a vast improvement, but is not currently available.

The Skyray, Henschel and Viking were all new to the range. The Henschel was briefly re-released in the 1990s, but otherwise these have not been seen for many years.

Airfix announced a new range of 1:48 scale aircraft. This scale was very popular in the United States, where it was also known as 'quarter scale'. The models chosen to launch the range were very famous aircraft, although the first didn't appear until 1979. The Mosquito was originally intended to be modelled to 1:24 scale, but Airfix abandoned it when the costs escalated too much. Hornby launched a 1:24 Mosquito in 2009 to show that Airfix was back!

The Spitfire and Mosquito both had extra parts added over the years to make further versions. The Spitfire was replaced by an all-new kit in 2014.

The USS *Forrestal* was a replica of the first big US aircraft carrier. It has appeared occasionally over the years. *Suffolk* and *Prinz Eugen* were additions to the 1:1200 Waterline Warships range, which was themed around the hunt for the *Bismarck*. The range of 1:1200 kits was unavailable for years until Hornby released them all in a 'Sink the *Bismarck*' set in 2011.

The *Golden Hind* was the large-scale version of the original Airfix kit produced in the early 1950s. It was moulded to 1:72 scale and featured crew figures. The box-top painting was by Geoff Hunt, who had replaced Brian Knight as the main painter for the large sailing ships. Geoff Hunt would later become famous for painting the covers to the Patrick O'Brian novels about Jack Aubrey, played by Russell Crowe in the film *Master and Commander*.

The Bengal Lancer was the second and last of the 54mm kits to be produced at 1:12 scale. Three more 54mm were announced covering the English Civil War. The mounted figure was cleverly designed so that either a Cavalier or Roundhead figure could be completed. They were out of production for many years, but in 2007 were all released in an 'English Civil War Collection', which included two

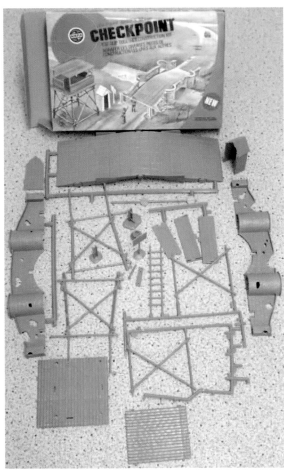

LEFT: *1977 'Checkpoint' kit.*

BELOW LEFT: *From the Collector's Series, 'English Pikemen 1642' from 1977.*

BELOW RIGHT: *First edition of the 1977 leaflet.*

mounted figure kits to enable all the options to be modelled.

Three more sets of Multipose figures were listed, and like the first two sets, were very well detailed. The second of the Wildlife kits was issued, being a model of a pair of Blue Tits. An exciting new range of kits for younger modellers was announced with the release of two kits of Dinosaur models. They were all to different scales. Thirty years later, six were released again in two sets of three models.

The 1:32 scale soldiers saw the addition of a set of Gurkhas and, surprisingly, a set of Modern German Infantry. Quite who the Germans were meant to fight I do not know, but they were very well moulded. They have not been seen for many years.

Finally in 1:76 scale, a scaled-down Jungle Outpost kit was revealed which included a vacuum-formed base. A second-edition set of British Commandos replaced the original 1968 set. Unfortunately the tool appears to have been lost, as the original tool is the one that is in use today.

1978

A total of thirty new kits was announced in 1978, and twenty-five new kits were released:

01064	Focke-Wulf Fw 190D	1:72
01065	Supermarine Spitfire Mk Ia	1:72
01068	MBB BO 105C Helicopter	1:72
02049	Junkers Ju 87B-2 *Stuka*	1:72
02065	Boeing Sea Knight Helicopter	1:72
02066	North American P-51B Mustang	1:72
02067	Hawker Hurricane Mk I	1:72
03030	Junkers Ju 87B/R *Stuka*	1:72
04022	Dassault Mirage F.1C	1:72
05015	F-15A/B Eagle	1:72
06177	McDD DC10-30	1:144
10170	Space Shuttle	1:144
05175	Pan-Am Orion 2001	N/A
07170	Starcruiser 1	N/A
06404	Stutz Bearcat	1:25
08440	1932 Chrysler Imperial	1:25
04585	World War II British Infantry	1:32
04586	World War II US Infantry (Europe)	1:32
08369	Dodge 3/4-ton Ambulance	1:35
08370	Steyr Tractor and *Nebelwerfer*	1:35
08371	US Army 2.5-ton Truck	1:35
04382	North African Outpost	1:76
05281	RAF Rescue Launch	1:72
04380	Robins	1:1
03802	Ankylosaurus	N/A
03803	Stegosaurus	N/A
03804	Corythosaurus	N/A
03805	Dimetrodon	N/A
01756	Waterloo Prussian Infantry	1:76
51474	Medieval Foot Soldiers	1:32

The Focke-Wulf and two *Stukas* were designed to replace the 1950s models.

The two *Stuka* kits were separate moulds, but the Series 3 kit contained extra parts to make the 'R' version, along with two sets of decals. Both have appeared regularly over the years.

The Mustang, Spitfire and Hurricane were all early versions of the existing Airfix kits and did not replace them. In 2010, Airfix produced a new Spitfire Ia, and an early Mk I Hurricane was released late in 2013. The Spitfire was similar to the 1974 Mk Vb, and it has been suggested that it is the top-selling Airfix kit of all time.

The BO 105C was a new helicopter to the range, but the Sea Knight was a revision of the old Vertol 107-11 from 1965.

The Mirage F.1C and F-15A/B Eagle were models of two new aircraft. The F-15 was later upgraded to the F-15E Strike Eagle in 1993. Both are currently out of production.

Two new 1:144 kits were revealed: the DC10-30 was first issued in British Caledonian markings; and the Space Shuttle was reissued for the twenty-fifth anniversary, and was in the range until 2014.

Two 'sci-fi' kits were added: the Orion was a re-issue of the 1969 kit, and the Starcruiser was one of a small range of Airfix-designed 'sci-fi' kits. The Orion was sold as a 'SNAPnglue' kit in 1981 and released as recently as 2000.

The third kit in the range of 1:72 fast patrol boats was revealed as the RAF Rescue Launch. It is currently in the range again. Airfix was well advanced with plans to make a US PT boat and a replica of the Fairmile 'D' fast patrol boat, but sadly these were cancelled shortly before Airfix went under.

Two more 1:25 cars were introduced from MPC moulds: the Stutz Bearcat and Chrysler Imperial. A further three ex-MAX 1:35 AFV kits were listed, but although decals, instructions and boxes were prepared, I don't think they were ever released by Airfix.

What were to be the final two multipose kits, the British and US Infantry sets,

were released. Possibly poor sales put paid to future sets, but I would have loved to have seen sets of Napoleonic figures produced in the multipose format.

The 1975 Desert Outpost was scaled down to 1:76 scale and issued as the North African Outpost with a vacuum-formed base. Recent releases of the 1:76 buildings have not included the bases. A set of Waterloo Prussian Infantry increased to nine the number of Waterloo figure sets in 1:76 scale. They were last issued in the 2008 Waterloo Battle Set. Also released and using the same box illustration was a new set of US Marines to 1:76 scale. They were not advertised. A similar new set of Foreign Legion figures had earlier been released, probably in 1972, and again used the existing illustration. It was by chance that I discovered these new sets.

For the latest set of 1:32 figures, Airfix moved from the safe option of World War II soldiers to produce a set of medieval men-at-arms. They were reissued briefly in 1995 in a bag of six figures.

A pair of robins became the third set of British birds to be announced, and four more dinosaurs joined the first two prehistoric monsters.

It was also announced that as from the October 1978 issue of *Airfix Magazine*,

Gresham Books would take over the publication of the magazine. PSL, which had been printing *Airfix Magazine* for eleven years, would continue to publish its range of modelling books, but there would be no more books published in conjunction with Airfix.

1979

In 1979 only nine new kits were announced, although some twenty-five were actually released, which reduced the backlog. The new releases consisted of the following:

03035	Alpha Jet	1:72
04023	McDonnell F2H Banshee	1:72
08173	Braniff 'Big Orange' Boeing 747	1:144
10171	'Moonraker' Space Shuttle	1:144
09259	HMS *Bounty*	1:87
20480	Norton 'Commando'	1:8
20481	BMW R75/5	1:8
02315	Opel *Blitz* and Pak 40 Gun	1:76
03651	Platform Figures	1:76

The Alpha Jet and Banshee were both new moulds. The Alpha Jet, which was the main competitor to the BAe Hawk, has been issued occasionally over the years, but the

Banshee has not been seen for many years. The Banshee was apparently chosen for production instead of the Sea Vixen, probably with an eye on the US market.

The 'Big Orange' 747 was the standard 747 kit but with Braniff's unusual orange scheme applied. The kit was known at Airfix as the 'Big Banana' because the illustration appeared to show the fuselage curved like a banana! The 'Moonraker' Space Shuttle was a version of this space craft, which featured decals to match the ones used in the James Bond film of the same name. As a film tie-in, it had a brief life, but of course the Space Shuttle was unaffected by this.

HMS *Bounty* was to be the last of the large sailing ships produced by Airfix. It was noted by the designers of the kit that the hull shape and dimensions were very close to those of the *Endeavour*, Airfix's first large sailing ship kit. Work on a replica of the *Santa Maria* was well advanced, but it was cancelled as the financial situation worsened.

The two motorcycles were produced from moulds purchased from Heller. Two variants would follow in 1980, but none is currently available.

The Opel *Blitz* and Pak 40 Gun was a decent model of the German World War

The 1979 Braniff 'Big Orange' Boeing 747 kit. AIRFIX

Junkers Ju 87B Stuka *from 1979.*

II combination. It is the only one of the 1980 introductions which is still in the catalogue.

Finally, Airfix released the first of two sets of figures to go with its new Train sets and existing Trackside kits. The two sets were later sold to Dapol, which company produces them today.

The big news for 1979, however, was the decision to rotate many of the older moulds. A great many shops found they could not stock the entire range of Airfix kits as there were simply too many of them. Some older kits were advertised in the catalogue each year but were not actually issued at that time.

So Airfix decided to withdraw many of its older kits to leave a core range, and then rotate the withdrawn moulds on a three-year cycle. This immediately reduced the number of kits in the range and meant that when models did return they could receive new colours and squadron markings. Virtually all the existing kits had for the previous twenty years used the same

LEFT: *Geoff Hunt's artwork for the 1979 release of the HMS* Cambeltown *model.* Cambeltown *was the destroyer packed with explosives and then deliberately crashed into the dry dock at St Nazaire in the daring raid of 28 March 1942.*

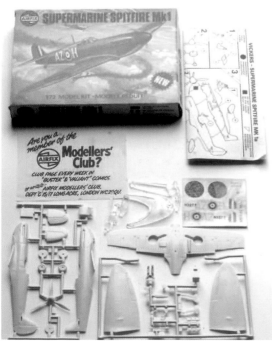

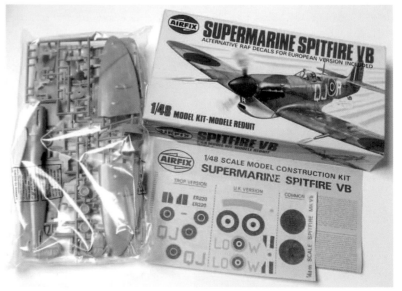

Spitfire Mk Ia and MkVB kits, 1979.

decals and colours. Airfix referred to these re-released kits, including the non-aircraft kits, as 'new squadron' releases.

The change of markings meant that the existing illustrations could not be used, so the likes of Ken McDonough and Ron Jobson would repaint the box tops for a 'new squadron' release. Thereafter it has been the policy of Airfix to offer a core range of kits each year, with certain kits making a come-back for a short period. Some kits turn up regularly, but others disappeared from the range for twenty or more years, or have not yet reappeared.

Thus 1979 was not a very exciting year for Airfix modellers, although the release of many of the previous year's new models would keep most of them happy.

Grumman Avenger box from 1979.

1980

Things looked up in 1980, when thirty new kits were announced and thirty-three were released. The new additions were as follows:

03036	MiG-23 Flogger	1:72
08002	Avro Lancaster BIII	1:72
04102	Hawker Hurricane Mk I	1:48
04103	Hawker Fury Mk I	1:48
16001	Focke-Wulf Fw 190A-8/F	1:24
06179	McDD DC10-30 – (SAS)	1:144
05174	Starcruiser Interceptor	N/A
08175	Cosmic Clipper	N/A
06405	Lancia Stratos	1:24
06406	Triumph TR7	1:24
06407	Ferrari 365 Boxer	1:24
06408	Porsche 934/5	1:24
06409	Datsun 280Z	1:24
06410	Mustang Cobra II	1:24
06412	Lamborghini Countach L500S	1:24
07401	Maserati Merak	1:24
07402	Lotus Elite	1:24
07404	BMW M1 Coupé	1:24
16401	Ford C900 Tractor and 40in Trailer	1:32
20482	Norton SS	1:8
20483	BMW Polizei	1:8
06361	17-Pdr Anti-Tank Gun and Crew 1:32	
51494	World War I British Infantry	1:32
51575	World War II British Infantry	1:32
51576	World War II Italian Infantry	1:32
51514	Sherman Tank	1:32
01757	World War II Italian Infantry	1:76
03628	Railway Workers	1:76
04831	Kingfisher	1:1
03806	Pteranodon	N/A

The 'Flogger' was a nicely detailed model of the then current Russian fighter, but it

Ken McDonough's Spitfire Mk.Ia artwork from 1979.

has not been seen for a few years. The Lancaster was the eagerly awaited replacement for the first of Airfix's large aircraft kits released in 1958. It was a magnificent model, and over the next thirty years would also be sold as a Dambusters and Grand Slam variant. Despite recent releases from other manufacturers, it was still considered superior in some areas. In 2013, in time for the seventieth anniversary of the Dambusters raid, a brand new tool was released: it is so far available in Dambusters, BIII and BII variants. It is an exceptionally fine model, and now also appears in the Battle of Britain Memorial Flight sets.

A good replica of the Hurricane Mk I joined the 1:48 range, and is still in production today. In 2015, Airfix is to release a new Hurricane Mk I. The Hawker Fury was an unfinished mould that was bought from Merit and then finished by Airfix. It is the only pre-World War II aircraft in the 1:48 range, and was still in the catalogue in 2014.

The Focke-Wulf Fw 190A-8/F was the last of the 1:24 superkits to be designed by Airfix before the 1981 closure. It was slightly simplified but had very good surface detail. It is still in the catalogue in 2014, but now has an Adam Tooby box top.

The DC10 was an accurate replica of the TriStar's main rival, and the kit has been released regularly over the years. Two sci-fi kits were released, but these only had a short life.

Airfix had bought the moulds for around a dozen Japanese-designed car and lorry kits, and released them as a fairly economical way of expanding the range. They were later released by Humbrol. Two further 1:8 motorcycles were released using the moulds previously bought from Heller.

One of the most exciting kits to be announced was a 1:32 scale model of the famous British 17-pounder field gun. It was a highly accurate model and came with a set of figures to fire it. Unfortunately, due to budget restrictions, a set of British

ABOVE: *Airfix Lancia Stratos and Triumph TR7 from 1980.* AIRFIX

LEFT: *1980 Lesser Spotted Woodpecker kit.* AIRFIX

Infantry multipose figures was included rather than specially designed figures. This tended to show the versatility of the 'multipose' concept, as the parts could be used to make gunners for the kit. However, it was still a very nice model which is today sought-after due to its comparatively short production life. Airfix had exciting plans for new 1:76 and 1:32 AFVs and tanks, but again the deteriorating financial position meant that work on them was stopped or slowed right down.

A long-awaited set of World War II British Infantry was released alongside a set of Italian Infantry in 1:32 scale. The first of what was expected to be the up-scaling of the 1:76 World War I figures was announced but never actually released; I don't think they were ever tooled. The Italians were also released at 1:76 scale and these are still available today.

The Railway Workers was the second set of railway figures to be released at this time by Airfix, and there were plans to release all the train and Trackside kits in 1981 – but as we now know, this was not to happen.

The Sherman Tank was the latest in the range of 'polyprop' 1:32 AFVs, but was not released by Airfix. It was later released by Classic Toy Soldiers in the US, for which company it was manufactured by Humbrol.

A 'life-size' kit of the kingfisher bird was added to the range. Since it was larger than the other birds, only one bird was included, but there was a nice log with a fish in the bird's mouth to make a mini diorama.

For dinosaur enthusiasts a model of the pteranodon joined the small range of dinosaur models.

This was an interesting selection, but not so great once the purchased moulds are removed. However, there were some very expensive tools in there, which showed that Airfix was still committed to developing its large kit range. The payback time for tool costs was increasing alarmingly and many small kits would now require several years, even decades, to reach profitability – a far cry from the heady days of the 1950s and 1960s when the initial Woolworth's order paid for the development cost. The much higher selling price of the large kits meant that the money could be recouped in a much shorter time, but the problem with large kits was that the initial outlay was considerably higher, and reduced cash flow meant that they couldn't always be produced.

Had Airfix survived the events of 1981, it is likely that several of these kits might still have not repaid their tooling costs by today, such is the effect of the downturn in the kit market that was starting to appear in the late 1970s. However, it would have had a back catalogue of 500 to 600 'paid for' kits to sustain it and generate money for new models.

LEFT: *December 1980 advert for the new SNAPnglue range.*

BELOW LEFT: *17-Pounder gun and crew kit from 1980.*

BELOW RIGHT: *Type 6 box of Japanese infantry figures, 1980.*

BOTTOM RIGHT: *1980's Starcruiser Interceptor SNAPnglue kit.*

1981

A thinner catalogue devoted to 1981's new releases was produced, but very few were distributed before Airfix went into receivership during the January 1981 Toy Fair: a cruel irony. Forty models were announced, but twenty-four were cars or vehicles produced from moulds either bought by Airfix or 'polybagged' in.

04024	McDD F-18A Hornet	1:72
04025	F-16A/B Fighting Falcon	1:72
06003	HH-53C Super Jolly Green Giant	1:72
06004	CH-53G/CH-53D Helicopter	1:72
05100	Junkers Ju 87B *Stuka*	1:48
16001	Focke-Wulf Fw 190A-5	1:24
06205	HMS *Repulse*	1:600
96206	HMS *King George V*	1:600
01758	NATO Ground Crew	1:76
51577	Space Warriors	1:32
04382	Lesser Spotted Woodpecker	1:1
06360	Little Owl	1:1

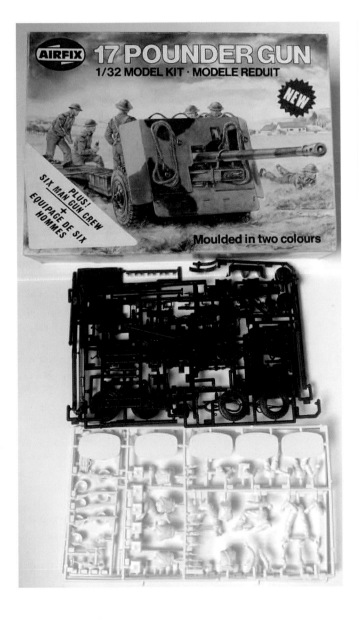

Type 6 box, containing 1980's MiG-23 Flogger kit.

04800	Brontosaurus	N/A
09174	Cosmic Starship	N/A
04213	Nautilus	N/A
04401	Kansas Kruiser	1:32
04402	Night Prowler	1:32
04403	Krackle Kat	1:32
04404	Rebel Rouser	1:32
14401	Ford C-800 Truck	1:32
04851?	Orange Tip Butterfly	1:1
04851?	Peacock Butterfly	1:1
06413	Maserati Bora	1:24
06414	Mazda RX7	1:24
06415	Porsche 935 Turbo	1:24
06416	Turbo Firebird	1:24
06417	Turbo-Vette	1:24
06418	Mustang Cobra	1:24
06419	Camaro Z28	1:24
06420	Firebird Type K Sportwagon	1:24
06421	Custom Mustang	1:24
06422	Camaro Ultra Z	1:24
06423	Custom Corvette	1:24
06424	Renault Alpine	1:24
06425	Maserati Boomerang	1:24
06426	BMW 3.5CSL	1:24
06427	De Tomaso Pantera	1:24
07406	Datsun 280ZX	1:24

I did not acquire my copy of the catalogue until nearly twenty years after, and today copies of the 1981 catalogue are very hard to come by.

The four new 1:72 aircraft kits were very attractive replicas of the latest US Air Force and Navy combat aircraft. The two fighters would be upgraded and new decals added over the years. The two large helicopters were in fact one mould that was released as two separate variants. It was part of the new policy to maximize the returns on a new mould. In the past Airfix had tended to mould one variant of an aircraft or tank; now they would be able to sell two models from the one mould. In recent years, Hornby has tooled up a basic mould to make a particular aircraft and then produced smaller tools to make further variants. It is a very cost-effective idea and means that multiple variants can be sold at relatively little extra cost.

As mentioned earlier, the main problem facing Airfix was that the time taken to recover the mould cost had increased dramatically, and the number of kits produced at each production run was steadily falling. Where once it had taken just a year or so to recoup the cost of production, now it was slipping into years and sometimes decades.

The *Stuka* was the latest in the new range of 1:48 aircraft kits, and was a very fine model that had benefited from the work done on the 1:24 kit. It would not be released until after the Palitoy takeover.

The Focke-Wulf Fw190A kit had been released just before Christmas, but was officially unveiled in the new catalogue. It is often regarded as Airfix's 'swan song' – and not a bad one at that.

Airfix had not been producing many new 1:600 warships, but surprised us all by announcing the introduction of fine models of HMS *King George V* and HMS *Repulse*, both involved in the *Bismarck* chase. Plans to release a model of HMS *Sheffield* were scuttled at the last moment. Again the ships would not be released until after Palitoy took over.

The OO/HO range of figures would see an attractive set of modern NATO Airfield Personnel added to the range to join the three earlier World War II sets. There was no mention of the 1:32 World War I British Infantry, but in their place was a set of Space Warriors. These figures seemed to be based on 1940s and 1950s sci-fi characters, and even included a female warrior in a short skirt! They have only appeared briefly once since, when Humbrol released six figures in a bag.

Two more single birds and a dinosaur kit were introduced. The bird kits have not been produced since the early 1980s, although they have been released by Gunze Sanyko in Japan on two separate occasions.

Along with the Space Warriors, Airfix proposed to release several kits from the realms of fantasy. The Cosmic Starship was an Airfix design, and the Nautilus was based on the ship in the Walt Disney film *Twenty Thousand Leagues under the Sea*. It does seem a strange choice, but presumably the tooling costs were low and they hoped to sell plenty of kits. It was finally tooled by Palitoy, but it was decided not to release it. Comet Miniatures did release a resin version produced using a test shot; the whereabouts of the mould is not known, but it was probably scrapped.

The four modern cars are interesting. The original kits were of modern cars of the 1960s, but by 1979 they were in a state of limbo, being no longer 'modern' but not old enough to be 'classic' or 'vintage'. Humbrol and Hornby have been able to re-release them as they are now considered to be classic cars of the 1960s! Sales were tailing off considerably, so Airfix asked toy designer Graham Westoll to look at ways of making the moulds relevant to the 1980s and thereby squeezing a few more sales out of them. His solution was to convert an initial four kits to 'hot rod' or 'streetwise' cars with colour schemes and decals to make them 'cool'. This involved some revision to the moulds, but Airfix felt that the existing kits were 'dead in the water' anyway so they had nothing to lose. In the end only three were actually released, and then only for a short while. They command high prices when they do turn up on eBay. They are unlikely to be re-released, but you never know.

Finally from its own moulds, Airfix proposed to release kits of butterflies to go with its bird kits. A swallow was under way, and artwork was prepared for a red squirrel. The moulds for the butterflies and their transparent wings were made and are now with Hornby, but the butterflies never emerged from their cocoons.

The rest of the kits were releases of the ex-Japanese tools Airfix had recently acquired. They were also re-released by USAirfix, which produced much needed license income for Airfix.

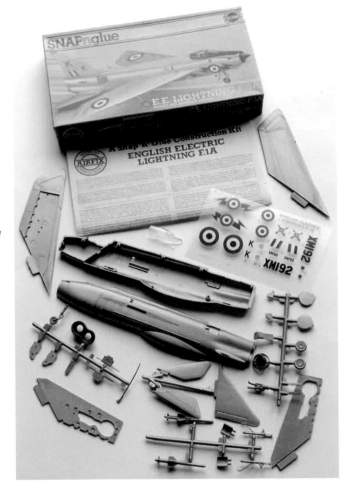

1981's Lighting F.1A kit.

buyout was proposed, and Peter Allen says that many of the employees got out their chequebooks in anticipation. In the end the receivers announced that the bid from General Mills of the United States had been accepted. Humbrol, which was keen to buy Airfix, was 'pipped to the post' but would get another chance in 1986.

Thus the large Airfix company that many of us had grown up with was no more. In the last year or so Airfix had sold its packaging and houseware divisions to help reduce its bank borrowings. Meccano, the losses at which were largely responsible for the poor state of the group's finances, had also been closed. Palitoy, General Mills' British subsidiary, absorbed the Great Model Railways into its Mainline range, and later sold the Trackside kits to Dapol, which continues to produce them. Airfix/MRRC racing sets were taken over by MRRC and moved to Jersey. Just as the Airfield Control Tower was the only Trackside kit not sold to Dapol, the Austin Mini was the only modern car kit that was sold to MRRC.

The Arts and Crafts and Toys were closed down, and the licensed toys such as Weebles returned to their license holders, where they are still produced.

I confess that following the January announcement, I largely lost interest in Airfix and stopped keeping records of kit production. The fact that Airfix was now American-owned didn't help: it was akin to learning that the football team you had eagerly supported from childhood had folded and been sold to the Americans. A large and important chunk of your childhood seemed to be gone forever.

For the next ten years, Airfix kits were not easy to come by. Most of the 'other' shops that had sold Airfix kits no longer sold them. Model shops, which were now the only real source of Airfix kits, were reportedly having difficulties obtaining the models, and an increasing number of shops were closing down. It seems that the disappearance of Airfix kits, which had revitalized a lot of toy and model shops in the 1960s and 1970s, was now to lead to their decline. I certainly never saw any Palitoy catalogues until years later.

So nearly thirty years after their first appearance, the kits were still considered the 'jewels in the crown' and have continued to be produced ever since. The golden age of Airfix kits had lasted for just over twenty-five years, and we would have to wait another twenty-five for the second golden age to appear.

The Jolly Green Giant helicopter kit from 1981.

Following the announcement of the closure of Airfix in late January 1981, things ground to a halt whilst the receiver sought a buyer or buyers. Limited production of kits was authorized, but only those new kits that were actually ready to go were produced. Thus in the first four

months we saw several new kits released, but it was clearly up to the new owners to decide which of the other 'new' releases would be completed.

Several companies were interested in buying the Airfix kit division, which was still proving to be profitable. A management

CHAPTER THREE

The General Mills/Palitoy Years, 1981–1986

1982

Following its acquisition of the Airfix kits division from the receiver, General Mills put Airfix under its British subsidiary, Palitoy. The design office was moved to Palitoy's UK headquarters in Coalville, Leicester. The moulds were shipped to its Miro-Meccano subsidiary in Calais, France. Humbrol, which had also tried to buy Airfix, went on to buy the French kit company Heller, but would return in 1986.

Once everything was in place, Palitoy concentrated on putting the existing kits back into production. Those that were almost ready were completed and released. The computerized numbering system was retained, but most kit numbers were now prefixed with a '9'. A 1982 catalogue was issued which featured a new logo, Type 8. Around forty 'new' models were announced: twelve of those were from the 1981 catalogue, the remainder were vehicles from the MPC range, which was also owned by General Mills. A range of *Star Wars* kits was included.

The models from the 1981 catalogue were as follows:

04024	McDD F-18A Hornet	1:72
04025	F-16A/B Fighting Falcon	1:72
06004	Sikorsky CH-53G/CH-53D	1:72
05100	Junkers Ju 87B *Stuka*	1:48
06205	HMS *King George V*	1:600
06206	HMS *Repulse*	1:600
04800	Brontosaurus	N/A
04832	Lesser Spotted Woodpecker	1:1
51577	Space Warriors	1:32
01758	NATO Ground Crew	1:76
16402	Lamborghini Countach	1:16
07171	Flying Saucer Cosmic Starship	N/A

These completed the models that were at an advanced stage when Airfix went into receivership. The other 'new' models were brought-in kits rather than new Airfix moulds. They included:

1:25 Vehicles

9-06431	Wild Breed Mustang	1:25
9-06432	Ford Express	1:25
9-06433	Chevy Cavalier	1:25
9-06444	Dodge Omni Sidewinder	1:25
9-06445	Ford Mark IV	1:25
9-06446	Brute Force Dragster	1:25
9-06447	Squad Rod Nova	1:25
9-06448	Black Belt Firebird FC	1:25
9-06449	Burnout Bird Firebird FC	1:25
9-06450	Night Stalker	1:25
9-06451	Blackbird	1:25

1:25 Off-Road Vehicles

9-06452	Mountain Goat O/R Jeep	1:25
9-06453	Swamp Rat Jeep CJ	1:25
9-06454	Freedom Rider	1:25
9-07407	Chevrolet 'Rolling Thunder'	1:25
9-07408	Ford Bronco 'Saddle Tramp'	1:25
9-07409	Chevrolet 'Ground Shaker'	1:25

1:16 Cars

9-14404	Firebird Turbo Blackbird	1:16

1:25 Super Trucks and Vans

9-07410	Ford Bronco 'Dust Devil'	1:25
9-07411	Dodge 'Bad Company'	1:25
9-07413	Dodge 'Thunders-Truck'	1:25

1:20 Cars

9-08442	McLaren MK-8D	1:20
9-08443	Corvette 'Sabre Vette'	1:20
9-08444	Corvette 'Class Act Vette'	1:20

'Dukes of Hazard' Vehicles

9-04405	Dukes Digger	1:25
9-04406	Boss Hogg's Hauler	1:25
9-04407	Cooter's Cruiser	1:25
9-06430	General Lee Charger	1:25
9-08445	Cooter's Tow Truck	1:25

Other Vehicles

9-20441	'The General' Steam Loco	1:25
9-20442	1911 Christie Fire Engine	1:12

'The Empire Strikes Back' – Space

9-10172	Rebel Snow Speeder
9-10173	Battle on Planet Hoth
9-10174	Encounter with Yoda

SNAPfix Flying Saucer kit, 1982.

July 1982 Battle *comic advert.*

9-10175   AT-AT
9-12101   Imperial Star Destroyer
9-18101   Millennium Falcon

The Airfix releases comprised some of the most exciting kits to come from Airfix. The two jets were the initial versions of the two latest US fighters; both were upgraded over the years, but are currently not available. Now Hornby would be more likely to mould a new kit of the latest version rather than try to convert the old tools. The large Sikorsky helicopter was the second of two kits to come from the same mould; however, it has not been released for some time. The *Stuka* was based on its larger 1:24 sibling and was an excellent kit; it remains in production today.

The two 1:600 warships were particularly welcome. Having dallied with US and Russian aircraft carriers, Airfix returned to its roots and produced excellent replicas of the battleship *King George V* and battle-cruiser *Repulse*, both of which took part in the *Bismarck* chase. They were produced sporadically in the years after, but were both retired in the 2014 catalogue.

The remaining models were not terribly exciting but all complemented the series for which they were designed. The Brontosaurus made a brief return in a dinosaur set, but the Woodpecker, like the other birds, has not been re-released by Airfix.

Neither the Space Warriors and Flying Saucer were re-released, but the Space Warriors made a brief appearance in a bag in 1995! The Countach is owned by Airfix but I don't think has been released since.

The NATO Ground Crew was sold in a Modern Jet Airfield Set in the early 2000s, and in 2013 was released separately to complement the three earlier World War II Airfield Personnel figure sets, but it was not in the 2014 range.

The MPC kits and the *Star Wars* kits were all, I think, released, but returned to the US after Humbrol bought Airfix. Many are available today in their US boxings. The emphasis on American vehicles and *Star Wars* did change the feel of the Airfix range. If nothing else, the release of a lot of cars and trucks showed that Airfix was back!

1983

For 1983, Palitoy issued a new style of catalogue and announced thirty-nine new kits. A new type of packaging was introduced, Type 8, with photographs of the completed models on the box tops:

9-02073	Hawker Hunter FGA.9	1:72
9-02074	NA OV-10D Bronco	1:72
9-03040	Northrop F-5E Tiger II	1:72
9-03041	Kaman SH-2F Seasprite	1:72
9-03042	Kamov Ka-25 Hormone A/C	1:72

9-04026	BAC VC10 K.1 Refuelling	1:144
9-04027	Panavia Tornado GR.1	1:72
9-04028	Lockheed U-2 B/C/D	1:72
9-05016	Republic F-105F Thunderchief	1:72
9-05017	Mil-24 Hind	1:72
9-06005	Republic A-10 Thunderbolt II	1:72
9-09002	Avro Vulcan B.2	1:72
9-12003	Rockwell B-1B Bomber	1:72
9-03180	Boeing 727-200	1:144
9-05101	HS Sea Harrier FRS.1	1:48
9-07101	Hughes AH-64 Apache	1:48
9-08176	Grumman EA-6B Prowler	1:48
9-01759	Modern US NATO Infantry	1:76
9-01760	Modern Russian Infantry	1:76
9-51578	SAS Figures	1:32
9-51579	Modern US NATO Infantry	1:32
9-51580	Modern Russian Infantry	1:32

Star Wars Kits

9-10176	Rebel Base
9-10177	X-Wing Fighter
9-10178	Bobba Fett's *Slave 1*
9-10179	Jabba the Hutt's Throne Room
9-10180	Speeder Bike
9-12102	Imperial Shuttle Tydirium

Car and Truck Kits

9-03413	Porsche 935 (SNAPfix)	1:32
9-03414	Ford Escort (SNAPfix)	1:32
9-03415	Supercharged Dragster (SNAPfix)	1:32?
9-06436	Indy Pace Car Camaro	1:25
9-06446	Brute Force Dragster	1:25
9-06449	Burnout Bird Firebird FC	1:20
9-06457	1983 Corvette	1:25
9-06458	Toyota Supra	1:25
9-07414	'Fall Guy' Camaro	1:25
9-08446	'Fall Guy' Truck	1:25
9-06434	Rosco's Police Car	1:25

From the United States came a new range of kits of *Star Wars* licensed space machines. Also a further 'Dukes of Hazzard' vehicle, and two vehicles from the new *Fall Guy* television series. Several cars were added. Following the sale to Humbrol in 1986, the US imports all returned Stateside. Many are still available today, and Airfix-badged examples are quite popular with collectors.

The most interesting releases and the longest lasting were the Airfix-originated kits. They consisted of five kits that were modifications or updates of existing kits. The Hunter, Bronco and Tornado were modified from the earlier 1:72 kits. The Boeing 727 received a new fuselage to make the much more successful 200 Series aircraft. To extend the life of the VC10 kit

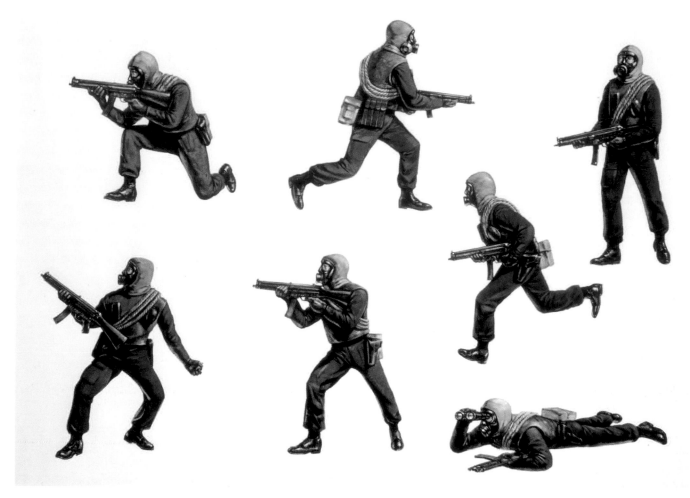

SAS 1:32 figures from 1983. AIRFIX

Avro Vulcan model from 1983.

AIRFIX | OV-10 D BRONCO | 1:72 MODEL KIT MODÈLE RÉDUIT MODELLBAUSATZ SERIES 2

LEFT: *Rockwell OV-10 D Bronco, 1983.*

BELOW: The Model World of Airfix, *published in 1984.*

the mould was modified into the tanker variant, which unfortunately meant it could no longer be sold as the airliner. These kits have all been available at various times over the last thirty years.

The remaining eight aircraft had all either been started by the original Airfix team, or had been cancelled shortly before Airfix went under and were revived by Palitoy. Since the core of the new design team was the old Airfix team, this was a logical action.

Currently only the Vulcan, Boeing 727-200 and Sea Harrier are in the 2014 range. The Vulcan was a surprise release since the production of one by Airfix had always been vetoed by John Gray. Shortly after General Mills took over it was suggested that Airfix tool a Rockwell B-1B Bomber for MPC in the States and as quid-pro-quo, Airfix was allowed to tool the Vulcan for Airfix. At the Toy Fair, a visiting John Gray remarked to the sales team that they had finally got it past him!

Many of the other ranges were culled, with a number of kits disappearing for good or at least a very long time. The figure sets were expanded, however. The SAS figures were released in 1:32 scale, and Palitoy announced it was to concentrate on modern military figures; therefore sets of modern US and Russian Infantry were moulded. In both cases a common set of masters or 'patterns' was made, from which the sets could be pantographed down to either scale. Sadly, the patterns for all the figure sets appear to have been 'lost' following the sale to Humbrol, which makes any modification to those sets very difficult.

The SAS figures have returned to the 2014 range, but the others are presumably not 'modern' enough to come back.

1984

By 1984, Palitoy was well into its stride and less dependent on US imports to fill the catalogue, but the new releases showed very few new kits. Those kits listed as new were as follows:

9-01761	SAS Figures	1:76
9-03181	Sikorsky Sea King	1:72
9-03182	Hawker Hurricane IIB	1:72
9-03183	NA P-51D Mustang	1:72
9-05017	Mil 24 Hind	1:72
9-05018	Martin B-57B Canberra	1:72
9-06006	Boeing Chinook	1:72
9-06821	Handley Page 0/400	1:72
9-09003	Lockheed AC-130H Gunship	1:72
9-07101	Hughes AH-64 Apache	1:48
9-07102	Panavia Tornado F.2	1:48

Day One Kits

9-60264	Agile Combat Aircraft (ACA)	1:72
9-60265	Nautilus	N/A

Star Wars Kits (SNAPfix)

9-06900	X-Wing Fighter	
9-06901	A-Wing Fighter	
9-06902	TIE Interceptor	
9-06903	B-Wing Fighter	

Car and Truck Kits

9-06459	Hardcastle and McCormick Car	N/A
9-06460	Knight Rider 2000	1:25
9-06461	Jody's Firebird	N/A
9-06462	'New Car'	N/A

The *Star Wars* and car kits were all from the States, and I don't think all the car kits were released through Airfix; they all returned to their originators in 1986. Many of the 1982 and 1983 cars were dropped from the range.

The remaining kits were largely re-releases, and only seven could be classed as new; the others were either announced in 1983 or were proposed re-releases.

The SAS figures were based on the 1:32 figures but were never moulded and released. Neither was the Chinook moulded. Recently Airfix has relied on releasing an Italeri mould. Similarly the ACA and Jules Verne's *Nautilus* were never released; the Nautilus was tooled but was only ever available as a resin kit made from a test shot. The Agile Combat Aircraft was the UK's forerunner of the Eurofighter, later to be renamed Typhoon, which was later tooled by Airfix.

Three racing cars and three aircraft were to be released in sets of two under the 'Day One' label, but like the ACA and *Nautilus*, they were in fact never issued. Three compendium sets, including three kits and paints, were issued and are quite highly sought after today.

The Hind and Apache were both announced in 1983 and are not currently available. The 0/400 does feature in the 2014 range and will probably be there until at least 2018!

The Tornado F.2 was a new mould and would later spawn other variants. The Martin B-57B was a drastic modification to the existing Canberra kit, and whilst it solved the problem of the 'dodgy' nose on that kit, it also meant that Airfix no longer had a BAC Canberra in its range. This was largely rectified in 2009 when Hornby released two new Canberra kits in 1:72 scale.

The Hercules Gunship was, like the VC10 and Canberra models, a major revision of the earlier kit: it was hoped that by modifying a slow-selling kit it would revitalize sales. In recent years the earlier kits have become more popular, but they are no longer available. Recently Airfix has had to borrow a kit from another manufacturer to have a standard Hercules in its range.

The three remaining 'new' kits were not released until Humbrol took over.

Back in the USA, General Mills was looking at withdrawing from the toy market in Europe. Arthur Ward wrote in *The Boys' Book of Airfix* that in 1984 Airfix's research and design department was closed and the staff made redundant, which of course explains the lack of new models for 1986 and 1987. Humbrol would have to start from scratch.

1985

By 1985, General Mills had decided to withdraw from the toy market in Europe and so its Palitoy subsidiary was put up for sale. A very simple catalogue running to sixteen pages was issued for 1985, which was first available in the February 1985 issue of *Airfix Magazine*. It listed several 'new' releases, but mostly they were all re-issues of existing kits, or kits that had been announced in the 1984 catalogue. I did not see any of the separate issue catalogues until many years later.

The only new models announced – and they were all ex-American tools – were as follows:

Star Wars 'Structors' Kits:

9-06501	C3-PO
9-06502	AT-AT
9-06503	Scout Walker
9-06504	R2-D2

Star Wars Kits:

9-60276	AT-ST Scout Walker
9-60277	Y-Wing Fighter

Cars and Trucks:

9-60134	Hardcastle and McCormick 'Pick-up'
9-60135	Streethawk Car
9-60136	Streethawk Motorcycle

I believe only the two *Star Wars* kits were actually released. Airfix kits were becoming harder to find as Palitoy was winding down kit production as the operation was put up for sale again.

We had had high hopes for the development of the Airfix range under General Mills, and for a short while we had received some exciting new kits. Now it seemed we were in for another period of stagnation whilst the ownership of Airfix was sorted out. Certainly in the shops, Airfix kits were hard to come by and it did look as if Airfix was finally going to disappear.

Whereas Palitoy had inherited a lot of Airfix kits in development to initiate its new range, all new development work had ceased, and so any new buyer would find itself starting from scratch as regards new models. Effectively, the modeller would be in for at least three years with little or no production of new kits from 1985. Whoever bought Airfix would have its work cut out for the first couple of years.

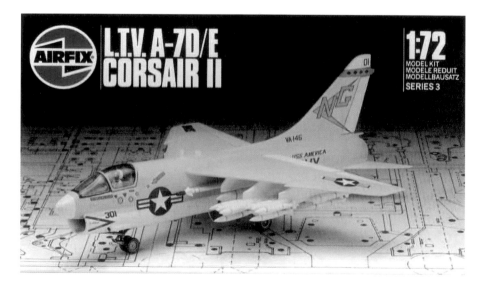

1984's A-7D Corsair II.

CHAPTER FOUR

The Humbrol Years, 1986–2006

1986

Humbrol purchased Airfix in February 1986. It had tried to buy Airfix in 1981, but was beaten by General Mills. Humbrol was founded as the Humber Oil Company, based in Kingston-upon-Hull, and was owned by the American chemical company Borden UK. Humbrol already owned the French kit company Heller, so Airfix was seen as a perfect fit. The archives and everything else at Coalville was moved to Humbrol's headquarters at Marfleet, Kingston-upon-Hull. The moulds were moved from Calais to Trun, where Heller was based, and future Airfix production was centred on Trun. Twenty years later this decision was to prove the downfall of Humbrol.

At this point it seems that most, if not all, of the original artwork was lost, or given away by Palitoy. Some very early artwork and other records were given to the Bethnal Green Museum of Childhood. Some of this original artwork was displayed at RAF Hendon from June 2013 to May 2014.

A simple twelve-page, A4-size catalogue was issued and contained the following statement:

> The acquisition of Airfix by Humbrol in February 1986 marks the dawn of a new era in the model kit industry. Possibly the world's most famous name in model kits is now owned, managed and serviced by a company dedicated to the model kit industry, with all the expertise and professionalism required to maintain Airfix in a position of brand leadership.
>
> Over the next few years, Humbrol will develop Airfix considerably, whilst preserving the character and individuality of the brand.
>
> The Airfix re-launch, available in mid-1986, offers a balanced selection of high quality, popular kits, and a wide choice of attractive price points. During 1986 and 1987, the range will be increased by the addition of new kits and some long-awaited re-releases.
>
> Model paints and adhesives are a further essential element of the Airfix re-launch, and both products have totally new packaging for 1986. The Airfix paint range has been substantially revised to a new, improved formulation and to offer modern and comprehensive colour selection, with many unique shades.
>
> Airfix is back – in force!

A second four-page leaflet was available later in the year and listed 'Forty New Items'. All were re-issues. The style was reminiscent of the later Palitoy ones.

So Airfix was once again in British hands, and the signs for the future were looking good. Humbrol was a known and respected name in the modelling world, so we all looked forward to new models being produced.

What we didn't realize at the time was that the research and development side of Airfix had been closed in 1984, which meant that Humbrol was going to have to start with a new team and a lack of 'work in progress' models. It had only acquired the name and the existing stock and moulds. Fortunately, the person in charge of research and development at Humbrol, Trevor Snowden, was a keen modeller and he was tasked with bringing the range back to the market place and preparing new moulds for the future. Consequently, we would have to wait until 1988 to see the first new moulds from Humbrol.

Several kits were released to tie in with the movie Top Gun *in 1987. The 'MiG' kit was actually an F-5 kit, as F-5s represented MiGs in the film.*

1987

In 1987 the first proper catalogue was produced by Humbrol. It had a white cover, which showed the new packaging style to be used by Humbrol, Type 9, and ran to twenty-four pages. The 'new' releases were shown by box-top artwork rather than photographs of the models. Some of the models were shown in a further style, which became Type 10.

However, there were not, as yet, any new tools. Around twenty figure sets and thirty-four aircraft were reintroduced. World War I aircraft, airliners, historic cars and sailing ships returned and were boxed as 'special editions' in the Type 10 packaging. The Tornado AFV2 from 1984 was announced as an AFV3 variant.

The only totally new items were three aircraft that were packaged as aircraft from the recent movie *Top Gun* starring Tom Cruise. They were, however, only minimum change variants of three existing kits, but given new decals to approximate the actual aircraft from the film. They were:

00501	Jester's A-4 Skyhawk	1:72
00502	'The MiG' (F-5E Tiger II)	1:72
00503	Maverick's F-14A Tomcat	1:72

The Tomcat and Tiger II were both fairly recent kits, but the Skyhawk was the very old and basic kit dating from 1958. Being licensed items, they were only available for a year or two, but did help to show that Airfix was looking ahead.

1988

Humbrol was now well into its stride, and models were appearing in the new, 'lighter' packagings. Several kits were added to the existing ranges, and some of the 'new' aircraft kits were given new decals and illustrations to match. Humbrol was now using the likes of James Goulding and Anthony Sturgess to paint the aircraft boxes, whilst Paul Monteagle was producing new artwork for the vintage aircraft and cars. Humbrol returned to the earlier catalogue number system, and dispensed with the '9' prefix used by Palitoy.

Five aircraft received a 'makeover': these were:

01054	DHC Chipmunk	1:72
01059	Westland SA341 Gazelle	1:72
02012	Dassault Mirage IIIC	1:72
02013	Ilyushin IL-2M3 Stormavik	1:72
04020	Dornier Do 217E/J	1:72

New releases for 1988.

Ten more new aircraft were announced, but they were all modifications of existing kits and consequently received new catalogue numbers:

02080	BAC Lightning F.3	1:72
03054	Westland Navy Lynx HAS.2	1:72
03055	HS Buccaneer S.2B	1:72
03056	BAe/McDD Goshawk	1:72
03057	Northrop RF-5E 'Tiger Eye'	1:72
04035	Panavia Tornado F.3	1:72
05023	Mil Mi-24 Hind A	1:72
05024	Republic F-105G 'Wild Weasel'	1:72
05102	BAe Harrier GR.3	1:48
06012	A-10 + Maverick Missiles	1:72

The Lightning was modified with a new tailfin and other parts, and would soldier on until a new Lightning F.2A was announced in 2013. The original Navy Lynx was upgraded to the then current standard, and then upgraded again in 2001 to HMA.8 standard.

The Buccaneer was virtually a new kit with only the undercarriage, tailplane and airbrakes surviving from the old NA-39 kit from 1960. It was still in Series 3 and was a tight fit in the box! In 2009, Hornby added additional weapons so that all the Series 2 variants could be made, and a year later moved it into Series 4.

The Goshawk was a proposed model of the US Navy's carrier-borne trainer built in the USA by McDonnell-Douglas and based on the BAe Hawk trainer. Like the Buccaneer, it could probably have used only a small part of the Hawk kit, and in the end it was not tooled. The RF-5E 'Tiger Eye' was a modification of the 1983 Tiger II. The Tornado F.3 was a major modification of the earlier Tornado GR.1 kit.

*1988's Harrier
GR.3 kit (Type 10).*

The Mil Mi-24, F-105G and A-10 were all variants of the earlier kits, and mainly had extra missiles added. The only one of the new kits still in the catalogue is the 1:48 Harrier GR.3, which relied heavily on the Sea Harrier of 1983.

For those who were looking for brand new tooling, 1988 looked promising; but in 1989 that promise seemed to disappear.

1989

Although there were around thirty new announcements in the 1989 catalogue, they were all re-issues of existing kits. The Goshawk was noticeable by its absence, as were the 'Top Gun' kits.

The models listed as 'new' included the following:

01052	Hawker Demon	1:72
01060	MDD DO 105C	1:72

02042	Hawker Hurricane Mk I/IIB	1:72
02057	North American Harvard	1:72
01087	Hellcat – Aircraft of Aces	1:72
02088	P-38 – Aircraft of Aces	1:72
02089	P-51D – Aircraft of Aces	1:72
02090	F4U-1D – Aircraft of Aces	1:72
03019	DH Mosquito	1:72
03049	BAC Jet Provost/Strikemaster	1:72
03051	Boeing-Vertol Sea Knight	1:72
03055	HS Buccaneer S.2B	1:72
03058	Kamov Ka-25B Hormone	1:72
04035	Panavia Tornado F.3	1:72
04103	Hawker Fury	1:48
12002	Messerschmitt Bf 109E	1:24
05280	Vosper MTB	1:72
01305	25-Pdr Field Gun & Quad	1:76
01314	Matador and 5.5in Gun	1:76
01317	Lee/Grant Tank	1:76
02046	Aston Martin DB5	1:32
02415	Jaguar 'E' Type	1:32
02420	MGB	1:32
03800	Tyrannosaurus Rex	N/A

03801	Triceratops	N/A
03803	Stegosaurus	N/A
03805	Dimetrodon	N/A

The new kits announced the year before, and the new aircraft and cars, were presented using their new artwork, but all the rest of the kits used their old paintings. They all appeared in the new Type 9 or 10 packaging.

Three or so models were added to the Vintage aircraft and World War II 'Aircraft of the Aces' series and had new paintings by Paul Monteagle, James Goulding and Anthony Sturgess. The MGB, Aston Martin DB5 and 'E'-Type Jaguar were added to the Vintage Cars series, painted by Paul Monteagle. The 'E'-Type and DB5 are still in the catalogue today. Four of the dinosaurs made a brief return.

To further add to modellers' woes, Humbrol suffered a serious fire in a

*Type 9 Triceratops
kit from 1989.*

1989 RELEASE PROGRAMME

CODE No.	SUBJECT	SCALE	RELEASE DATE					
			APR	MAY	JUN	JUL	AUG	SEPT
	SERIES 1 MILITARY AIRCRAFT							
01052	Hawker Demon	1:72				★		
01059	Westland Aérospatiale SA 341 Gazelle	1:72	★					
01068	MBB Bo 105C	1:72				★		
	SERIES 1 MILITARY VEHICLES							
01305	25 pdr Field Gun and Quad	HO/OO	★					
01314	Matador and 5.5 in gun	HO/OO	★					
01317	Lee/Grant Tank	HO/OO	★					
	SERIES 2 MILITARY AIRCRAFT							
02012	Dassault Mirage III C	1:72	★					
02042	Hawker Hurricane Mk I/IIB	1:72						★
02057	North American Harvard	1:72						★
	SERIES 2 AIRCRAFT OF THE ACES							
02087	Grumman F6F Hellcat	1:72				★		
02088	Lockheed P-38 Lightning	1:72				★		
02089	North American P-51D Mustang	1:72				★		
02090	Vought F4U Corsair	1:72				★		
	SERIES 2 HISTORIC CARS							
02406	Aston Martin DB5	1:32			★			
02415	Jaguar 'E' Type	1:32			★			
02420	MGB	1:32			★			
	SERIES 3 MILITARY AIRCRAFT							
03019	De Havilland Mosquito Mk II/VI/XVIII	1:72						★
03049	BAC Jet Provost T5/Strikemaster	1:72				★		
03051	Boeing Vertol Sea Knight	1:72				★		
03055	Hawker Siddeley Buccaneer S.2B	1:72			★			
03058	Kamov Ka 25B Hormone	1:72						★
	SERIES 3 DINOSAURS							
03800	Tyrannosaurus Rex			★				
03801	Triceratops			★				
03803	Stegosaurus			★				
03805	Dimetrodon			★				
	SERIES 4 MILITARY AIRCRAFT							
04035	Panavia Tornado F3	1:72					★	
04103	Hawker Fury Biplane	1:48			★			
	SERIES 5 SHIPS							
05280	Vosper Motor Torpedo Boat	1:72		★				
	SERIES 6 MILITARY AIRCRAFT							
06012	Fairchild A10 Thunderbolt II +Maverick missiles	1:72	★					
	SERIES 6 MODERN AIRLINERS							
06180	McDonnell-Douglas DC10	1:144	★					
06181	BAC Aérospatiale Concorde	1:144	★					
	SERIES 12 MILITARY AIRCRAFT							
12002	Messerschmitt Bf109E	1:24						★

★ = Proposed release date – final dates to be confirmed during 1989

ABOVE: *The 'World War II Aircraft of the Aces' kits (1989).* AIRFIX

LEFT: *Humbrol's 1989 release programme.*

A selection of kits from 1989.

warehouse in 1989 and much existing stock was destroyed. Water damage also affected some of the artwork, necessitating a lot of repainting.

It seems that the 'promises' of 1986 were not being lived up to, and though many older kits were being represented in new and exciting ways, there was no sign of the new tools that had been promised.

1990

1990 saw a significant change at Airfix. The catalogue was much thicker and contained a great deal of lovely artwork, with only a few models still appearing in the photographic box tops. More impor-

tantly there were twelve 'new' kits in addition to the re-issues. The new kits comprised the following:

03059	Shorts Tucano T.1	1:72
03060	Dassault Super Etendard	1:72
03061	Dassault Mirage 2000	1:72
04036	EFA Eurofighter	1:72
04037	MiG-29	1:72
05025	Sukhoi Su-27A	1:72
02091	Yakovlev Yak-3	1:72
02092	Messerschmitt Bf 109K	1:72
02093	Mitsubishi A6M2 Zero	1:72
02094	Hawker Tempest V	1:72
02095	Supermarine Spitfire Mk IIa	1:72
02096	Hawker Hurricane Mk IIC	1:72
10999	Battle of Britain 50th Set	1:72

The totally new moulds, of which there were actually six, were all tooled at Heller's Trun factory and produced there. The Tucano and Eurofighter were Airfix designs, as France was not a buyer of Tucanos or Eurofighters. The Etendard and Mirage 2000 were Heller kits, but sold by Airfix, which also paid half the mould cost. The Russian jets were part of a new agreement whereby Heller would market the trainer variants and Airfix the fighters, again with Airfix paying half the mould cost.

They were basically good models with fine raised and inscribed detail. The Eurofighter has been upgraded over the years to the current Typhoon variant. All have featured in the catalogue in recent years.

The Yak-3, Bf 109K and Tempest were ex-SMER kits bought in to go in the 'Aircraft of the Aces' range. The Zero was the old Airfix kit. None is currently available. The Spitfire and Hurricane were fitted into a fiftieth anniversary Battle of Britain Museum Flight Set, which also included the Lancaster. They were all available separately. The Spitfire was the Airfix Mk Ia kit, and the Hurricane was a Heller model as Airfix did not make a Mk IIC at that time.

Among the reissues, Airfix re-released six of the seven sets of multipose figures, the Japanese, oddly, not appearing. This time two shots of the mould were packaged so that twelve, rather than six, different figures could be made. This was most welcome, as the kits originally contained instructions for twelve figures to be made from the six figures provided.

Other kits returning included the Dennis Fire Engine and the magnificent 1:12 scale Bentley, which is still in the range today.

1991

The 1991 catalogue was a simple affair running to twenty pages and entitled *Airfix New Releases*. As such, it was similar to the 1981 *New Releases* catalogue. Thirty-five new additions were announced, though over half of these were reintroductions. The sixteen new kits were a mixture of two old kits refreshed, nine cars produced from other kit manufacturers, and five new moulds developed with Heller.

The new kits were as follows:

02071	Fairey Swordfish	1:72
02097	AW Seahawk	1:72

The commemorative set released to mark the fiftieth anniversary of the Battle of Britain.

04038	BAe Harrier GR.5	1:72
04039	BAe Harrier GR.7	1:72
04040	BAe Harrier T.10	1:72
07102	Dassault Etendard IVP	1:48
12004	Boeing AWACS E-3D Sentry	1:72
06412	Jaguar E-Type	1:24
06413	Mercedes 170	1:24
06414	Mercedes 500K	1:24
06415	Bugatti T50	1:24
06416	Alfa Romeo	1:24

Hi-Tech Series

17001	Ferrari 250 GTO	1:24
17002	Triumph TR2	1:24
17003	Austin Healey Sprite	1:24
22001	Jaguar XK-E Hardtop	1:24

The Swordfish and Seahawk were the old kits but were given new FAA decals to represent aircraft flown by the FAA Historic Flight at Yeovilton.

The three Harriers were all tooled together and used some common runners; they represented the new Harrier variants just entering service. Like the models from the previous year, they were similar in design and construction. As the GR.5 variant was quickly replaced by the GR.7/9 variant in RAF service, this model was not available for long. The kits all used rather mediocre illustrations, which were later replaced by much better airbrush paintings. Hornby tooled a new GR.7/9 just as the aircraft was leaving service. Heller sold the aircraft in their US Marine Corps colours and designations of AV-8B and TAV-8B.

The Sentry was a conversion of the earlier Heller Boeing 707 kit but with new engines and the radome added. Finally, the Etendard IVP was tooled by Heller, but also used by Airfix. Again it was a fine model and was a worthy addition to the 1:48 range.

The five 1:24 car kits were Heller moulds that were used by Airfix. The 'Hi-Tech' car kits were produced by the Japanese company Gunze Sanyo, but sold by Airfix for a few years. Airfix had had an arrangement with Gunze Sanyo dating back to the late 1970s, when Airfix had 'loaned' some of their bird moulds to Gunze to produce in Japan. The new Hi-Tech kits included white metal and photo-etched parts to make a more detailed model. The artwork for the cars was executed by Gavin McLeod, who would create some lovely airbrush art for many Airfix kits.

Four warships were reintroduced, and they were still in the range until 2013; however, the eight Waterloo 54mm kits were only in the range again for a few years.

1992

A new catalogue was produced in 1992. Forty-six new models were listed but only thirty-five were actually new moulds or kits new to the Airfix range.

05026	F-117A Stealth	1:72
05027	YF-22 Lightning II	1:72
05103	MiG-17F	1:48
07103	Dassault Mirage 2000B	1:48
09176	Tornado GR.1/GR.1A	1:48
09177	Tornado GR.1/GR.1A (Gulf)	1:48

Hi-Tech Aircraft

04041	Weapons Kit	1:72
10005	BAe Harrier GR.7	1:72
10006	Tornado GR.1	1:72
10007	MiG-29 Fulcrum	1:72
10008	Supermarine Spitfire Vb	1:72
10009	F-15A/B Eagle	1:72

Cars and Trucks

10401	Scania Eurotruck	1:24
10402	Refrigerated Trailer	1:24
10403	Semi Trailer	1:24
05401	BMW M1	1:24
05402	Maserati Bora	1:24
05403	Renault Alpine	1:24
05404	Lamborghini Countach	1:24

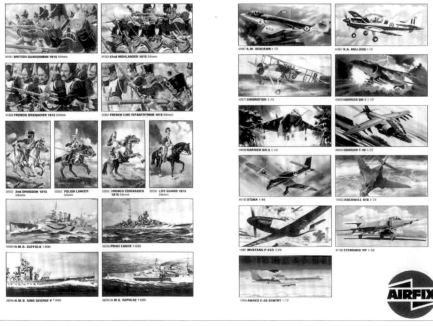

Additions to the programme in 1991.

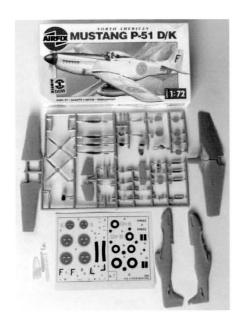

Swedish Mustang kit, 1992.

05405	De Tomaso Pantera	1:24
05406	Ferrari Rainbow	1:24
05407	Maserati Boomerang	1:24
05408	Lotus Esprit	1:24
05409	Lamborghini Jota	1:24
05410	Corvette	1:24
05411	Triumph TR7	1:24
05412	Maserati Merak	1:24
06401	Dino Ferrari	1:24
06402	BMW 3.5 CSL	1:24
06403	Mercedes 300SL Gullwing	1:24
06404	Lamborghini Countach LP500S	1:24
06405	Ferrari Daytona 365 GTB/4	1:24
06406	Porsche 928 S4	1:24

06417	Citroën 2CV	1:24
06419	Peugeot 905 EV1	1:24
06420	Bugatti EB110	1:24

The five new aircraft were again all tooled by Heller for use by Airfix. The Mirage 2000B was a Heller kit. The two Tornados were developed from the earlier Tornado ADV kit to make the bomber version that was in service with the RAF and German AF. A boxing that included Gulf War decals was also made for a limited period; later on, Humbrol would update this kit to GR.4/4A standard. The MiG-17F was an ex-SMER kit sold for only a couple of years.

The 'Hi-Tech' kits were the basic kits, but with photo-etched parts and white metal parts included to enable a higher quality model to be made. The Weapons kit was a new mould of the latest weapons which could be used with the Hi-Tech and other modern aircraft kits.

The three trucks were Heller kits, and the other car kits were a mixture of Heller and Italeri moulds. This was a fairly cost-effective way of adding to the range for a short period without the expense of costly new moulds.

Several other Airfix kits were reintro-duced, some with new decals. It was becoming apparent that Humbrol was not investing the money into new moulds that it had earlier said it would, but was relying on plenty of Heller kits and 'poly-bag' kits from other kit manufacturers.

1993

The main feature of the 1993 range seems to be that the Airfix catalogue was now combined with the Heller catalogue. This made sense, since many Airfix kits were now sold by Heller. There were many deletions and fewer additions. The additions amounted to nineteen models, of which one, the Tornado, was announced the previous year. Unlike Hornby where the new additions are described as 'new tool' for new mouldings or 'new for 2014' for old favourites returning with a new look, Humbrol usually referred to any new addition to that year as a 'totally new kit'. This was rather confusing to the buyer, but it hid the fact that there were not many totally new models!

The new additions were:

02099	Commonwealth Boomerang	1:72
03001	DH Heron II	1:72
04009	Ford 5-AT Tri-motor	1:72
04042	Gloster Javelin T.3	1:72
05028	McDD F-15E Strike Eagle	1:72
98004	Lancaster BIII 'Dambuster'	1:72
09176	Tornado GR.1/GR.1A	1:48
03171	Vickers Vanguard	1:144
03174	HP 42 Heracles	1:144
04170	Boeing 707-420C	1:144
06360	Rommel's Half-Track	1:32
01305	25-Pounder Field Gun Set 1:76	
06701	Fort Sahara	1:76
06702	Sherwood Castle	1:76
06703	Fort Apache	1:76
06704	Roman Fort	1:76

Spitfire and Bulldog kits from 1992, shown with a range of Humbrol paints.

RIGHT: *1993's kit of the 1962 Vickers Vanguard.*

BELOW: *Two 500-piece puzzles from 1993.*

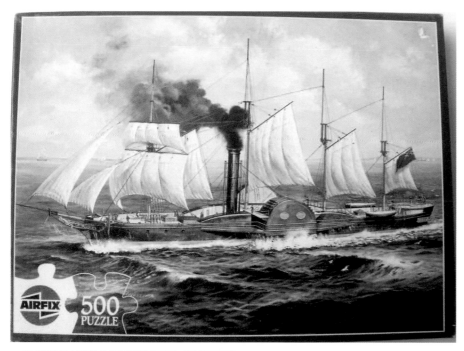

Four playsets returned with new illustrations, and at the time they were the only way that the modeller could access the figure sets that went with them. The original paintings for these sets had all been 'thrown away' by Palitoy, so new ones were commissioned.

Only two new moulds were announced, and these were both modifications to existing moulds. The 1980 F-15A/B was updated to the latest F-15E Strike Eagle variant and the latest weapons added. It made a useful addition to the range of modern jet fighters. However, it has not been available for a few years, and I suspect if Hornby wanted to sell a version of the latest F-15 it would probably tool a new kit.

The 1980 Lancaster kit was modified and extra parts added to enable the 'Dam Buster' variant to be made as well as the standard Lancaster kit. The 1980 Lancaster kit was always one of the best Lancaster kits, and this and a later modification got the best out of the mould. The fuselage halves were modified by inserting a removable mould section into the area where the mid-upper turret was moulded, so when a Dambuster or standard Lancaster was to be run, the relevant turret or non-turret section was fitted into the mould. Both Lancaster kits were replaced in 2013 by a new mould kit, which has replaced the old Lancaster in the Battle of Britain Memorial Flight sets.

One further kit appeared unannounced in the shops, and this was the old Heller kit of the Javelin T.3. It was a very good kit of this 1950s delta-winged fighter, which had previously not featured in the Airfix range. The detail was fine, and after a short run the mould was altered to make the more aggressive FAW.9/9R variant. It did not appear in any catalogues.

During 1993 Airfix decided to release, at short notice, three Luftwaffe aircraft. They were poorly illustrated and did not appear in any catalogues. They were:

03028	Henschel Hs 126A1/B1	1:72
03053	Focke-Wulf Fw 189	1:72
04004	Heinkel He 111H-20	1:72

Unless you actually have one of these four models it is easy to miss them.

On the whole 1993 was a poor year for Airfix models, and there was little sign that things were going to improve.

1994

In 1994 the second of the joint Airfix/Heller catalogues was issued, with half being devoted to Airfix and the other half to Heller kits. The Humbrol paints section was included at the end of the Airfix section. The second half was printed upside down so it could be sold the right way up in France! It was also available as an Airfix and Humbrol-only catalogue without the Heller section.

In 1994, Borden sold Hobby Products Group, as its Humbrol subsidiary was known, to Allen, McGuire & Partners Ltd, an Irish investment company. The new company was now under the Humbrol banner.

Fifteen 'new' releases were announced, but only two were actually new moulds. One of the remaining thirteen kits was a tool modification of the recently released Heller Javelin, and most of the rest were re-releases to go with the fiftieth anniversary of D-Day, which Airfix was celebrating.

The three new models were:

04045	Gloster Javelin FAW.9/9R	1:72
07014	Sepecat Jaguar GR.1A	1:48
08100	HS Buccaneer S.2B	1:48

Other 'new' kits were:

02050	Brewster F2A-2 Buffalo	1:72
04015	Martin B26 C Marauder	1:72
05011	Douglas A26 B/C Invader	1:72
04175	SE210 Caravelle	1:144
04176	DH Comet 4B	1:144
07251	*Endeavour* Bark 1768	1:120
01309	Bren Carrier and 6-Pounder AT Gun	1:76
02302	Buffalo Amphibian and Jeep	1:76
02316	DUKW	1:76

Various trainers in 'Historic Collection' boxing, 1994.

Selection of Starter Sets and Gift Sets.

The first starter sets, 1994.

03301	LCMIII and Sherman Tank	1:76
06704	Gun Emplacement	1:76
06706	Coastal Defence Fort	1:76

The Javelin was a rework of the Heller T. 3 released the previous year. Modellers were urged to buy the initial T. 3 because it was revealed that the mould was to be altered, and so the T. 3 variant would be a limited issue. The T. 3 consisted of three runners moulded in light grey plastic with fine raised detail and restrained engraved detail for the control surfaces. The runners had the Heller release number '346' moulded on to them. The FAW.9/9R was moulded in a silvery-coloured plastic and was now stamped 'Gloster Javelin 4045'. It is, I think, the only example of an existing mould being irreversibly altered by Humbrol/Airfix, whose policy was one of adding extra runners to make new variants.

The Jaguar had been first mooted in 1:48 scale by Airfix in the late 1970s but was never proceeded with because of a lack of money. Being an Anglo-French aircraft used by both countries and based on an original Bregeut design, the Jaguar was a logical choice for the new Anglo-French kit company. Airfix only ever sold the single-seat variant in its RAF colours. Two-seater and Aeronavale variants were available from Heller. Interestingly, in late 2006 when Hornby acquired Humbrol and of course Airfix, the 1:48 Jaguar kit was, I think, the only mould that was not included in the Airfix tool bank. There remains the possibility that Airfix can 'polybag' it in the future, but it does not look likely that Heller wishes to relinquish the mould!

The Buccaneer was a surprise but a very welcome one. Used by only the British and South African air forces and navy, it probably only had limited appeal worldwide as a kit. Some of the detail was somewhat heavy, and there were a few complaints about the fit of parts, but a truly awesome kit of the 'flying brick' could be achieved. The kit was of the RAF's S.2B variant which was in use at the time. The following year would see the naval and South African variants released.

The Marauder was the superb 1973 kit with its beautiful smooth finish. The Invader and Buffalo were fine models, but unfortunately were festooned with the rivets that Airfix was wont to put on its early models. The two airliners were the original two aircraft in the 1:144 range, and were now elevated from Series 2 and

3 to Series 4! They were included in the 'rustic' style packaging Airfix was then using for its airliner re-releases.

The AFVs were all D-Day orientated, and the two playforts included two sets of OO/HO figures each, one to attack and one to defend. These two forts were released as part of the 2014 seventieth anniversary of the D-Day landings.

The *Endeavour* was the first of Airfix's large sailing ships and appeared again for a limited time.

1994 was a good year for enthusiasts of large jet fighters and bombers, but offered little else to other enthusiasts. Tucked away in the back of the catalogue was a page of 'starter' and 'gift' sets. In the early 1980s Airfix had sold a few sets of three or four kits in a box complete with paint and brushes, and three new sets were announced. More importantly, single kits were now fitted into 'blister' packs, which included glue brushes and paint so that younger modellers could get everything they needed in one package to complete a reasonable model. It also meant that smaller retail outlets could now stock several kits without also having to stock all the paints and so on to complete them. It was a good idea, and one that

Airfix has steadily expanded and developed over the years. The following year would see the big launch of this new range.

1995

Apart from the release of the starter sets, little else took place in 1995. Three new kits were released, but they were all modifications of existing kits:

03062	DH Mosquito NF.XIX/J.30	1:72
08101	Buccaneer S.2, S.2D, SMk50	1:48
08102	Panavia Tornado GR.1B	1:48

The Mosquito was a modification of the 1972 multi-variant kit, which was always one of the finest Mosquito kits on the market. A runner containing four-bladed propellers, a new blunt-looking nose and several other parts to make a night fighter and a Swedish Air Force variant was included. Sweden had always been a good market for Airfix kits, and so Airfix often included Swedish markings in its releases. Gavin McLeod painted a lovely box top of the Swedish aircraft flying over lakes. The standard Mosquito was put into one of the new 'all-in-one' sets.

9509 *THE HISTORIC CAR COLLECTION*

9510 *THE V.E. DAY COMMEMORATIVE COLLECTION*

Two Historic Collection kits from 1995: The Historic Car Collection and The VE Day Commemorative Collection.

The Buccaneer was the second of the two new 1:48 kits to be released. It contained the basic kit plus extra runners to enable the modeller to make the two remaining S.2 variants and the South African variant. Decals were provided for all three, and the box top showed a naval variant taking off. In 2005, both kits were combined into one release in Series 9, and it seems that a misunderstanding at the packing station meant that many of the kits had two complete kits in the box. Exceptional value if you were lucky to get one!

The final new kit was a small upgrade to the Panavia Tornado GR.1/GR.1A kit to the then current GR.1B version. The kit was released in Series 8, making it cheaper than the earlier GR.1A kit. In 2003 it would be updated again to GR.4/GR.4A standard.

The starter sets and three gift sets announced the year before were repackaged to match the current style, and several more sets were added. Basically, the existing boxed kit was fitted into the 'blister' pack. The prefix 9 instead of 0 denoted a set, and the other numbers were the standard catalogue numbers for each kit. The initial sets had the single kit fitted into a basic 'blister' pack, which helped to use up stocks of each kit.

Since then, the concept of the starter set with everything included to complete a basic model has been heartily embraced by Airfix. It has also enabled Hornby/Airfix to offer a different set of decals with a new illustration, thereby increasing sales of the standard kit. The new range for 1995 comprised the following:

Starter Sets

91036	Red Arrows Gnat	1:72
91071	Supermarine Spitfire Mk I	1:72
91072	Messerschmitt Bf 109G-6	1:72
92024	MiG-21	1:72
92083	NA P-51B Mustang	1:72
92406	Aston Martin DB5	1:32

All-in-One Sets

93011	BAC Jaguar GR.1	1:72
93019	DH Mosquito Mk II/VI/XVIII	1:72
93025	Westland Army Lynx	1:72
94001	VA Wellington BIII	1:72
94013	McDonnell F-4 Phantom	1:72
94027	Panavia Tornado GR.1	1:72
95005	Boeing B-17G Flying Fortress	1:72
93205	HMS *Fearless*	1:600

Premier Collections

| 98004 | Lancaster BIII Dambuster | 1:72 |
| 99177 | Desert Storm Tornado GR.1/1A | 1:48 |

Historic Collection

| 9509 | The Historic Car Collection (MGB, DB5 and E-Type) | 1:32 |
| 9510 | VE Day Commemorative Set (Spitfire IX, Me 262 and P-51D) | 1:72 |

Action Figures

51550	British Paratroopers	1:32
51565	Cowboys	1:32
51566	Indians	1:32
51567	German Paratroopers	1:32
51574	Medieval Figures	1:32
51577	Space Warriors	1:32

The starter and all-in-one sets tended to be of models that were in production, and meant that some of the latest run of each kit was diverted to the blister packs. The Premier Collection consisted of two specialized large kits. The Historic Collection comprised three models plus the paints and glue. The standard boxing of these latter sets meant that Airfix could vary the contents easily.

Finally, some of the 1:32 figures made a welcome return, but they were now packed in small bags similar to the ones used for sweets! There were six figures in each set, and since the full sets normally had seven different poses, this seems rather odd. However, the full sets had several duplicates in them, and it was only the 'officer' figure that was single.

Again, it was not a very exciting year, but one that laid the groundwork for a very successful range of models for Airfix

1996

In 1996 the starter sets were expanded further, with several new additions. A couple of old kits, the Superfreighter and Rotodyne, were reintroduced and it was nice to see them back in the range again. The Superfreighter had a new illustration and decals. We had been led to believe that the Superfreighter mould was badly worn, but the kits appeared quite fresh. The Battle of Waterloo Farm House returned, but there were no soldiers to fight over it!

However, two entirely new kits were released, and they were 1:48 models of a Spitfire F.22/24 and a Seafire FR.46/47. They were magnificent models and were designed using the same method of tool manufacture that was employed by the

Fairey Rotodyne and Bristol Superfreighter, both 1996 releases.

likes of Tamiya. The detail was exquisite, and they were the first Airfix kits that could match the more expensive Tamiya models. The Seafire appears in the 2014 catalogue but is now in Series 6.

The common parts of both aircraft were moulded on one or two runners, and the parts particular to each variant were moulded on separate runners. This cut down the cost of producing each kit, as the cost could be recouped over two kits rather than one. Even so it took longer to recoup the cost, which is probably why, after the Lightnings, Airfix returned to the cheaper method of mould production.

Only within the last two or three years have we seen kits emerging from Airfix with similar levels of detail, but now with much reduced tooling costs. The new kits announced in 1996 were:

07105	Supermarine Spitfire F.22/24	1:48
07106	Supermarine Seafire FR.46/47	1:48

Starter Sets

91028	Mitsubishi A6M2 Zero	1:72
91030	Messerschmitt Me 262A	1:72
92023	Grumman F6F-3 Hellcat	1:72
92054	Vought F4U-1D Corsair	1:72
92415	Jaguar E-Type	1:32
92420	MGB	1:32

All-in-One Sets

93026	Red Arrows Hawk	1:72
93043	Westland Sea King	1:72
94039	BAe Harrier GR.7	1:72
95026	Lockheed F-117A Stealth	1:72

Historic Collection

9511	World War II Fighter Classics	1:72
9512	Pacific Conflict Collection	1:72

As kits were deleted from the catalogue and new ones added, the contents of some of the collections would reflect that.

1997

Like the previous year, 1997 saw a further expansion of the various sets, although one or two were quietly dropped. The big news was the announcement of two new 1:48 kits of the English Electric Lightning, covering all single-seat variants. A new range of kits was introduced for younger modellers known as 'Battlezone', or Junior Airfix. These were largely snap-together models. Several individual kits returned briefly to the range. The new additions comprised the following:

06100	HS Sea Harrier FA.2	1:48
09178	EE Lightning F.2A/F.6	1:48
09179	EE Lightning F.1/F.1A/ F.2/F.3	1:48

Junior Airfix (Battlezone)

04900	Night Owl	N/A
04901	Black Widow	N/A
04902	Phantom	N/A
04903	Eclipse	N/A
04910	Gladiator	N/A
04911	Vigilante	N/A
04912	Crusader	N/A
04913	Liberator	N/A

Starter Sets

91027	Hawker Typhoon IB	1:72
91038	Curtiss P-40E Kittyhawk	1:72

Three alternative treatments possible with the 1997 kit of the ever-popular English Electric Lightning.

92042	Hawker Hurricane Mk I/IIB	1:72
92072	Hawker Harrier GR.3	1:72
92419	Triumph TR4A	1:32

All-in-One Sets

93055	HS Buccaneer S.2B	1:72
94100	Supermarine Spitfire Mk VB	1:48
94212	HMS *Belfast*	1:600
95013	Grumman F-14A Tomcat	1:72

Historic Collection

9513	Sports Cars – New Selection	1:32
9514	World War II Fighters – New Selection	1:72
9515	Historic Tank Collection	1:76
9518	RN Historic Flight Collection	1:72

Premier Collection

| 97105 | Supermarine Spitfire F.22/24 | 1:48 |
| 99252 | HMS *Victory*, 1765 | 1:180 |

The Lightnings were designed around the same time as the Spitfires and to the same standard. They were magnificent models, with much finer detail than the Buccaneers and Tornados. We would not see Airfix producing such fine quality moulds until very recently. The F.2A/F.6 model is in the 2014 catalogue.

The Sea Harrier FA.2 was a modification of the FRS.1 tool, itself a modification of the GR.3 tool, enabling the latest Sea Harrier version to be built. The original FRS.1 version could still be built, and today the GR.3 and FRS.1 are both in the catalogue, but the FA.2 is not.

The Battlezone models were developed by Heller and were known previously as 'Clic/Clac'. One of several ideas for simple kits for younger modellers, they were clip-together kits that required no painting and the decals were of the 'peel and stick' variety. They were aimed at the seven to eleven age group, and were seen as a way of getting the youngsters into the kit-building habit. A similar idea would be tried several times over the next few years. They were not entirely successful and tended to be around for only a year or two.

By this time the moulds were being produced in the Far East, particularly Korea. In the 1970s, Airfix had been using the 'spark-eroded' process, which enabled inscribed panel lines to be cut into the mould, but they were quite coarse and deep. The Japanese had developed the beryllium copper process, whereby a heated male pattern is pressed into molten female beryllium copper to make the female half of the mould. It produced much finer detail than before, but was

more expensive. Trevor Snowden estimated that an average tool cost roughly £1,000 per component. It is easy to see how a small Series 1 kit could cost a lot, and it could take many years at the reduced runs being made at the time to recoup the cost. Better, then, to mould a large-scale aircraft where the extra parts could be covered by the greatly increased selling price.

Money, or lack of it, always seemed to be a problem during the Humbrol years, and Trevor is to be congratulated for producing those kits he managed to during his time at Humbrol.

1998

The 1998 catalogue proudly announced the addition of no fewer than forty 'brand new' items, although in fact the only ones that could be described as 'new' were the ships in bottles, as they had never been in the Airfix range before. Interestingly they may have been the inspiration for the original Airfix sailing ships. The *Charles Morgan* whaler, however, was a subject that had not been moulded by Airfix before.

Several new sets were announced, along with the return of quite a few old kits. James Bond and Oddjob made a welcome return, but being a licensed product it would only appear briefly. The similar James Bond Autogyro was sold in a starter set. Three Heller 1:43 cars entered the range, and the Heller DH Vampire FB.5 would be in the range for several years. In 2013, Hornby produced its own Vampire kit. Several 'set' kits were released singly. Over thirty kits were deleted from the range to make way for the new additions.

The 'new' kits, including those put into sets, were as follows:

Starter Sets

| 92416 | VW Beetle | 1:32 |
| 92421 | Austin Healey Sprite Mk 1 | 1:32 |

All-in-One Sets

93407	Ferrari 250 LM	1:32
93409	Gulf Porsche 917	1:32
94401	James Bond Autogyro	1:24

Make and Paint – Historical Figures

| 92501 | Henry VIII | 1:12 |
| 92502 | Anne Boleyn | 1:12 |

Dogfight Doubles/Classic Conflicts

| 93141 | Spitfire IX and Bf 110C/D | 1:72 |
| 93340 | Tiger Tank and Sherman Tank | 1:76 |

Premier Collection

| 99178 | EE Lightning F.2A/F.6 | 1:48 |

Ships in Bottles

60001	*Mayflower*	N/A
60002	*Charles Morgan* Whaler	N/A
60003	*Cutty Sark*	N/A

Individual Kits

01411	Land Rover	1:43
01412	Mini	1:43
01413	Jaguar XJS	1:43
03064	DH Vampire FB.5	1:72
04402	James Bond and Oddjob	1:12
08181	Concorde (New Decals)	1:144
05201	SS *Canberra*	1:600

This was not a very inspiring year. Money was apparently tight at Humbrol, and there was very little for new moulds, hence the reliance on using Heller moulds and the expansion of the sets.

Kits of old models were often released when the original kits were fetching high prices, and this seems to have been the *raison d'être* for the James Bond kits. However, the boxes featured scans of posters rather than the original Roy Cross artwork, and this seems to have blunted sales.

The cars were produced by Heller to the odd scale of 1:43, which has traditionally been used for die-cast cars. Over the next few years several Heller racing cars and rally cars to 1:43 scale would join the Airfix range.

The old 'Dogfight Double' concept was revived, initially using the original pairings and illustrations. This idea was extended to tanks, and the best-selling, though dated, kits of the Tiger and Sherman tanks were put together as 'Classic Conflicts'.

Three Series 1 aircraft were released, as were three sailing ships in Series 0, in smaller boxes and slightly cheaper. But on the whole there was very little to excite modellers as far as Airfix was concerned.

1999

In 1999 a modified logo was introduced, and the catalogue told us it was the '50th Anniversary of Airfix: 1949–1999'. 1949 was in fact when the Ferguson Tractor was first issued, but it made a convenient point to celebrate the initiation of the kit range.

Only two new Airfix moulds were announced; the rest were 'polybagged' kits from other manufacturers. The new models consisted of the following:

Anne Boleyn 'Make and Paint' release from 1998.

'Ships in Bottles', 1998.

LEFT: *A 'James Bond' starter set from 1998, based on the character's appearance in 1964's* Goldfinger.

Web Warriors

20001	Web Warrior Byte	N/A
20002	Web Warrior Ram	N/A
20003	Web Warrior Drive	N/A
20004	Web Warrior Icon	N/A
20005	Web Warrior Bug	N/A
20006	Web Warrior Virus	N/A
20007	Web Warrior Glitch	N/A
20008	Web Warrior Crash	N/A

Wallace and Gromit

51100	Motorbike and Sidecar Model Kit	N/A
51101	Aeroplane Model Kit	N/A

Authentic Collectors Sets

9401	Red Arrows Gnat Video Set	1:72
9402	Supermarine Spitfire Video Set	1:72

LEFT: *1999's AWACS kit.*

BELOW: *The Series 0 kits from 1999.*

Present Sets

9520	1960s Sports Car Present Set	1:32
9521	Fast Jets Present Set	1:72
9522	Classic Cars Present Set	1:32

Premier Collection

| 98005 | B-17G Flying Fortress | 1:72 |

Mini Starter Sets

90013	DH Comet	1:72
90017	MiG 15	1:72
90022	A4D-1 Skyhawk	1:72
90100	F-4E Phantom II	1:144
90101	MiG-21PF Fishbed D	1:144
90102	MiG-23BN Flogger H	1:144
90103	Northrop F 20 Tiger Shark	1:144
90104	General Dynamics F-16 XL	1:144
90264	*Golden Hind*	N/A
90267	HMS *Victory*	N/A
90269	*Mayflower*	N/A

Small Starter Sets

91411	Land Rover	1:43
91412	Mini	1:43
91413	Jaguar XJS	1:43
92003	Bristol Beaufighter TF.X	1:72
92073	Hawker Hunter FGA.9	1:72
92088	Lockheed P-38F/H Lightning	1:72

Medium Starter Sets

93181	Boeing 737-200	1:144
93184	Boeing 777	1:300
93185	Boeing 747-400	1:300
93204	HMS *Ajax*	1:600

Large Starter Sets

95104	NA P-51D Mustang	1:48
95105	Focke-Wulf Fw 190A-8	1:48
95106	Vought F4U-1A Corsair	1:48

Individual Kits

| 00100 | F-4E Phantom II | 1:144 |
| 00101 | MiG-21 | 1:144 |

SERIES 0 KITS	Outer Pack Qty.	Outer Pack Size m³	Outer Pack Weight kg	EAN
900100 F4 Phantom	96	0.069⁵	5.2 kg	50-14429-01118-4
900101 MiG 21	96	0.069⁵	5.2 kg	50-14429-01119-1
900102 MiG 23	96	0.069⁵	5.2 kg	50-14429-01120-7
900103 F20 Tiger	96	0.069⁵	5.2 kg	50-14429-01121-4
900104 F16 XL	96	0.069⁵	5.2 kg	50-14429-01122-1

00102	MiG-23	1:144
00103	Northrop F-20 Tiger Shark	1:144
01084	Fiat G91 'Frecce Tricolori'	1:72

08005	B-17G Flying Fortress	1:72
12004	Boeing AWACS E-3D Sentry	1:72
05104	NA P-51D Mustang	1:48

05105	Focke-Wulf Fw 190A-8	1:48
05106	Vought F4U-1A Corsair	1:48
03184	Boeing 777	1:300
03185	Boeing 747-400	1:300
03541	Skeleton	1:6

Several other old favourites also returned, while twenty or so kits were removed from the range.

The Web Warriors was another set of kits designed with the young modeller in mind. They were Transformer-like kits designed by Academy. However, along with the Battlezone range they disappeared from the 2000 catalogue.

Wallace and Gromit were licensed models from the very successful *Wallace & Gromit* films produced by Nick Park. The kits were designed by Airfix and would be one of three successful collaborations with other television films and series over the following ten years. They were the only new Airfix moulds that year.

Two sets containing a kit, video, paints and brushes were introduced, and three new present sets, which included three kits, were released.

The very successful B-17G kit, which dated from 1962, was finally retired and replaced by a 'polybagged' model from Academy. We are told that around four million of the old B-17G had been made over the years, and despite several inaccuracies, it is doubtful whether any other manufacturer of B-17s will ever come anywhere close to this production record; such was the dominance of Airfix in the popular market in the last millennium. The Sentry was a conversion of the Heller kit, and the Fiat G91 received new decals.

The Series 0 range was expanded by the inclusion of several more ex-Series 1 kits, and a new range of 1:144 Chinese kits appeared in Series 0. Most went into the Mini Starter Sets as well.

Two 'polybagged' 1:300 scale kits of airliners were also added, but due to their small size they were a bit of an oddity and didn't last long.

1:48 was continuing to prove popular with modellers, but Humbrol could not, it seems, afford the mould costs, so a series of ex-Arii kits was introduced over the following two years. They were generally well detailed kits.

Finally the old Skeleton kit returned, but this time with 'glow in the dark' paints. As a second coming it was short-lived.

The following year would see the new millennium, so hopes were high for new kits.

2000

The aptly titled 'Millennium Edition' catalogue was 70 per cent smaller than its predecessors at A5-size. The contents looked as if they had been reduced from A4, and some writing was quite small as a result. New additions included the following:

Individual Kits

00105	SAAB Viggen	1:144
00106	F-104 Starfighter	1:144
00033	Hawker P.1127	1:72
00060	Piper Cherokee Arrow	1:72
00061	SA Bulldog	1:72
02048	Messerschmitt Bf 109E	1:72
02051	Henschel Hs 123A-1	1:72
03030	Junkers Ju 87B	1:72
05107	Spitfire Mk VIIIc	1:48
05108	Grumman F6F-3 Hellcat	1:48

2000's 'Dogfighter' computer game.

05109	Curtiss Kittyhawk Mk Ia	1:48
03178	BAC One-Eleven	1:144
18003	Harrier GR.3/AV-8A/AV-8S	1:24
06201	RMS *Queen Elizabeth*	1:600
01741	Astronauts	1:76
01744	Waterloo French Infantry	1:76
01745	Waterloo British Infantry	1:76
01758	NATO Ground Crew	1:76
01759	US NATO (Europe)	1:76
02552	2nd Dragoon (Scots Greys)	54mm
02553	Polish Lancer	54mm
02555	French Cuirassier	54mm
02556	Lifeguard	54mm
03383	Pontoon Bridge	1:76
03013	Apollo Lunar Module	1:72
06171	Orion 2001 Spacecraft	1:144
09170	Apollo Saturn V	1:144
10170	Space Shuttle	1:144

Sets

| 10999 | B-of-B Memorial Flight Set | 1:72 |

A lot of old models returned to the range, including some that had not been issued for many years such as the Hawker P.1127, first released in 1963. The BAC One-Eleven later appeared in a starter set. The Bulldog received new Swedish decals.

Three more ex-Arii 1:48 kits were issued, and a 'Battle of Britain Memorial Flight' Set was released to celebrate the sixtieth anniversary of the Battle of Britain. It contained the Lancaster, Spitfire Ia (decaled as an IIa) and the Heller Hurricane IIc. Over the years the contents would vary to reflect those aircraft and colour schemes flown by the RAF Battle of Britain Memorial Flight.

The final two 1:144 fighters were added. Several space models were re-released, and were also released in the US by the Space Agency.

The only kit that could be classed as a new Airfix kit was the 1:24 Harrier. The original kit had been released in 1974, and now several extra parts were moulded so that you could make the RAF's GR.3 and the AV-8A and AV-8S as flown by the US Marine Corps and Spanish Navy. Decals were provided for four aircraft, and it was still possible to make the GR.1, because the basic mould had not been altered. Some cutting was required, but if you could afford the price and build such a complex model, then a little deft use of a razor saw should not be beyond you. The kit still features in the 2014 catalogue.

The various sets that had been introduced over the previous few years were drastically cut back until only thirty or so small and medium starter sets remained.

A full page was devoted to the recently published book by Arthur Ward – *Celebrating 50 Years of the Greatest Plastic Kits in the World!* But without substantial investment in new moulds it was doubtful whether Airfix would survive another fifty years. Frank Martin, CEO of Humbrol, left to join Hornby, but would be reunited with Airfix and Humbrol six years later. Also Allen, McGuire & Partners had re-financed the company, borrowing heavily from Royal Bank of Scotland to do so, and now took a back seat whilst the bank became more involved.

2001

The 2001 catalogue was bigger, literally mid-way in size between A5 and A4. The remaining range of sets was deleted, and a whole new range introduced. A new modified logo and packaging were also introduced. Several kits were brought in from Heller or other kit manufacturers, and there were four modified tools.

The new additions were as follows:

Inclusive Collections

Small Starter Sets

90059	Westland Gazelle	1:72
91036	Red Arrows Gnat	1:72
91042	Westland Scout	1:72
91071	Supermarine Spitfire	1:72
91412	Mini	1:43

91423	Jaguar XJS	1:43
91414	McLaren F1	1:43
91415	Williams F1	1:43
91416	Citroen Xsara T4	1:43
91417	Subaru Impreza WRC	1:43
91418	Peugeot 206 WRC	1:43
92058	Messerschmitt Bf 109E	1:72
02072	Harrier GR.3	1:72
92082	Hawker Hurricane Mk I	1:72
92416	VW Beetle	1:32

Medium Starter Sets

93019	DH Mosquito Mk II/VI/XVIII	1:72
93026	Red Arrows Hawk	1:72
93043	Westland Sea King	1:72
93063	Westland Navy Lynx Mk 8	1:72
93205	HMS *Fearless*	1:600
93407	Ferrari 250 LM	1:32

Junior Airfix

04914	Construction Skip Transporter	N/A
04915	Construction Mixer	N/A
04916	Safari Land Rover	N/A
04917	Safari Helicopter	N/A
04918	Delta Force Phantom	N/A
04919	Delta Force Liberator	N/A

Gift Packs

74025	F-16A/B Fighting Falcon	1:72
74026	F-117A Stealth	1:72
74036	Eurofighter Typhoon	1:72
74039	BAe Harrier GR.7	1:72
74212	HMS *Belfast*	1:600
75028	F-15E Strike Eagle	1:72

2001's 'Junior Airfix' kits.

04918 Delta Force Phantom

04919 Delta Force Liberator

04914 Construction Skip Transporter

04915 Construction Mixer

04916 Safari Land Rover

04917 Safari Helicopter

A starter kit of the BAC One-Eleven, 2001.

Premier Collections

97400	Rav 4	1:24
97403	Citroen Xsara T4 WRC	1:24
97404	Peugeot 206 WRC	1:24

Dogfight Doubles/Classic Conflicts

93141	Spitfire IX and Bf 110C/D	1:72
93142	Camel and Albatross	1:72
93143	Beaufighter and Bf 109G-6	1:72
93144	Bristol F2B and Fokker DR1	1:72
93340	Tiger 1 and Sherman Mk 1 Tank	1:76

Present Sets

9521	Fast Jets × 3	1:72
9522	Classic Cars × 3	1:43
51100	Wallace and Gromit Motorbike	N/A
51101	Wallace and Gromit Aeroplane	N/A

Individual Kits

03063	Westland Navy Lynx Mk 8	1:72
04043	SAAB JAS 39 Gripen	1:72
05029	Dornier Do 217 Mistel	1:72
05030	Boeing Chinook	1:72
05031	Douglas DC-3 Dakota	1:72
08006	Lancaster BI 'Grand Slam'	1:72
09003	Lockheed C-130E Hercules	1:72
12005	Supermarine Spitfire Mk Vb	1:24
01414	McLaren F1	1:43
01415	Williams F1	1:43
01416	Citroën Xsara T4 WRC	1:43
01417	Subaru Impreza	1:43
01418	Peugeot 206 WRC	1:43
07400	Rav 4	1:24

07401	MGB	1:24
07402	Aston Martin DB5	1:24
07403	Citroen Xsara T4 WRC	1:24
07404	Peugeot 206 WRC	1:24

In addition several other 'golden oldies' rejoined the range for a couple of years. Three of the 1:24 cars were ex-Japanese and the others were Heller kits often produced in two scales!

The sets used a standard packaging into which were inserted the paints and the standard kit box, which enabled Airfix to run them for as long as they had supplies of the standard kit. This meant there was a rapid turnover of the sets.

Junior Airfix was reintroduced, with six more ex-Heller 'snap-together' kits. Again these had a short life.

Three further Dogfight Doubles from the 1960s were revived, but this time included paints and so on.

The individual 'new' aircraft kits consisted of several 'polybagged' kits from other manufacturers, and four modified Airfix kits. Having irrevocably modified its Hercules into a gunship in the 1980s, Airfix had to import a kit if it wanted to have a standard Hercules in the catalogue, as it did with the Dakota, which had also been converted to a gunship. In 2014, Airfix released a new tool, C-47/DC-3, to much acclaim and is now able to offer various versions without having to resort

to buying-in a competitor's kit. Airfix had proposed a Chinook back in the 1980s but had not gone ahead, and so needed to 'borrow' one if it wanted to have one in the catalogue.

The new Airfix kits consisted of the Navy Lynx Mk 8, itself a modification of the original HAS.2 from 1977. The new kit used the old kit but had extra runners to make a model of the current RN helicopter. The existing upgraded version, the HAS.3, 03054, was still available.

The Dornier Do 217 was the old kit with extra parts moulded and a Me 328 jet, sourced from MPM, to ride 'piggyback' on the top.

The Lancaster 'Grand Slam' was the excellent Lancaster kit with an extra runner to provide the 'Grand Slam' bomb.

Finally, extra parts were moulded for the 1:24 Spitfire Mk Ia kit, so the modeller was now able to model a Mk V with alternative tropical filter.

In each case it was still possible to make the original and both Spitfires are currently in the catalogue.

2002

2002 saw a return to a full-size A4 catalogue. Around thirty 'new' models were announced, plus eight new sets, though only two could be considered new Airfix kits. Seven more Heller car and motorcycle kits were added, and a couple of 1:48 jets were 'polybagged' from other companies. Several aircraft returned with new decals and illustrations, and the old Airfix Hercules Gunship made a brief comeback. It was now possible to compare the old Airfix Hercules with the standard Hercules by Italeri, which was still in the catalogue.

Some new starter sets were added. The 'new' models included:

Small Starter Sets

92482	Honda 500cc	1:24
92483	Suzuki 500cc	1:24
92484	Yamaha 500cc	1:24
91419	Ford Focus WRC	1:43
91420	Mitsubishi WRC	1:43

Present Sets:

N/A	Rally Car Set 1 × 3 cars	1:43
N/A	Rally Car Set 2 × 3 cars	1:43
N/A	Bike Set × 3 Bikes	1:24

Individual Kits

03059	Shorts Tucano	1:72
04040	BAe/McDD Harrier TAV-8B/T.10	1:72

Small Present Set from 2002, featuring models of the Hawker Hurricane and Lockheed P-38 Lightning.

2002's kit of the Focke Wulf Fw 190A/F.

09002	Avro Vulcan B.2	1:72
09004	AC-130H Hercules 'Gunship'	1:72
05101	BAe Sea Harrier FRS.1	1:48
05102	BAe Harrier GR3	1:48
05110	Spitfire Mk Vc / Seafire III	1:48
07104	Sepecat Jaguar GR.3	1:48
07107	SAAB JA-37 Viggen	1:48
07108	Super Etendard	1:48
20001	BAe Sea Harrier FRS.1	1:24
05204	World War II Destroyer Set	1:600
06203	*Queen Elizabeth 2*	1:600
01419	Ford Focus WRC	1:43
01420	Mitsubishi WRC	1:43
07405	Mitsubishi WRC	1:24
07406	Subaru Impreza WRC	1:24
02482	Honda 500cc	1:24

02483	Suzuki 500cc	1:24
02484	Yamaha 500cc	1:24
01736	Waterloo French Cavalry	1:76
01743	Waterloo British Cavalry	1:76
01744	Waterloo French Infantry	1:76
01745	Waterloo British Infantry	1:76
01756	Waterloo Prussian Infantry	1:76

The starter and present sets included the new and recently released Heller-designed vehicle kits. The car kits were designed and then produced in two scales, which helped to reduce the design costs by spreading each one over two kits. Following the sale of Humbrol and Airfix to Hornby in 2006, these moulds stayed with Heller.

The three present sets were not actually allocated catalogue numbers; certainly none appeared in the catalogue, and they used the standard tray, which did not have any numbers on.

As I mentioned earlier, several old favourites were reintroduced, some without alteration and some with new decals and illustrations. The F-16A/B, F-18A and F-14A all received new decals. In the 1:144 civil airliners the TriStar, A300B and DC-10 returned. The Tucano made a comeback with a striking new colour scheme and artwork; and that perennial favourite, the Vulcan reappeared with a new Gavin McLeod painting showing it flying above the runway at Port Stanley. Those listed are the ones that were reissued as another mark or were a more interesting reissue.

The two-seat Harrier had originally been issued as the RAF trainer but this release saw the US Marine Corps decals included. A much improved illustration was used. In 1:48 scale the Harrier GR.3 and Sea Harrier FRS.1 both received new decals and excellent new artwork.

The original 1969 Hercules kit had been re-released in 1977 as a C-130E, and then in 1984 the mould had been irreversibly altered to make the AC-130H model, with various Gatling guns moulded separately to make a 'gunship', similar to the earlier Dakota conversion.

I had written some years before in *Constant Scale* that it was a great shame that moulds such as the Hercules, VC10 and Canberra had been irreversibly altered so that the original version could no longer be made. Peter Allen, who was a designer at both Airfix and Palitoy / Airfix, wrote back pointing out that kit companies were in the end there to make money. If a kit's sales were trailing off and it was thought likely to rejuvenate sales by producing a different version, then the mould would be altered at a lower cost than a new mould, and that cost could be recouped by the extra sales. This made commercial sense, but the Humbrol philosophy was to add extra runners to make a conversion without altering the mould.

This approach is best seen in the kit of the Spitfire Mk Vc and Seafire III. Trevor Snowden, chief designer at Humbrol/ Airfix and a confirmed Spitfire enthusiast, elected to produce a kit that covered most of the early marks of Spitfire. To achieve this he virtually moulded a new kit with new fuselages, wings and many smaller parts. These new runners were crammed into a box containing the original Mk V kit. A handful of small parts were still used from the old kit, but it did mean that the Spitfire Vb could still be sold as a stand-alone kit. In 2014, Airfix released a new tool of the Spitfire Vb, but the old tool will still be available to make the Seafire kit, until Hornby moulds a new Seafire III.

The main drawback to this approach, which was largely dictated by financial considerations prevailing at Humbrol, is that the resulting kit can be expensive to produce. The Seafire and 2003 Mosquito kits all require practically two complete kits to make them, which impacts seriously on the profitability unless the price is raised, which would blunt sales. Hornby is more likely to mould new multi-version kits of the Seafire and Mosquito in the future.

The Jaguar GR.1a was released as a GR.3 and Jaguar ES. New decals and box top were included. An ex-Esci Viggen and a Heller Super Etendard also joined the range of 1:48 aircraft.

The other new Airfix kit was a release of the Sea Harrier FRS.1 in 1:24 scale. It was the second of three proposed modifications to the standard Harrier GR.1 kit released in 1974. Like the real thing, which was a conversion from the RAF Harrier GR.3, this kit was similar. Enough extra parts were moulded to make the Sea Harrier, including a new cockpit, nose and canopy. The inside of the forward fuselage was 'scored' into the mould, and the existing nose had to be cut off to fit the new nose. Both kits are still in the catalogue today.

Trevor was also working on a conversion to produce the Sea Harrier FA.2 model. As well as a new nose, this version required an extended rear fuselage, which on the real thing needed the fuselage aft of the wing to be separated and a parallel section inserted. Since it was much more likely that a modeller would not make an accurate cut, it was proposed that after moulding, the fuselage halves would be cut in the factory, thus making the conversion much easier for modellers. In the end, I believe cost put paid to this conversion. Nowadays I suspect it would be cheaper to mould new fuselage halves and thus avoid all the complicated 'surgery'. However, I am told that CAD-designed parts do not really fit into the old moulded parts, so this option may not be viable.

Given the cheaper cost of CAD-designing, if Hornby wanted to have a

This 2002 kit could be assembled as a Spitfire Vc or a Seafire IIIc.

range of 1:24 Sea Harriers in its catalogue, it would probably opt to produce a basic Harrier mould with extra runners to provide for the different fuselages and weapons. The GR versions could also be factored in at little extra cost.

Five sets of Waterloo figures were re-released, but the Farm House was not, so they had nothing to fight over!

The other interesting release was a boxed set of the four World War II destroyers in 1:600 scale. These had long been out of production, and this was considered to be a cost-effective way of re-releasing them. Like the original Dogfight Doubles where two kits could be released for less than the cost of both, by putting them into one box they could be sold at a much lower price than individually. The kits included the *Narvik* Class Destroyer and HMS *Hotspur*, *Cossack* and *Campbeltown*. Later the remaining small ships, HMS *Daring* and HMS *Leander*, would be combined in sets with a larger ship.

In 2003 these ideas of conversions and combining kits were further extended.

2003

The 2003 catalogue was preceded by a leaflet issued at the toy fairs. 2003 was going to be a good year for modellers, with several Heller kits joining the range, but more importantly new moulds of the Hawk and Mosquito in 1:48 scale! In the leaflet these new kits were shown at

Series 7 and 8 respectively, but when the catalogue arrived they had been lowered to Series 5 and 7, which was good news. The usual crop of old moulds returned but they were refreshed by new decals and illustrations. The new kits were as follows:

Small Starter Sets

92020	Northrop F-5E Tiger II	1:72
92036	NA F-86E Sabre	1:72
92080	BAC Lightning F.3	1:72
92099	CA 13 Boomerang	1:72
92485	Honda RC211V	1:24

Medium Starter Sets

93015	SAAB Viggen	1:72
93025	Westland Army Lynx	1:72

Large Gift Sets

74025	F-16A/B Fighting Falcon	1:72
74027	Panavia Tornado GR.1	1:72
74032	McDD F-18A Hornet	1:72
74039	BAe Harrier II GR.7	1:72
74100	Supermarine Spitfire Mk Vb	1:48
74212	HMS *Belfast*	1:600

Gift Sets

93302	RAF Diorama Set	1:72
95450	Le Mans Car Collection × 4	1:43
96450	World Rally Car Collection × 3	1:43
96499	Racing Motorbikes × 3	1:24
98099	Navy Firepower × 3 Aircraft	1:72
95111	Red Arrows Hawk Gift Set	1:48
97111	DH Mosquito NF.30 Gift Set	1:48
10998	617 Sqn 60th Anniversary Set	1:72

Tornado GR4/4A			08105	
Scale	Length	Width	Pieces	Skill
1:48	348	290	132	4

Tornado GR.4 kit from 2003.

D.H. Mosquito NF30			07111	
Scale	Length	Width	Pieces	Skill
1:48	257	343	127	3

D H Mosquito B MkXVI/PR XVI			07112	
Scale	Length	Width	Pieces	Skill
1:48	257	343	127	3

2003 also offered both fighter and bomber versions of the de Havilland Mosquito.

Individual Kits

02020	Northrop F-5E Tiger II	1:72
02036	NA F-86F Sabre	1:72
02080	BAC Lightning F.3	1:72
02099	CA 13 Boomerang	1:72
04026	VC10 Tanker	1:144
04035	Panavia Tornado F.3	1:72
05111	BAe Red Arrows Hawk	1:48
05112	BAe Hawk 100	1:48
07111	DH Mosquito NF.30	1:48
07112	DH Mosquito B Mk XIV/PRXVI	1:48
08105	Panavia Tornado GR.4/4A	1:48
04213	HMS *Tiger* and *Daring* Set	1:600
01421	Subaru Impreza WRC'02	1:43
07407	Ford Focus WRC'02	1:24
07108	Peugeot 206 WRC'02 'Safari'	1:24
02485	Honda RC211V	1:24
07480	Honda RC211V	1:12
07481	Yamaha YZR-M1	1:12
01707	Cowboys	1:76
01708	American Indians	1:76
01715	Wagon Train	1:76
01722	US Cavalry	1:76
01750	World War II Australian Infantry	1:76

The starter sets mainly used the new and re-released kits in them, as it was an ideal way to maximize sales of the basic kit. The large gift sets were used as a way to group kits together or make a specialist set. The RAF Diorama Set was not advertised but included the Mosquito and Refuelling Set.

The Navy Firepower Set comprised a US Navy Tomcat, Hornet and Royal Navy Lynx. The 617 Squadron Set gave the modeller the Dambusters' Lancaster with a Tornado GR.4/4A, the first and the last, so to speak.

Among the individual kits there were two brand new tools and two heavily modified tools. The new kits were both variants of the BAe Hawk in 1:48 scale. The Red Arrows' Hawk was produced from the same mould as the Hawk 100 Lead-In Fighter Trainer. They were really nice models although some of the inscribed detail was a little heavy. Several updated and 'special' colour scheme variants have been added over the years since.

The Mosquito, which was first released in 1980, was always a very good model as it was based on the work done for the proposed 1:24 kit before that kit was abandoned. Trevor's idea was to add sufficient extra runners to enable two different Mosquitoes to be made. Both new kits were supplied with the standard Mosquito kit, 07100, which was unaltered, plus the extra runners to make the particular variant. A fault with the original Mosquito was the rather heavy main spar, which stood proud of the upper wing. This was overcome by moulding new wings. The three kits have been variously available since, and the PR.XVI (07112) was reintroduced in 2014 with new decals and artwork.

The cars and motorbikes were all Heller-designed kits. The F-86F Sabre kit was a Heller model and appeared for a few years. Airfix had produced a model of the Sabre Dog back in 1975, but this was the first real Sabre to appear in the range. In 2010, Hornby produced the first of two Sabre models to replace the Heller kit.

Following on from the Destroyers Set, Airfix released HMS *Daring* in a boxing with HMS *Tiger*. The original painting of HMS *Tiger* was executed by William Howard Jarvis and was recently on view at RAF Hendon as art of the exhibition of original Airfix artwork. It is about 3 × 4ft, somewhat larger than the box top! It is an exceptionally good painting with incredible detail. The box size enabled a much better view of the painting than the earlier 'letterbox' size used for the original releases.

Finally, Airfix re-released the Australians and the four 'Wild West' sets of figures in OO/HO scale. New artwork was needed for the Wagon Train because the original transparency was missing.

Airfix seemed to be spending more money on new moulds, which was very encouraging and led us to hope that we would see many more new moulds coming out.

2004

As in 2003, Airfix produced a leaflet for 2004 entitled *New Inspirations*, which showed the proposed releases for 2004 prior to the catalogue appearing. The catalogue was arranged in themes, which was slightly confusing as some of the new kits intended for a particular theme did not appear in it! There were about ten 'new' kits, and the starter sets were relaunched. The new 'gift sets' comprised the following:

Range A

00015G	DH Tiger Moth	1:72
01071G	Spitfire Mk Ia	1:72
01036G	Red Arrows Gnat	1:72
01417G	Subaru Impreza	1:43
01064G	Focke-Wulf Fw 190D	1:72
01302G	Panther Tank	1:76

Range B

01419G	Ford Focus WRC	1:43
01420G	Mitsubishi Lancer Evo	1:43
01421G	Subaru WRC 02	1:43
01422G	Peugeot 206 WRC	1:43
01423G	Citroen Xsara	1:43
02483G	Suzuki 500cc	1:24
02484G	Yamaha 500cc	1:24
02485G	Honda RC211V	1:24

Two 'Ninety Years of Fighters' triple packs from 2004.

02486G	Ducati	1:24	03146G	Red Arrows Hawk and Gnat	1:72	
01303G	M4 Sherman Mk 1 Tank	1:76	04208G	HMS *Ark Royal*	1:600	
01308G	Tiger I Tank	1:76	04212G	HMS *Belfast*	1:600	
02020G	Northrop F-5E Tiger II	1:72	04027G	Panavia Tornado GR.1	1:72	
02039G	SAAB Draken	1:72	04039G	Harrier GR.7	1:72	
02042G	Hawker Hurricane Mk I	1:72	05013G	Grumman F-14A Tomcat	1:72	
02046G	Spitfire Mk Vb	1:72	05026G	F-177A Stealth	1:72	
02048G	Messerschmitt Bf 109E	1:72	04100G	Spitfire Mk Vb	1:48	
02072G	BAe Harrier GR.3	1:72				
03043G	Westland Sea King	1:72				

07480	Honda RC211V	1:12	
07481	Yamaha YZR-M1	1:12	
07482	Ducati	1:12	

Range E

06101G	Spitfire F.22/F.24	1:48
07101G	Hughes AH-64A Apache	1:48
07104G	Sepecat Jaguar GR.3	1:48
07111G	DH Mosquito NF.30	1:48
07360G	Challenger II Tank	1:35

Range C

03026G	Red Arrows' Hawk	1:48
03141G	Spitfire IX and Bf 110C/D	1:72
03143G	Beaufighter and Bf 109G-6	1:72

Range D

07405	Mitsubishi WRC	1:24
07407	Ford Focus WRC'02	1:24
07408	Subaru Impreza	1:24
07409	Peugeot 206	1:24
07410	Citroën Xsara	1:24

Themed Gift Sets

10010G	Frontline Fighters × 2	1:48
10300G	D-Day 60th Anniversary	1:72
10400G	Rally Car Collection	1:43

10404G	Racing Motorbikes	
	Collection	1:24
11050G	Concorde	1:72
12250G	*Queen Mary 2*	1:600
98098G	RAF Firepower × 3	1:72
95450G	Le Mans Car Collection × 4	1:43
09750G	Red Arrows 40th Season Set	1:72
09252G	Classic HMS *Victory*	1:180

Many of the sets were repackaged from earlier sets. and, of course, new releases featured prominently. The main packaging was also altered to a more dedicated type and moved away from the earlier idea of 'blistering' a standard kit.

The new and reissued kits included the following:

01023	Auster Antarctic	1:72
01048	Avro 504K	1:72
03011	BAC Jaguar GR.3	1:72
03021	SA330 Puma	1:72
04007	Savoia-Marchetti SM79	1:72
04041	Tornado GR.4/4A	1:72
04044	AH-64D Apache Longbow	1:72
04046	Bell AH-1T Sea Cobra	1:72
05025	Sukhoi Su-27 Flanker B	1:72
06101	Spitfire F.22/F.24	1:48
09175	Panavia Tornado F.3/EF.3	1:48
11050	BAC-Aerospatiale Concorde	1:72
05205	Falklands Warships	1:600
12250	*Queen Mary 2*	1:600
01321	LCVP Landing Craft	1:76
01322	Willy's Jeep	1:76

01323	GMC Truck	1:76
07360	Challenger II Tank	1:35
07361	Abrams M1A2 Tank	1:35
07362	GMC DUKW	1:35
01732	British Commandos	1:76
02441	1933 Alfa Romeo 8c	1:32
02446	1930 Bentley	1:32
02451	Bugatti 35B	1:32
F1001	England Football Stars Set 1	N/A
F1002	England Football Stars Set 2	N/A
F1003	England Football Stars Set 3	N/A

Twelve aircraft were added, of which five were welcome reissues, two were 'poly-bagged' – Apache and Sea Cobra – four were upgrades and one was a new mould.

The Auster, Avro 504K and SM79 all returned with their original paintings. The Su-27 and Spitfire F.22/F.24 had new paintings by Humbrol's current artist, John D. Jones, who also painted the other box tops.

The Apache and Sea Cobra were both produced from moulds made by Ki-Tech and were only available for a couple of years. The upgraded kits all contained the standard model with several new runners added to make the latest version. Thus the old Jaguar GR.1 kit, which had had a laser nose added in 1977, had sufficient extra parts added to make the then current GR.3 variant. The Puma was upgraded to the latest standard, and the Tornado GR.1 from 1983 now became the latest GR.4/4A variant. Finally, the large Tornado, upgraded in 1987, could now be made as the EF.3 version. This was a relatively cost-effective way of prolonging the life of these kits until the actual aircraft left service.

The totally new mould was a large 1:72 model of the Anglo-French Concorde. It was tooled by Heller. The long fuselage was made in three pieces, but the level of detail was not very great, and the panel lines were quite wide and deep. Concorde was known to expand by several inches when flying supersonically, but the depth and width of the panel lines was a little overdone!

Airfix produced its final set of small ships when it produced the Falklands Warship Set. Back in the 1980s, Airfix had moulded Exocet and other missiles to fit its two old warships, HMS *Devonshire* and *Leander*. HMS *Amazon* was fine for a Falklands ship. Since they were unlikely to be released singly again, this grouping was a sensible and profitable way of using the moulds.

The three high-speed launches in 1:72 scale were re-released along with USS *Forrestal*.

Airfix's first new liner since the *QE2* was the *Queen Mary 2*, again tooled in France, where the original was actually built. It was a much better model than the Concorde, and built up into a sizable model.

Three of Airfix's 1930s vintage cars were released again and all used their original illustrations.

Airfix went to town on the sixtieth anniversary of D-Day, with three new AFV kits released in 1:76 scale. The 'Higgins' LCVP boat, a Willy's Jeep and GMC truck were all tooled by Heller, which had previously modelled some of them in 1:35 scale. After a break of twenty-five years it was good to see Airfix making new AFV kits again. Airfix had made a jeep many years before, but it was included in the Buffalo kit, which made it an expensive way to build a collection of jeeps. In 2014, Hornby decided to tool new models of the LCVP and Jeep for the seventieth anniversary of D-Day range.

Three recent kits from Trumpeter and Italeri to 1:35 scale were brought into the range. They were all good kits and made reasonable replicas, but their scale of 1:35 did not fit into the Airfix range which was 1:32, and anyway was not currently available. The DUKW was relevant to D-Day, of course, but again there was nothing else in the range to go with it.

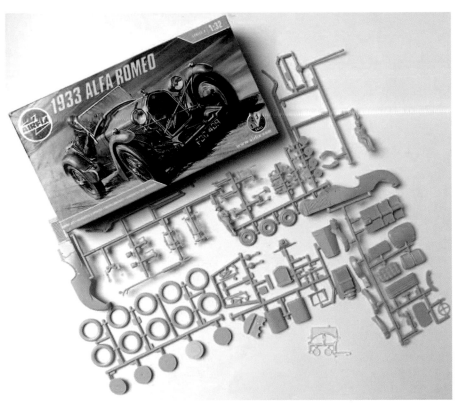

1969 Alfa Romeo in Type 14 packaging, 2004.

Three Vintage cars were re-released, all in Series 2. They all used their original illustrations.

The British Commandos returned, but were still the original figures as the mould for the newer set could not be found.

The big surprise of the year was the release of three sets of footballers! The figures were around 10in tall, which made them a rather odd scale. There were enough parts to construct four footballers in each box, and four heads, made out of a rubbery kind of compound, moulded to represent four members of the England football team. The other two boxes contained the same kit parts but four different heads. In all, twelve footballers could be made. They were released to coincide with the Euro Cup in June and the World Cup qualifier later. As we now know, England was knocked out fairly

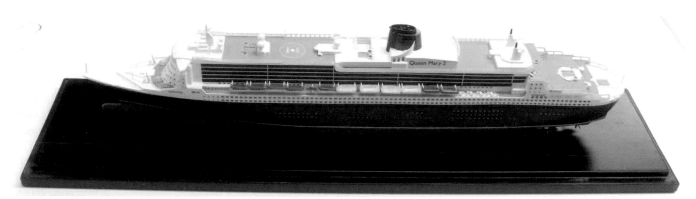

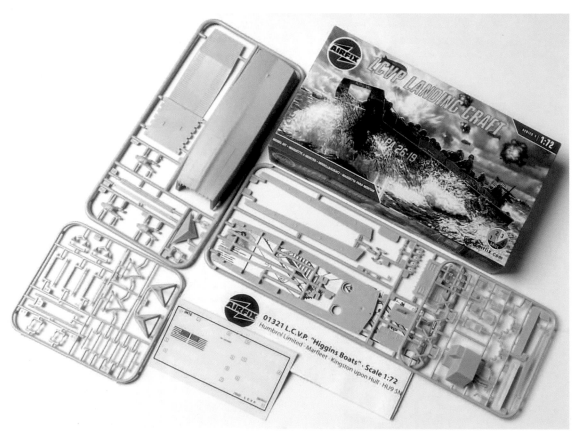

TOP: *2004's Churchill Tank set.*

ABOVE: *The Queen Mary 2 model from 2004.*

LEFT: *LCVP Landing Craft kit, 2004.*

quickly, which can't have helped sales! With the rapid turnover of players and David Beckham's haircut over the years, the chances of seeing them again are not great. Even if new heads could be moulded, the actual football kit has probably changed enough.

Also released that year were six jigsaw puzzles based on box-top artwork. Three were sold in tubes, and three larger ones in boxes.

Therefore 2004 was a good year overall, and one felt that Humbrol, or at least its bankers, was beginning to spend a little more money on Airfix.

2005

Three new kits were announced for 2005, although strictly speaking one was a Heller kit, six kits were modified, and the usual crop of reissues appeared as 'new' kits. Heller was sold to its own management, although it continued to make kits for Airfix. In fact the majority of kits produced by Heller were Airfix kits. The new kits included the following:

Gift Sets – Range A

01017G	MiG-15	1:72
01030G	Messerschmitt Me 262A	1:72
01043G	F-5A Freedom Fighter	1:72
01059G	Westland Gazelle	1:72
01267G	HMS *Victory*	N/A

Gift Sets – Range B

01424G	Peugeot 307 WRC	1:43
02486G	Ducati	1:24
02487G	Yamaha 500cc	1:24

Gift Sets – Range C

03147G	Hurricane IIb and Junkers Ju 88	1:72

03148G	Meteor III and V1 Flying Bomb	1:72
05032G	F-117A Stealth	1:72
04042G	Panavia Tornado GR.4/4A	1:72

Gift Sets – Range D

07412G	Peugeot 307	1:24

Themed Gift Sets

08666	Concorde	1:144
08667	Dinosaurs Set 1 × 3	N/A
08668	Sea Rescue Set	1:72
09750	Red Arrows Anniversary Set	1:72
10301	VE-Day Anniversary Set	1:72
08672	VJ-Day Anniversary Set	1:72
11999	HMS *Victory* – 200 Years	1:100

Boxed Sets

04214	HMS *Manxman and Suffolk*	1:600
12201	Kriegsmarine	1:400
09441	Dennis Fire Engine and Omnibus	1:32
08366	World War II Desert Rat Set	1:32
12301	1945 – Road to Berlin	1:72

Individual Kits

01085	Avro 504K	1:72
02040	Supermarine Spitfire Mk Vc	1:72
03009	HS Dominie T.1	1:72
03065	SAAB S/J-29 Tunnan	1:72
03066	NA T-6G Texan	1:72
04028	Lockheed U-2 B/C/D	1:72
05033	F-117A Stealth	1:72
06012	Fairchild A-10 Thunderbolt	1:72
06013	HP Halifax BIII	1:72
07004	BAC TSR2	1:72
08007	Avro Lancaster 'G' for George	1:72
05113	Supermarine Spitfire Mk IXc	1:48
05114	BAe Hawk 100 Series	1:48
09180	Buccaneer S.2/B-C-D S Mk50	1:48

14003	NA P-51K Mustang	1:24
16002	Hawker Hurricane Mk IIc	1:24
06280	RNLI Severn Class Lifeboat	1:72
02320	Sherman 'Crab' Tank	1:76
02321	Churchill 'Crocodile' Tank	1:76
03580/6	7 × Multipose Sets	1:32

Extras

J4102	Hurricane Mk I – Jigsaw	
J9252	HMS *Victory* – Jigsaw	
J9256	*Wasa* – Jigsaw	
61601	Airfix Diecast Fighters × 2	1:72
61602	Airfix Diecast Rally Cars × 3	1:43

The gift sets had the usual new releases added to them, and two new Dogfight Doubles were included. The Meteor had a V1 Flying Bomb borrowed from another manufacturer.

The themed gift sets saw the new Lifeboat in a box with the Sea King helicopter. The Red Arrows Anniversary Set contained a Hawk and two Gnats. One of the Gnats came with the colours of the 'Yellowjacks', which was the forerunner of the Red Arrows.

The Dinosaurs Set included three of the original dinosaur kits in one boxing, being the Tyrannosaurus Rex, Stegosaurus and Triceratops. The set did not appear in the catalogue until 2006 but was released in 2005, along with Wallace and Gromit's Anti-Pesto Van.

The VE Anniversary Set contained a variety of 1:72/1:76 kits appropriate to the end of the war in Europe. The VJ-Day Anniversary Set did the same for the Japanese war. Finally the 200 Years – HMS *Victory* Set had the large 1:100 Heller kit complete with paints and historical details.

One or two individual kits returned unaltered, but all the rest were either ex-Heller or had decal and illustration

Various World War II fighting men kits from 2005.

changes. The Avro 504K from 2004 had a new set of decals added and was allocated a new catalogue number.

The Spitfire Vc kit was the old Spitfire V kit with extra parts added to make the Vc version. The Dominie had not been released since Humbrol bought Airfix in 1986 so it was pleasing to see it back again; it had all new decals and box artwork.

The SAAB and the Texan were both Heller kits. The Texan was a slightly different version to the old Airfix Harvard and was an infinitely better model. The Heller models disappeared after the Hornby takeover in 2006.

The U-2 kit was issued in all its versions, and it and the F-117A Stealth and Thunderbolts all received new decals and illustrations.

The Halifax and Lancaster both received new decals and illustrations. In the case of the Lancaster, the markings used for the first Lancaster kit were applied, and the iconic Roy Cross painting of the Lancaster coming into land with a burning engine was used. This painting is a favourite of many older modellers.

The two Buccaneer kits were re-released in one boxing, and due to a mix-up, many of the early ones contained two complete kits!

The other aircraft kits were largely upgrades of existing kits. The Supermarine Spitfire contained the existing Mk V kit,

with sufficient extra parts to make the Mk IX version. Like the earlier Seafire Mk VIII, the box was crammed with virtually two kits. The Hawk 100 was released with extra decals for a South African Air Force aircraft and given a new catalogue number.

The Mustang was the old P-51D kit, but with an extra runner to make the K version. This option had been available on the small P-51D/K kit, and it enabled Airfix to offer its big brother in the same way. The large Hurricane was more interesting. Again, extra parts were to be moulded, but it was also proposed to mould one fuselage half in clear plastic so the inside could be viewed. When Airfix proposed the idea to its retailers it met a lukewarm response, so the conversion was quietly dropped.

The new aircraft kit was a 1:72 model of the ill-fated TSR2 bomber which was cancelled in 1965 and has remained a cult figure ever since. Airfix had progressed

Dinosaurs set from 2005, including Tyrannosaurus Rex, Stegosaurus and Triceratops.

quite far with a kit in the early 1960s, but apparently had to abandon it after concerns from the MoD that it might give secrets away! Airfix had always tried to keep ahead of the competition by producing kits of aircraft that were only prototypes at the time. Some would go on to be updated to production standard, whilst others remained as prototypes. The TSR2 was probably the only aircraft that never made it into production, but was constantly requested by model makers. It was released as a 'limited production' kit, with enough manufactured to cover the costs. In fact it was so popular that Airfix went on to produce a 1:48 kit. The limited production status meant it was difficult for Airfix to release it as a mainstream kit for a few years, but it has been available in the Japanese Stratos four boxings.

Manxman and *Suffolk* were put together in the last of three boxings of smaller ship kits. Recently *Suffolk* was released on its own. The Kriegsmarine Set was a collection of several small ships from the Heller 1:400 range. It would pave the way for the introduction of several capital ships from that range.

For the other new mould, Airfix returned to its range of 1:72 fast boats, only this time the subject was the civilian RNLI lifeboat. The three earlier military boats had all been excellent models and were in the catalogue for 2014. This model

Avro Lancaster 'G-For George' in Type 15 boxing, 2005.

TOP LEFT: *2005's VJ-Day set.*

MIDDLE LEFT: *Halifax B III from 2005.*

BOTTOM LEFT: *2005's Lockheed U-2 kit.*

2005's set of the fast minelayer HMS Manxman *and the cruiser HMS* Suffolk.

Dennis Fire Engine & Omnibus set, 2005.

was equally good, and made up into a very compact and interesting model. The pairing with the Sea King enabled modellers to build dioramas incorporating the two main methods of rescuing mariners at sea. A portion of the proceeds of each sale was given to the RNLI.

Humbrol had always been strapped for cash, and so the updating of old moulds by adding new parts seemed the best that modellers were likely to get, along with the occasional new mould. Aircraft and the occasional warship had received this treatment, but in this year Humbrol announced the first two of several proposed updates to its top-selling AFV range in 1:76 scale.

The first two 'mods' were to the Sherman and Churchill tanks, both first released in 1961. Over the last fifty or so years the Sherman in particular has been criticised for not being very accurate, but it continues to be a consistent best seller. Apart from adding a little extra detail in the mid-1960s, both kits are unaltered.

For both kits Airfix added extra runners, which provided the parts to make a flailing mine clearer or 'Crab' for the Sherman, and a trailing bowser and other parts to make a flame-throwing 'Crocodile' for the Churchill. Both kits were released in Series 2 and included the original kit with the extra parts. To wargamers and younger modellers, who were not so concerned with 100 per cent accuracy, it was a fairly cheap way of adding extra tanks to one's arsenal.

A further playset, '1945 – The Road to Berlin' was issued, and included several figures, tanks and aircraft to celebrate the sixtieth anniversary of the end of the European War.

In 1:32 scale, the seven multipose sets were released again, along with a Desert Rat Set. This included the Crusader Tank and a set of 8th Army and Afrika Korps multipose figures.

The Dennis Fire Engine and 'B'-type bus were put into a single box and sold as a pair.

On the non-kit side, two more jigsaws were released in boxes, and two sets of diecast cars and aircraft were sold. These were only available for a limited period.

Things were finally starting to look up at Humbrol, and modellers were looking forward to more exciting new moulds in the following year.

CHAPTER FIVE

Airfix as Part of Hornby, 2006–2015

2006

2006 was indeed a momentous year for Airfix. At IPMS Modelworld at Telford in November 2005, Airfix had revealed that 2006 would see the release of a model of the Nimrod maritime patrol aircraft in 1:72 scale, and no fewer than four Canberras in 1:48 scale! There was the usual crop of reintroductions and upgrades, but significantly in the catalogue they were now referred to as 'new to Airfix', 'new kit' or 'back by popular demand', which helped newer modellers distinguish between the new moulds and the older kits. The new additions for 2006 consisted of the following:

Themed Gift Sets

08252G	Great Western Gift Set	1:180
08678	Spitfire Commemorative Set	1:72
08679	Spitfire Commemorative Set	1:48
08680	Dinosaurs 2 Set × 3	N/A
10170G	Space Shuttle 25th Anniversary	1:144
07901	Classic Cars × 3	1:32
10405	Rally Cars – Updated Set	1:43
10406	Racing Bikes – Updated Set	1:24
50100	Wallace and Gromit Anti-pesto	1:12
50101	Wallace and Gromit Collection	N/A
06501	English Civil War Collection	54mm
06901	World War II RAF Airfield Set	1:72
06902	World War II Luftwaffe Airfield Set	1:72
06903	World War II US Airfield Set	1:72
06904	Modern RAF Airfield Set	1:72

Individual Kits

12050	BAe Nimrod MR.1/MR.2/ 2P/R.1	1:72
10101	EE Canberra B.2, B.20	1:48
10102	EE Canberra B(I).8, B(I).12	1:48
10103	EE Canberra PR.9	1:48
10104	Martin B-57B, RB-57E/G	1:48
03067	BN-2A Islander/Defender	1:72
04015	Martin B-26C Marauder	1:72
04047	DH Dragon Rapide	1:72
05034	Lockheed Hudson 1	1:72
04048	Sea King HAS.5, AEW.2A	1:72
08008	Lockheed Super Constellation	1:72
08009	Civil Aircraft Collection	1:72
03177	Sud SE-210 Caravelle	1:144
02309	Bristol Bloodhound	1:76
02315	Opel Blitz and PAK 40 Gun	1:76
03301	LCM III and Sherman Tank	1:76
03306	Matilda 'Hedgehog' Tank	1:76
03307	Sherman 'Calliope' Tank	1:76
04301	Churchill Bridge Layer	1:76
01718	World War II Japanese Infantry	1:76
01754	World War II Gurkhas	1:76
01757	World War II Italian Infantry	1:76
08202	HMS *Hood*	1:400
08203	HMS *King George V*	1:400
08204	*Scharnhorst* or *Gneisenau*	1:400
08205	*Bismarck* or *Tirpitz*	1:400

The main activity with the sets was in the large number of themed sets that were added. The 200th anniversary of Brunel's birth was celebrated with the re-release of his Great Western ship model. For the seventieth anniversary of the first flight of the Spitfire two sets were announced but only the 1:72 scale set was actually released. The 1:48 set was to include an exclusive tool modification to make a Mk Ia, but the events of the summer meant this set was not released. A private company, ATP Promotions, released a 1:72 Spitfire Mk Ia and S6B in a tin as a limited run of 2,000 sets to mark the anniversary.

The second of the dinosaur sets was released, and I am not aware of there being plans to release the remaining three dinosaurs. The twenty-fifth anniversary of the Space Shuttle made a further gift set.

The Classic Car Set was basically an update of an earlier set. It included three cars: the Ford Escort, the Triumph Herald and the Vauxhall Viva. Since some of these cars were unlikely to be sold singly again, this was a good way of collecting them. However, the Triumph Herald was made available in a starter set in 2014.

The Rally Cars and Bikes sets were announced as 'updated sets', but I don't think they made it to production. Wallace and Gromit's anti-pesto van used in the film *The Curse of the Were-rabbit* was an all-new mould designed to 1:12 scale. At the same time the earlier two kits were combined into one set. A 1:12 scale Reliant Robin for an *Only Fools and Horses* license kit was proposed internally but not proceeded with.

The last 54mm figures to be released were figures from the English Civil War. The mounted figure could be made into a choice of two soldiers, one Royalist and the other a Roundhead. Two of these were included, with one each of the foot soldiers to make four figures, two from either side.

Finally, Airfix announced four Airfield sets. Each set had a different vac-formed base, an aircraft, a set of Airfield figures and a relevant AFV kit. Airfix had produced four sets of airfield personnel over the years, so this was a very effective way of using them.

Nimrod, the 'mighty hunter' of the Book of Genesis, was captured in this large model of the RAF's jet maritime surveillance aircraft. The kit included sufficient parts to make each of the versions operated by the RAF. The inscribed panel lines were a little deep, but did not detract from what was to be an awesome model.

The Canberra, modelled by Airfix many years previously and then altered irreversibly to a B-57, was now given the full treatment but in 1:48 scale. The kit was designed with two or three runners of parts that were common to all Canberras and B-57s, then separate runners were moulded for each kit, and these often included new fuselages and wings as well as the myriad other details for each variant. It was thus cheaper than four separate kits, and the costs could be recouped over four kits. Unfortunately, issuing all four kits in a year meant that the later kits tended to dilute sales of the core kit, and it thus took longer to repay the tooling costs. Nowadays Hornby try to issue the core kit in one year with variants following in the next, by which time the original has hopefully recouped its development costs.

The kits were very nicely detailed, although the engraved panel lines, like the Nimrod's, were deeper than we would have liked. However, it was great to see Canberras back in the Airfix catalogue.

The Islander and Marauder made welcome returns, resplendent in the original, lovely Roy Cross box tops. The Islander had been modified in 1977 to enable a Defender to be built, but when Humbrol wanted to release it, it was discovered that the clear canopy mould was missing, so a new mould was made. Strangely, some time later Airfix received an email from India questioning the mould sent to them for a Series 1 tank kit. The mould in question turned out to be the missing Islander windows, which it seems had been misfiled many years ago! The Dragon Rapide was the Heller model and was a decent representation of the original. Likewise the Super Constellation was a Heller model, and a large one too.

The Hudson had originally been released in 1963 and was elevated to Series 4 in 1986; it now rose to Series 5, but was given new decals and a painting by John D. Jones. The Sea King was the old kit, but was to have more runners added to make the Royal Navy's AEW variant.

The Caravelle returned, and three older 1:72 civil aircraft were released in a box as a set: they were the Heron, Ford Trimotor and Beaver.

Three old AFVs returned, and three new modifications were proposed. The Matilda and Sherman both had extra parts added to make rocket-firing versions. The Churchill had enough parts moulded to make a bridge layer using the existing kit. A Churchill 'carpet layer' was also proposed internally, but never featured in any catalogue. Three sets of World War II infantry joined the OO/HO figures.

The final new kits were the addition of four kits from Heller's 1:400 range. Each kit, apart from *Hood*, was capable of being built as two sister ships.

Also announced were the distribution rights to Robogear, a range of models for fantasy wargamers.

There were the usual deletions, including the TSR2 which Humbrol could not release again in the immediate future because of its 'limited production' status.

The two 1945 Anniversary sets disappeared, along with the entire range of jigsaws and diecast models.

However, further good news came in a press release on 6 February, which stated:

Airfix Humbrol has just received a welcome boost to its future with the arrival of a new top management team. Len Kalkum has taken over as Chief Operating Officer, while Colin Summerbell heads up Sales and Marketing and Peter Jones is the new Supply Director. This team of ex-Corgi fame is led by Chris Guest as Chairman. Jointly they represent one of the most experienced and successful teams in the hobby trade, and they are confident that they herald a turnaround in the Group's fortunes.

The new team is wholeheartedly committed to supporting the core Airfix modeller with increased investment in classic models, and additionally investing in new growth areas such as civil aviation; this will broaden the appeal of the brand. Much of this development is already in the pipeline, ensuring a steady stream of new Airfix products and concepts throughout 2006.

The company has already concluded its first acquisition with Colin's company, 1st Choice Collectables, coming into the Airfix Humbrol fold. At one stroke this means the company has acquired distribution rights to a number of well-known brands, as well as Colin himself.

This new distribution strategy has brought several brands into the group. These include Gemini Jets, highly detailed die-cast aviation models; First Gear collectible diecast construction and truck ranges; William Britain's military figures, and many other new product ranges.

Colin Summerbell states: This is a very exciting time at Airfix. The opportunity for the trade has never been greater, as we bring a wealth of new lines with proven appeal and we begin to support the trade in the way they have the right to expect. This can only help to build overall sales and profit and allow us to pump more tooling into the classic Airfix range. This must be good news for modellers.'

This was excellent news for Airfix, as it had been languishing for several years following the purchase by an Irish group, Allan & McGuire, in the mid-1990s. The acquisition by Humbrol in 1986 was regarded with much optimism, but a lack of money meant this potential was never reached. Now at last Airfix and Humbrol appeared to have the money and

resources they desperately needed. We all looked forward to what the new management would achieve.

Everything looked good and we couldn't wait for the kits to arrive – but then everything went horribly wrong.

I arrived home on Wednesday 30 August at around 6.30pm. There was a message on my answering machine from a leading national newspaper asking if I was aware that Airfix had gone into administration as of 5.30pm that day. I promptly phoned my local Airfix representative, who confirmed the news.

It was in fact Hobbies Product Group Ltd, which owned Humbrol, that had gone into administration, which also meant that subsidiaries such as Airfix were shut down. It appeared that Heller SA had gone into French administration in July, and was now refusing to supply kits to Airfix. Heller was also apparently disputing ownership of the moulds held at Trun, and this dispute could take up to two years to resolve in the French courts. Therefore Humbrol went to their bankers to explain the situation.

The bank was fully behind Humbrol, which despite having lost a great deal of money over the previous few years, mainly under the management of the Irish partnership, had appeared to turn the corner. This was largely due to the arrival of the ex-Corgi Toy directors. They brought with them a sound knowledge of the toy/model business as well as the distribution rights to several brands, including William Britain's toy soldiers and the Skymark range of 1:200 airliners.

They had also reviewed all the new models being planned by Airfix. However, far from terminating the new models, work proceeded on them. The new directors also agreed a three-year business plan with the bank, which included, for Airfix, an exciting 2007 programme of new moulds, revisions to moulds and re-releases. The lifeboat was actually finished and ready to start production when Airfix fell. The mould was in Portugal and not subject to the Heller impasse, and it looked set to be the most wanted new mould from Airfix for decades. The Nimrod was in the Far East and nearly finished. The Canberras were also in the Far East, but not yet ready. The Airfield sets were packed and awaiting shipment. Thus Airfix's future and position in the market place seemed to be at its best for decades.

Unfortunately the bank could see no early resolution to the mould problem, and the debt had rapidly increased without access to new kits. The bank decided therefore to stem the losses and close Humbrol and consequently Airfix.

The following day for me was extraordinarily busy. I got up just before 7am so as to give a live interview on Radio Four, and the rest of the day was spent being telephoned by journalists and newscasters. BBC News came to my house and recorded an interview for the six o'clock news, and two other photographers and live television crews turned up. I even had to write a quick article for the *Birmingham Post*. On the Friday I gave two more radio interviews, as well as going out live on Australian Broadcasting News at 5am!

What all this did show was the depth of feeling held by many people in this country and abroad for Airfix and its unrivalled range of construction kits. People were not really interested in Humbrol, Corgi, or any of the other brands affected, just Airfix, and all the reporters and newscasters said that they had made Airfix kits in their youth. It was as if a large part of the nation's childhood had been taken away.

The situation with the moulds did cause much gloom concerning saving Airfix, because Airfix was now effectively a company without anything to sell! However, several parties quickly showed an interest. Hornby was a possible purchaser, which would mean that Airfix would probably remain in this country. Revell was also interested, but I doubt whether Airfix would have survived as a separate kit company. The Matchbox kits Revell had acquired were all incorporated into the Revell range.

We just had to wait and see. The big obstacle for anyone wanting to buy Airfix was that access to the moulds had to be agreed. One could not have a thriving company just selling lifeboats, however popular they might be.

Heller had recently bought itself out from Humbrol. I had read that a French source had stated that Humbrol had failed to make a payment to Heller, which precipitated its French administration. However, my sources at Humbrol indicate that this was not the case, but rather it was Heller's failure to find more business for its factory (Airfix was 70 per cent of Heller's production) that pushed it into French administration. When Airfix wanted smaller runs of particular kits to better match market needs (something which the digital printing of box tops would allow), Heller found that without other 'customers' its income would be hit. Heller had, however, continued to produce Heller kits (it apparently had six months from its administration to continue producing) and wanted to produce Airfix ones! This loophole had now been closed.

This was the third time that the famous range Airfix construction kits had been put up for sale and this time the future did not look bright. Then on 10 November it was announced that Hornby Hobbies Ltd had purchased Humbrol, Airfix and New Scientist for £2.6 million. Sales and Marketing were being relocated to Hornby's HQ in Margate, Kent, while all the Airfix moulds were to be successfully repatriated to Margate, and Hornby was urgently looking for sites to manufacture the kits. In the end, China was selected to make the moulds, with production in India, though inevitably there would be a hiatus in production whilst everything was sorted out.

Frank Martin, CEO of Hornby, had plans to develop the Airfix range, and he was no stranger to the brand, having previously been CEO at Humbrol. At last the brand seemed safe, and we could all look forward to exciting developments coming out of Margate.

2007

The 2007 catalogue was essentially a 'warmed over' 2006 one. The bulk of the old catalogue was reprinted, and in the centre was a sixteen-page insert entitled '2007 Early Programme', which gave us hope for more to come later in the year. Naturally, Hornby was concentrating on getting out all the kits that were in the old catalogue whilst it set to work on designing new models. A new cover showed the Air-Sea Rescue Set, the only new kit that was guaranteed to be available. Two pages of the insert were devoted to the Lifeboat and Air-Sea Rescue sets, which were both labelled 'Available early 2007'. Donations of 60p and £1 respectively were to be donated to the RNLI.

A range of ready-assembled and pre-painted mini kits at 1:100 and 1:144 scales was announced, and four pages were devoted to the four Airfield sets, clearly showing what each set was composed of. Modellers could now model an airfield scene from the main combatants from the European theatre of World War II and the modern-day NATO forces. Different vehicles and aircraft could be assembled and used with each set.

The twenty-fifth anniversary of the Falklands War was to be celebrated and several models were illustrated and stated to be available later. They included the *Queen Elizabeth 2* and *Canberra* liners.

The Battle of Britain Memorial Flight received new markings and a colour box top to represent the 2007 season. The only new kit was the Spitfire Mk I, which had been intended for the 1:48 Spitfire Gift Set. It was now to be released as an individual kit with the catalogue number 05115. It contained parts to make a Mk I, a Mk Ia and a Mk. IIa, with enough propellers and spinners to make all three versions. It was an excellent model, and representative of the latest standard achieved by Humbrol.

Finally two pages were given over to the new Humbrol acrylic paint range. Like the 2006 catalogue, the Humbrol enamel range was shown in a separate leaflet inside the back cover.

The three AFV conversions which I was told had been put on hold the previous year were confirmed as going ahead. The two smaller conversions were to be sold in Series 2, a welcome reduction in price.

In the main catalogue, several kits were still shown to be of 'limited availability', indicating that they were no longer in production but there were still stocks of the kit available. Interestingly, Robogear was also now shown as being of 'limited availability', which shows that Hornby was not taking over the distribution rights. Robogear fans would either have to buy quickly, or go to the original producer to complete their sets.

Shortly after Humbrol went into administration I had been told that Airfix was working on a model of the Vickers Valiant V-Bomber in 1:72 scale. I knew that Hornby was looking seriously at all of Humbrol's future plans, so it was very much a case of keeping one's fingers crossed and hoping. What we needed to know was what was going to rise from the ashes of Humbrol, and in what direction Airfix was now headed. All kinds of rumours were circulating. Hornby had acquired the services of several key Humbrol employees, though not the new management team, and these included Trevor Snowden, the Chief Designer, and Darrell Burge from marketing, which meant they were in a good position to understand what sold well at Airfix.

For Trevor, the twenty years or so that he had been in charge of new releases for

Humbrol must have been at times frustrating. He had proposed many interesting and exciting new models for Airfix, but often found that the money for their development was not there. His two finest kits, the 1:48 Spitfires and Lightnings, are a fitting legacy, but did take several years to recoup their cost of development. He was always hampered by high design costs and low production runs, and under the circumstances he did remarkably well; Airfix enthusiasts owe him a debt of gratitude. Now in the twilight of his working life, things were suddenly looking up. We looked forward to further announcements coming out of Margate!

2008

Just before Christmas 2007, Hornby revealed some of its plans for the relaunch of Airfix. Prominent was the release of new models of Doctor Who and Shaun the Sheep, which were to be the flagships of the new range. There was a larger than normal number of deletions, which included the new Nimrod kit, though fortunately there were a lot of new moulds to take their places. Many of the gift sets were deleted, and most of the ex-Heller kits disappeared.

Several older Airfix kits were re-released, but for the first time new additions outweighed the older kits. The new kits were either new moulds, existing kits with new parts added, or 'poly-bagged' kits from other manufacturers. The reissued kits tended to use either their old illustrations, or new ones by John D. Jones who was still the current Airfix artist. Several other artists were employed to paint the box tops for series such as the ex-JB Models, which Hornby was introducing.

Probably the most far-reaching decision was that of using computer-aided design, or CAD, for the new models. CAD was already used by Hornby Trains, and it promised to allow much greater detail and accuracy for the kits, as well as costing much less than the old method of making the moulds – that of draughtsmanship, pattern making and pantographing down. Fewer models would need to be sold to break even, which raised the prospect of paying for the new kits in one or two years.

Also Hornby had decided to utilize digital artwork for the new releases, which would bring uniformity to the box tops. The first kit to use the new digital artwork by Adam Tooby was the 1:48 TSR2, and it helped launch the 'new look' Airfix. Hornby was still using a modified Type 15 packaging, but coupled later with the new Type 16 boxes with their bright red colour and Type 13 logo, Airfix was back!

The new releases comprised the following:

Individual Kits

A02005	BAe Hawk – Red Arrows	1:72
A02008	Fairey Fulmar	1:72
A02045	Hawker Sea Fury FBII	1:72
A02065	Spitfire Mk IXc	1:72
A02094	Hawker Tempest IV	1:72
A03068	FMA IA 58A Pucara	1:72
A03072	Buccaneer S.2B/S.2C/D S Mk 50	1:72
A03073	BAe Hawk 128/132	1:72
A03076	Gloster Meteor F.8	1:72
A03077	AH-64A Apache Longbow	1:72
A04048	Sea King HAS.5/AEW.2	1:72
A05003	Fokker F-27 Friendship	1:72
A05035	Boeing Chinook	1:72
A05036	Horsa Glider	1:72
A05037	Vickers Wellington Mk Ic	1:72
A05038	EE Canberra B(I).8	1:72
A05039	EE Canberra PR.9	1:72
A05040	Fw Mistel (Ta 154 and Fw 190A)	1:72
A10105	BAC TSR2	1:48

The 2008 D-Day Collection.

Bedford 4-ton truck kit from 2008.

A20002	DH Mosquito (Fighter)	1:24
A03251	HMS *Montgomery*	1:400
A03252	HNoMS *St Albans*	1:400
A10281	U-Boat Type XXIII	1:72
A01762	World War II British Infantry	1:76
A05870	Beam Engine	N/A
A05871	1804 Steam Locomotive	N/A

Ex-JB Military Models

A02322	LWB Landrover ST and Trailer	1:76
A02323	M113 US ACAV	1:76
A02324	LWB Landrover HT and Trailer	1:76
A02325	Saladin Mk 11 Armoured Car	1:76
A02326	Bedford MK 4-Tonne Truck	1:76
A02327	M113 US Fire Support Version	1:76
A02328	Saracen APC Mk 1/2/3	1:76
A02329	Bedford MK Aircraft Refueller	1:76
A02330	Vickers Light Tank	1:76
A02331	Landrover 1-Tonne FC Truck	1:76
A02332	British M119 105mm Field Gun	1:76
A02333	Landrover 1-Tonne Ambulance	1:76

Mini Kits

A50024	Focke-Wulf Fw 190A	1:100
A50025	P-47 Thunderbolt	1:100
A50026	Mitsubishi Zero	1:100
A50072	Messerschmitt Bf 109F	1:100
A50073	Supermarine Spitfire Mk Vb	1:100
A50074	NA P-51D Mustang	1:100
A50027	McDD F-15 Eagle	1:144
A50067	McDD F-4 Phantom II	1:144
A50075	Grumman F-14 Tomcat	1:144
A50076	F-117A Nighthawk	1:144

Gift Sets

A50065	BBMF Five Fighter Set	1:72
A50028	BBMF Dakota 'Berlin Airlift'	1:72
A50055	BBMF Spitfire Mk Vb	1:24
A50029	RAF 90th Anniversary Set	1:72
A50031	BAe Red Arrows Hawk	1:48
A50056	IWM Collection	1:72
A50064	D-Day Collection	1:72
A50048	Waterloo Battle Set	1:76
A50049	Medieval Tournament	1:76
A50057	Science Museum: Flight	1:72
A50058	Science Museum: Automotive	1:32
A50044	*Wasa* Gift Set	1:144
A50045	*Cutty Sark* Gift Set	1:130
A50047	*Endeavour* Gift Set	1:120
A99262	HMS *Victory* Gift Set	1:180

Hanging Gift Sets

| A50051 | British Infantry MP | 1:32 |
| A50052 | 8th Army MP | 1:32 |

2008's 'Shaun the Sheep' tractor.

A50053	German Infantry MP	1:32
A50054	US Infantry MP	1:32
A50030	Red Arrows Hawk	1:72
A50032	Spitfire Mk IX	1:72
A50077	Spitfire Mk Ia	1:72
A50078	P-40E Kittyhawk	1:72
A50079	Hawker Typhoon 1B	1:72
A50082	Focke-Wulf Fw 190D	1:72
A50089	Aston Martin DB5	1:32
A50090	MGB	1:32
A50091	Ford Escort	1:32
A50092	VW Beetle	1:32
A50068	Mosquito and Me 262A	1:72
A50040	Typhoon and Spitfire	1:72
A50041	F-15 & P-51	1:72
A50043	F-18 Gift Set	1:72
A50071	HMS *Hood*	1:600

Licensed Gift Sets

A50006	Dr Who: Welcome Aboard	1:12
A50007	Dr Who: Dalek Encounter	1:12
A50008	Dr Who: Gridlock or Spacecraft	1:12
A50009	Dr Who: *Titanic* Kylie	1:12
A50018	Shaun the Sheep and Landrover	1:12
A50019	Shaun the Sheep * Tractor	1:12

Airfix Accessories

| A1004 | 1:24 Scale Electric Motor | N/A |

There were several kits advertised earlier that were shown as new, and all Hornby-released models now bore the 'A' prefix. Later, when a change of decals was proposed, the suffix 'A' was added to show that it was not a new model but a slightly altered one.

The really big news was the announcement of a 1:24 Mosquito kit. Airfix had originally designed a large Mosquito in the late 1970s, but costs escalated and finally it was released as a 1:48 model. Humbrol had moulded additional parts to make further variants of the Harrier, Spitfire and P-51D, but we believed that we would never again see a new 1:24 aircraft kit.

Shortly after the Hornby purchase, at a meeting to discuss the development of the Airfix range, Trevor Snowden was asked what model he would like to design to launch the new Airfix range and show that Hornby was serious in its desire to rejuvenate the Airfix brand. He replied that Hornby should do the 1:24 Mosquito that Airfix had never managed to complete. He expected the new owners to dismiss his suggestion, but instead the reply was 'OK, go ahead!' So he did.

Despite its size, many of the parts, such as the engines, undercarriage and tailplanes, are not 'handed', so it is possible to put these parts on one runner and then run it twice for each kit. Also Hornby was using computer-aided design, or CAD, to design its existing models, and this cut out a lot of the work required on patterns and drawings and was consequently cheaper. The whole design could now be done in one office at Margate, and the completed computer design sent out to China for mould preparation.

This kit helped to show that Airfix was back, and that the competition needed to take note. The kit was finally released in 2009 in Series 25 at a whopping £129.99, but went on to become Airfix's most successful model and quickly recouped its development cost.

Airfix also announced several new moulds of existing aircraft. The BAe Hawk kit that since 1975 had been a huge money-spinner for Airfix in its Red Arrows guise, was released as a new mould in Series 2. Reports that the old mould was damaged were untrue, but that kit had represented a pre-production aircraft and lacked many of the extras that were on the production aircraft. The new mould had engraved panel lines and more detail. The following year it was released in its more aggressive mode as the Lead-In Fighter Trainer (LIFT) variant.

A new Spitfire IX to replace the 1960 'JE-J' kit was revealed. It was a slightly simpler kit, but Airfix finally had an accurate Mark IX in its catalogue.

Also announced were two new Canberras in 1:72 scale. They were CAD kits, but nevertheless once again Airfix had Canberra kits in its 1:72 range.

Airfix had decided to gradually replace its earlier best-selling kits, and also to add new kits of aircraft that had not previously been made by them. So now, enthusiasts could look forward to seeing which old kits were going to be replaced, and which lesser known aircraft would join the range. Initially, though, all the new tools would be of aircraft, as this was still the most popular range of models, dating back to the launch of Spitfire BT-K in 1955.

The other new model was a 1:48 scale kit of the TSR2, and it made an impressive kit. It was also the first kit to have a box-top painting that differed from the previous ones. Hornby was still using the talents of John D. Jones to paint its box tops, but was approached by a young artist who was proficient in the use of digital artwork. Hornby so liked this artwork that it was felt that the Airfix range needed a combination of new, eye-catching artwork allied to a revised logo and box style to say that Airfix was back in force!

Kits would still be advertised in the catalogue with their old illustrations, but when they came out they would receive the Adam Tooby treatment. This seemed to say that the new Airfix range was thoroughly up-to-date.

Revised kits included an updated Buccaneer to make all the later models, and the long-awaited Sea King upgrade. Airfix could now offer the latest Search and Rescue Sea King as well as the AEW variant, with its huge external radar which pivoted out of the way. This was a good kit, but unfortunately the old Sea King was becoming worn, and it did not easily make a good model on which to hang the 'extras'. It took until 2010 to appear.

The Fokker F-27 Friendship, which had been released back in 1960 and converted to a troopship in 1979, was released now with an extra runner on which were new propellers, a nose and one or two other parts. The old kit made the early Series 100 variant, and now the kit could be assembled as a 100 or 200 Series aircraft. The number of airline liveries that could be applied was considerably enhanced as a result.

The rest of the new releases were 'polybagged' kits from other manufacturers, but all filled gaps in the Airfix range. Hopes that the Wellington was to be a new Airfix tool were dashed when it turned out to be the ex-MPM model. At the time of writing Airfix has yet to announce a new Wellington kit.

Two 1:400 destroyers joined the other 1:400 warships, and we were promised a 1:72 scale U-Boat – but in the end it failed to surface!

The mould for the OO/HO British Infantry had been lost many years before, and as an interim measure a set of ex-Esci figures was released.

The old Beam Engine and 1804 Locomotive were re-released in a range entitled 'The Golden Age of Steam': they hadn't been released for thirty years.

The three modified AFVs were released, along with the range of JB model kits. JB Models had been making a range of 1:76 armoured vehicles and trucks mainly from the post-war period. One kit, the Vickers Light Tank, came from the early 1930s. Airfix bought the JB moulds and released them all in the existing AFV ranges. In one go, Airfix had covered most of the period from 1960 to today. The models were very attractive, accurate models and all received new illustrations by Keith Woodcock.

The mini kits range was expanded, and the models all renumbered into the Hornby system.

Most of the gift sets were dropped and the range effectively re-launched. Several new sets were added. The entire range of Waterloo figures was released in a set that included the Farm House and Accessory Set. The Accessory set had been specially moulded for the 1975 release of the Waterloo set, and had never been sold separately. This new set included the Prussians.

Aircraft and cars from the Science Museum, Imperial War Museum and Battle of Britain Memorial Flight were put into sets with paints and brushes.

Another set entitled the Medieval Tournament was to use figures and buildings from other manufacturers; however, in the end it was not released.

Four sets of multipose figures were intended to be released in the hanging gift sets but again failed to materialize, although three sets would feature in the 2014 range. The Spitfire IX set was replaced by the Mk Ia kit. Two new sets, called 'Then and Now', paired a modern jet with a wartime fighter to show the differences, and another old Dogfight Double returned.

The other big news for 2008 was the increased range of licensed kits from three television series. 'Doctor Who' was expected to feature prominently in the new Airfix range. The first two sets included the TARDIS with a Dr Who figure (David Tennant) and his assistant; a Dalek was in the second set. Both were moulded to 1:12 scale, and others were planned.

Two sets of Shaun the Sheep, a Popular Aardman Animations series on the television, were produced; one set had a model tractor and the other a Land Rover to go with the figures of Shaun and Bitzer, the dog. The Wallace and Gromit sets were also available.

Although these television kits were very good and made into excellent models, they did not prove as successful as the basic aircraft models, and after a couple of years they quietly disappeared from the catalogue.

2009

Fourteen new moulds and two mould modifications were revealed for 2009. Some really exciting kits were announced, including the following:

Individual Kits

A02017	Spitfire PRXIX	1:72
A02029	Messerschmitt Bf 109G-6	1:72
A02037	MiG-15	1:72
A02096	Hawker Hurricane Mk IIc/d	1:72
A03078	BAe Sea Harrier FRS.1	1:72
A03079	BAe Sea Harrier FA.2	1:72

A05116	Spitfire Mk XVIe – Club Kit	1:48
A09181	HS Sea Vixen	1:48
A09170	Apollo Saturn V	1:144
A12202	HMS *Illustrious*	1:350
A50008	Vodafone McLaren Mercedes	1:32
A02037	World War I Female Tank	1:76

Mini Kits

| A50102 | F-18 Hornet | 1:144 |
| A50103 | Hughes AH-64 Apache | 1:144 |

Medium Gift Sets

A50092	Triumph TR4A	1:32
A50095	NA P-51D Mustang	1:72
A50096	Westland Whirlwind Mk I	1:72

Boxed Gift Sets

| A50038 | Junkers Ju 88 and Hurricane | 1:72 |

Gift Sets

A50105	Fly Navy 100	1:72
A50061	Dambusters	1:72
A50097	Vulcan to the Sky	1:72
A50046	*Golden Hind*	1:72
A50059	HMS *Illustrious*	1:350

A50104	RMS *Titanic*	1:700
A50060	World War I Western Front	1:76
A50106	One Small Step for Mankind	1:72

Young Scientist

| A20005 | Jet Engine | N/A |
| A42509 | Internal Combustion Engine | N/A |

It was now possible to see Hornby's plans for the development of the range. Several new tools of existing aircraft were announced and one or two new subjects were modelled for the first time by Airfix. One or two older kits had extra parts added to make them more accurate or make another version, and of course older kits were re-released with new decals and illustrations.

Three new kits of existing World War II aircraft were revealed. The Spitfire PRXIX was the late war photo reconnaissance variant that was unarmed and had not previously featured in the Airfix range. It was a very fine model and would later be released in 1:48 scale.

As mentioned earlier, Hornby had decided to employ CAD for its new kits because it was cheaper than the old process and allowed more detail to be incorporated. To that end, it had recruited a young team of post-graduates who had all studied CAD at university. Most knew very little about aircraft, cars or tanks but they did know how to use a CAD programme. Having designed one or two kits, they soon became very knowledgeable about aircraft or ships, and this is visible in the design of the more recent kits.

Some modellers did criticise the accuracy of the very early models, but they now find that the newest releases achieve a level of accuracy not previously seen in most Airfix kits. There were one or two errors in the Bf 109G-6 and Hurricane Mk II kits, but they were much superior to the kits they replaced. The young designers had to 'cut their teeth' on these early models, but as we have seen with the recent early Hurricane Mk 1 kits, they learned very quickly!

The MiG-15 replaced the very early fifty-year-old kit. The old kit had been a regular entry in the catalogue and was obviously a steady seller. The new kit would become a worthy opponent for the new Sabre kit to be announced in 2010. There were criticisms, however, from some modellers about the shape and size of the kit, but it was still a big improvement over the old kit. Since it is not really possible or viable to alter moulds to overcome size issues, as a popular subject that consistently sells well, it is in the realms of possibility that it could be re-tooled in a few years' time.

I am told that due to the cost advantages of using CAD to design new kits,

ABOVE: *Airfix Model Club limited edition set, 2009.*

RIGHT: *2009's Battlefront Gift Set.* HORNBY

and because it can recoup the investment in a much shorter time, typically a year or so, Airfix is more inclined to mould a new kit than 'mess about' with an old mould. At the end of the day, once a new tool has paid for itself, Airfix can look forward to possibly fifty years of useful life from a mould, whereas a modified old mould is still a fifty-year old mould.

Adding extra parts to an old kit to make a new or a more accurate version was still viable, and this can be seen in the World War I 'Female' Tank and the Apollo Saturn V. Both kits used the original kit but had extra runners included. The extra parts meant that the Female tank from World War I could be built, and in so doing Airfix doubled the number of World War I tanks in its range! The Saturn V had been criticised over the years for inaccuracies around the command module. Sufficient new parts were moulded to replace the inaccurate ones and thereby make a much better Saturn V kit. The existing mould was unaltered. The old Lunar Module kit was released in a set including the astronauts and a vac-formed moon landscape to celebrate the fortieth anniversary of the first moon landing. The other space kits would return the following year.

The other new aircraft kits consisted of a mould which would make a basic Sea Harrier kit. Extra runners were designed so that both the early FRS.1 version and the later FA.2 version could be made. The Sea Harrier had not featured in the Airfix range of 1:72 aircraft before, and was the beginning of a complete replacement of its Harrier range. There was an oddity in the FRS.1 version in that the pilot figure was actually not a jet pilot but a World War II pilot figure, probably included in error due to translation issues between Margate and China!

One aircraft that had never featured in the Airfix range was the DH Sea Vixen. A proposed 1:72 scale model lost out to the McDonnell Banshee kit in 1980, and although Airfix has yet to release a 1:72 scale Sea Vixen, it did announce a 1:48 scale model in 2009. It was an excellent kit with a wealth of internal detail and fine external detail. This level of detail in 1:48, Airfix was beginning to apply to its 1:72 kits.

One kit that was not announced and only ever appeared as a club kit, although it was allocated a catalogue number, was the Spitfire Mk XVIe in 1:48 scale. It was a tool modification but included new fuselage halves showing the cut-down rear fuselage of that variant. It was a lovely kit and could easily be released under its catalogue number of A05116.

Two other new moulds were also announced. Hornby had been keen to launch a large ship kit, and whilst I would

TOP: *Churchill bridge layer kit from 2009.*

ABOVE: *2009 MiG-15 kit.*

BELOW: *Mosquito model from 2009.* HORNBY

personally have preferred to see HMS *Warrior* modelled, Airfix had set its sights on a range of 1:350 modern Royal Navy vessels. The 'flagship' of this new fleet was to be HMS *Invincible*, but by the time it was announced it had been changed to HMS *Illustrious* which was still in commission. Airfix had been releasing the Heller 1:400 ships, and this range would not be compatible with them, but the new ships were to be of modern warships so the lack of commonality didn't really matter.

To celebrate Lewis Hamilton becoming the 2008 F1 World Champion, Airfix released a simplified model of his Vodafone McLaren Mercedes car to 1:32 scale. It was pre-painted and clipped together, and was based on a Scalextric model.

Two more mini kits were added, and several gift sets. An ex-Academy kit of the *Titanic* to 1:700 scale was issued, and a World War I set which included the two tanks and a vac-formed trench system was released.

Finally, the two Young Scientist kits produced by Humbrol were released as Airfix 'Engineer' kits. Both were still in production in 2014.

2010

Nineteen new tools, two tool modifications and four new resin buildings were announced for 2010. They included:

A01071A	Supermarine Spitfire Mk Ia	1:72
A03080	Messerschmitt Bf 110C/D	1:72
A03081	Messerschmitt BF 110E	1:72
A03082	NA F-86F Sabre	1:72
A03083	NA Sabre Mk 4 (Canadair)	1:72
A03085	BAe Hawk T.1	1:72
A04050	BAe Harrier GR.9	1:72
A11001	Vickers Valiant	1:72
A05117	Supermarine Spitfire Mk XII	1:48
A05120	Messerschmitt Bf 109E	1:48
A05122	Messerschmitt Bf 109E Tropical	1:48
A06102	Supermarine Seafire XVIIc	1:48
A08107	Westland Lynx HAM.8/Super	1:48
A08108	Westland Lynx AH.7	1:48
A03260	Trafalgar Class Submarine	1:350
A03410	Jaguar XKRGT3 APEX Racing	1:32
A03411	Aston Martin DBR9 Gulf	1:32
A03306	Bedford QL Trucks QLT and QLD	1:76
A01763	World War II British Infantry	1:76

Tool Modifications

A05121	BAe Hawk T.1	1:48
A11150	Saturn V Skylab	1:144

Ruined Buildings (Resin)

A75001	European Workshop	1:76
A75002	European Café	1:76
A75003	European Corner House	1:76
A75004	European Country House	1:76

Starter and Gift Sets

A50009	Battle Front	1:76
A50015	RAF Battle of Britain Airfield	1:72
A50022	B-o-B 70th Anniversary	1:72
A50098	Eurofighter Typhoon	1:72
A50109	Jaguar XKRGT3 APEX Racing	1:32
A50110	Aston Martin DBR9 Gulf	1:32
A50111	Jaguar XLRGT3 and AM DBR9	1:32
A50114	BAe Hawk T.1a	1:72
A50030	Douglas Bader's Spitfire Mk Va	1:48
A50021	Trafalgar Class Submarine	1:350
A50112	Westland Lynx HAS.3	1:48

Bedford QL trucks from 2010.
HORNBY

Dramatic colour schemes on two Messerschmitt Bf 110s from 2010.

A50017	BAe Sea Harrier FA.2	1:72
A50013	Westland Sea King HAR.5	1:72
A50010	BAe Sea Harrier FRS.1	1:24

Re-Releases

A01001	Spitfire Mk Ia – BT-K	1:72
A02044A	Vought Corsair F4U (FAA)	1:72
A02048A	Messerschmitt Bf 109E	1:72
A02082A	Hawker Hurricane Mk I	1:72
A03030A	Junkers Ju 87B	1:72
A04177	Boeing 727-200	1:144
A04178	Boeing 737-200	1:144
A05172	Vostok 1	1:144
A06172	Saturn 1B	1:144
A02710	World War II British Infantry Support	1:32
A02713	German Mountain Troops	1:32

Flipping through the catalogue, it now appeared as if we were in a new golden age of Airfix kits. There were new moulds of well known aircraft, plus a few not so well known ones. Perhaps more importantly, we had new kits from ranges other than aircraft.

Leading the new tools was a brand new Spitfire Mk Ia kit. It was designed to replace the old Mk Ia, which, we were told, was the best-selling Airfix kit: well, it was a Spitfire! However, the still lovely old kit was re-released in a bag with a header as 'BT-K', the one that started off the aircraft range fifty-five years ago. It was moulded in blue plastic, as was the original, but was intended to tie in with James May's recent television programme where he built a full-size replica of BT-K at RAF Cosford Museum.

Unlike the recent Spitfire Mk IX kit, which was somewhat simplified, this kit was fully detailed, particularly inside. The cockpit assembly mirrored that on the 1:24 kit and was simply incredible. Young modellers would be well advised to make up BT-K; it was a lot easier for them. It came in Series 1.

In the late 1990s, Humbrol had said that there was virtually no chance of new 1:72 kits and that the future lay in 1:48 where the higher price made it easier to recoup the development cost. Also, much more detail could be incorporated, which is what serious modellers wanted. However, Hornby found that CAD reduced the cost of design and so 1:72 became possible again. Often new aircraft were released in Series 1, with one set of decals and also in Series 2 with two decals. This undoubtedly helped sales to the 'pocket money' market, which would be the main market in a few years' time.

The Messerschmitt Bf 110 was one of the first Airfix twin-engined aircraft, and I always felt was a very nice model. The new Bf 110 was one tool but could be made into three variants, all from around the Battle of Britain, which was seventy years ago and meant that schoolboys could shoot them down with their new Spitfire Mk Ia kits!

The Sabre was designed as an opponent to the new MiG-15 and was sold as two kits. The previous Sabre kit was the later 'Sabre Dog' variant and not produced for many years. Obviously the ex-Heller Sabre would no longer be sold by Airfix.

The Hawk T.1 was a new mould but based on the recent Red Arrows model. Although Airfix had a recent Harrier GR.9 kit, it had been decided to renew the Harrier range and so the 2009 Sea Harriers were joined by a new GR.9 kit. A state-of-the-art model, it joined the range just as the 'real thing' left RAF service.

The big 1:72 kit was the Vickers Valiant, the first of Britain's V bombers. In the early 1980s, Palitoy had moulded a slightly simplified Vulcan kit, which was still a good seller. The Valiant had been in Humbrol's 2006 programme and Hornby felt it would be viable. The kit was large and very well detailed and covered the main bombing variant. The other lesser used variants would be catered for in a novel way later.

Seven new models were added in 1:48 scale. Two very fine models of late mark Spitfires and Seafires were included. Airfix was well on the way to moulding every variant of this iconic aircraft. The Battle of Britain Bf 109E was selected, and again it was one tool with sufficient parts to make two or possibly more kits.

The BAe Hawk T.1 was modelled by using the existing Red Arrows mould, but adding extra parts to make the RAF's trainer and light attack aircraft.

Two new helicopter kits were announced, making an Army and Navy Lynx. 1:48 scale would allow for a very high level of detail, and there would be quite a high degree of commonality in the moulds. The kits were released in Series 9 and 10. The Army Lynx was sold in the new 'Operation *Herrick*' range that Airfix was proposing to develop.

A 1:350 scale kit of the Royal Navy's 'Trafalgar' class submarine joined HMS *Illustrious*. Decals were provided for all members of the class.

The next four kits were in many ways the most interesting because they saw

Airfix revisiting ranges other than aircraft and producing new tools. The two cars were both supercars of the type much liked by the *Top Gear* presenters, and they would be sold as single kits, double kits and gift sets.

The OO/HO, 1:76 AFV kits were perennial favourites, and this year Airfix announced its first new tool kits in this range, which was a kit of the famous World War II Bedford QL truck. Sufficient parts were included to enable two kits to be made, covering the two main versions. The Bedford QL had been modelled earlier but as part of an Airfield kit. *Airfix Magazine* had devoted many articles to the myriad of conversion possibilities with these trucks, and now modellers would be able to buy the trucks without all the other vehicles. They would prove to be a very popular choice of new kit.

After a break of nearly thirty years Airfix would return to designing new OO/HO figure sets. One of the last sets to be moulded by the old Airfix team was a set of World War II British Infantry. This mould appears to have been lost around 1986, and so in 2008 Airfix had released a set of Esci figures. These were to be replaced by a new set. This was a new venture for the young team at Margate, and required the figures to be sculpted. Apparently the first set was not considered good, and another set was designed. The resulting set was not up to the standards of those designed by John Nibblett and Ron Cameron, who sadly died in 2013, but at least showed that Airfix was prepared to consider new figures again.

The other tool modification was the release of the recent Saturn V upgrade, which included extra parts to make a Skylab model.

An entirely new range for wargamers and military modellers was revealed. For some years Hornby Railways had modelled a range of Trackside buildings made out of resin and known as 'Skaledale'. This process would lead to a range of ruined buildings to be used alongside the figures and AFVs. The models were supplied unpainted, and overcame the main drawback of the plastic buildings, namely thin walls, but created a new problem of roof tiles which were the thickness of the walls! Probably experienced modellers would be able to overcome that detail. However, the resulting buildings did look very effective in dioramas. Perhaps the solution might be to mould the shell of the building out of resin with the roof tiles out of plastic?

Several older kits were reissued with new illustrations and decals. Two 1:144 aircraft were given a makeover and have received different decals since. The remaining spacecraft kits joined the fortieth anniversary range.

The 1:32 soldiers saw the British Infantry Support Group and German Ski Troops return. Initially advertised as Series 2 with fourteen figures, Airfix quickly realized that these sets could not be sold in the same way as the other sets, so they were released as complete sets but now in Series 4. They remain the most interesting of the military figure sets produced by Airfix.

The gift sets mainly used the new tools, which enabled Airfix to offer different decals and in some cases versions. The Navy Lynx was issued as the earlier HAS.3 variant. Douglas Bader's Spitfire used the old Spitfire V kit.

The Battle of Britain Airfield Set was basically the recent RAF World War II Airfield Set in a new box with a new painting.

After many years of seeing Airfix releasing 'warmed over' old kits, enthusiasts at model shows would now head straight to the Airfix stand to see all the new models and handle the test runners to view the incredible detail that Airfix was now incorporating into its new kits. They could also quiz the designers on the stand in the hopes of finding out if Airfix was planning to release a new Beaufighter or Defiant.

Airfix seemed to be selecting anniversary years for picking which models to tool, and we were all wondering what anniversaries Airfix would select in 2011.

2011

The 2011 catalogue revealed that the forthcoming seventieth anniversary of Pearl Harbor would provide the impetus to replace the venerable Mitsubishi Zero kit and mould a kit of the early Curtiss P-40, both of which had fought at Pearl Harbor.

Modellers were to be treated to fifteen new moulds and several welcome re-issues and interesting gift sets. The range for 2011 included the following:

A01003	Curtiss Warhawk P-40B	1:72
A01005	Mitsubishi A6M Zero	1:72
A01006	Folland Gnat	1:72
A02010	Spitfire Mk I/Mk IIa	1:72
A04053	Fairey Swordfish Mk I	1:72

A14101	AugustaWestland Merlin HC.1	1:48
A10201	HMS *Daring*	1:350
A02338	Cromwell Cruiser Tank	1:76
A06301	British Land Rover Twin Set	1:48
A02750	British Army Troops	1:48
A03412	BMW Mini RS56	1:32
A75005	European Town House	1:76
A75006	European Church	1:76
A75007	European Four-Storey Shop	1:76
A75008	European Brewery	1:76

Gift and Starter Sets

A55100	Spitfire Mk Ia	1:72
A55101	Curtiss Tomahawk IIB	1:72
A55102	Mitsubishi A6M Zero	1:72
A55200	'E' Type Jaguar	1:32
A55201	Triumph Herald	1:32
A55300	BAe Harrier GR.9	1:72
A55301	Panavia Tornado F.3	1:72
A50112	Westland Lynx HMA.8	1:48
A50120	'Sink the *Bismarck*' Set	1:1200
A50121	British Forces Land Rover Patrol	1:48
A50122	British Forces Helicopter Support	1:48
A50123	British Forces Patrol and Support	1:48
A50126	BMW Mini Twin Set	1:32
A50127	P-40B v. Zero Dogfight Double	1:72
A50128	Spitfire Mk Ia v. Bf 110	1:72
A50129	IWM Victoria Cross Icons	1:72
A50131	London Icons	1:12
A50132	HMS Daring Type 45	1:350
A50133	Fairey Swordfish Mk I	1:72

Re-Releases

A07006	Lancaster 'G for George'	1:72
A06103	Seafire FR.46/FR.47	1:48
A09178	EE Lightning F.2A/F.6	1:48

A02026	Angel Interceptor	1:72
A08011	Stratos 4/TSR2MS	1:72
A10170	Space Shuttle	1:144

Accessories

AF1005	Five-Up Stand	N/A
AF1006	Two-Up Stand	N/A
AF1007	1:24 Stand	1:24
AF1008	Assortment of Small Stands	1:72

For many years Airfix had models of the Mitsubishi Zero and P-40E Kittyhawk in its range, both of which were good likenesses and which sold consistently well. The P-40E was a later variant of the P-40 series. The two new models were produced to the very high standard that the new team at Hornby had reached. Both had fine inscribed panel lines and plenty of internal details. They were sold singly in Series 1 and also as a twin set in the 'Dogfight Doubles' range. Several older early World War II US and Japanese aircraft kits returned to the catalogue.

The Folland Gnat, which had enjoyed reasonable sales in the Airfix range in the 1960s, had been altered to a Red Arrows Gnat, and as such had never been out of the catalogue. Although the RAF had replaced the Gnat with the Hawk, British modellers kept on buying the Red Arrows Gnat kit, so a replacement was a shrewd move. The kit was initially released as the RAF's T.1 Trainer, but later in the year was released as a Red Arrows Gnat. With new tools of both the Hawk and Gnat, the possibility of new gift sets was high.

The Spitfire Mk I/Mk IIa was the new kit with extra decals to make further variants.

2011's Vickers Valiant.

The attack on Pearl Harbor had been based a lot on the earlier attack on the Italian battle fleet at Taranto by Swordfish aircraft. Airfix had had a Swordfish in its range, in Series 2, since 1958 and it had recently been sold as a Royal Navy historic aircraft. Tamiya had produced a 1:48 Swordfish that was considered to be exquisitely detailed but very expensive.

The new Airfix kit was in Series 4, but it would prove to be worth every penny! The cockpit detail was very comprehensive and the external detail very fine, and it resembled what modellers would have expected a Tamiya 1:72 scale version to look like. Airfix said that a floatplane version would soon be released.

The final new aircraft kit was a 1:48 model of the RAF's Merlin helicopter. It would be a large kit and was not to be released until 2012, but it gave modellers something to look forward to. It was part of Airfix's growing range of 'Operation *Herrick*' kits. The ground-based element of the Afghanistan operation saw the addition of models of the various Land Rovers used in that conflict; also a set of figures was moulded to fight alongside the helicopters and ground vehicles. The figures were basically a simplified multi-pose kit, with each soldier being made up of four or five parts. They would all be combined into various sets.

The new range of 1:350 modern Royal Navy vessels saw the new Type 45 destroyer added. Decals were provided for all six members of the '*Daring*' class ships, as had been widely predicted.

Following the success of the Bedford QL trucks, Airfix produced a model of the Cromwell tank, first used in 1944. Earlier tank kits had used separate flexible 'silver' tank tracks that were wound round the wheels and sprockets of the kits, and which modellers either loved or hated. This new kit had the tank tracks moulded in lengths of rigid plastic and were immediately popular. The old ones had tended to react with the plastic and gradually dissolve it. Modellers were looking forward to a suitable adversary being moulded by Airfix.

A kit of the modern BMW-built Mini was tooled, and it would also be available in a twin set. The Mini is a truly iconic car, and the original Mini kit had given good service to Airfix and its motor-racing sets for many years, but following the closure of Airfix in 1981, the mould for the car was sold to MRRC, which was then making the racing sets for Airfix. It is possible that Airfix may one day tool a new 'classic' Mini – particularly if we keep on watching the film *The Italian Job* on television!

Finally, Airfix added four more resin models of 'ruined' buildings. These were to OO/HO or 1:76 scale and again proved popular.

Most of the gift and other sets consisted of the new tools and gave modellers a further choice of decals and versions. Sets using older kits were being gradually withdrawn, so that Airfix could better showcase its new tools and thereby maximize sales.

The three 'Operation *Herrick*' sets carefully combined the new releases to make high-value sets which give modellers the necessary kits to model each scenario.

A set of four older Airfix kits of World War II aircraft was released with decals to make four aircraft flown by winners of the Victoria Cross. With the 2012 London Olympics looming, Airfix released the original three kits of 1:12 figures in a set called 'London Icons'. The first three kits were of ceremonial soldiers and comprised a Guardsman, a Lifeguard Trumpeter and a Yeoman of the Guard. The number of tourists in London and the rest of the country was expected to boost the sales of this boxing.

Two more Dogfight Doubles were released using the various new tools.

1941 was also the year of the sinking of the German battleship *Bismarck*, and several of the ship kits in 1:600 scale were re-released. Also the 1:1200 'Waterline Warships', which had been released in the late 1970s and intended to be released in a set, were now put into a set entitled 'Sink the *Bismarck*'. Thus all six kits could now be bought as one set, and a 'table-top' naval battle could once again be fought.

Among the re-releases were half a dozen that stood out. The 'G for George' Lancaster release, which had used Roy Cross's memorable painting, was released in Series 7; it had a new illustration by Adam Tooby that was similar to Roy's, but took it into the digital age. Like the Lancaster, the Seafire kit was reduced in a series, making it more affordable.

The superb late-mark Lightnings came back, and the Space Shuttle joined the other recently issued space kits. Science fiction was also catered for: in Japan, a series of cartoons had been made that utilized a spacecraft called the 'Stratos 4'; this was basically the BAC TSR2 aircraft with extra bits added on and a crew of attractive young female pilots. Airfix accordingly moulded an extra runner for its 1:72 kit to include the new parts, and made two kits available.

The 'limited production' status of the original 2007 TSR2 kit meant that we would not see that kit released again for a few years. However, an option in the new kits was to make the prototype of the TSR2 with the appropriate decals. I should imagine that a large number of those sold were made up as that aircraft.

Science fiction had always been a niche market for Airfix, and the kits seemed to date quickly. Many of the television science fiction programmes had actually used parts from Airfix models to make the spacecraft; I remember one of the Airfix designers inviting us to see how many parts of the new 1:24 Harrier kit could be seen in a particular television series! In the artist section of this book, Mike Trim explains how Airfix kits were used by Gerry Anderson in his early puppet sci-fi programmes.

A forerunner of 'Stratos 4' was 'Captain Scarlet', and Airfix had produced a nice model of the 'Angel Interceptor' used in that series. The aircraft was actually flown in the programme by attractive young female pilots, or 'angels'! It was released again and was still in the 2014 catalogue with its original Roy Cross painting. Sadly as I write this in June 2014, I have just read of the death of the actor Francis Matthews, who 'voiced' the puppet of Captain Scarlet using his version of the mid-Atlantic accent notably used by Cary Grant!

2011 was another excellent year for Airfix kits. Airfix was improving its range all round, and the new logo and box style, together with the new digital artwork, was making Airfix very prominent in the shops. The instruction sheets were being upgraded and appeared more professional. There had been criticisms of the decals used by Hornby at first, and so steps had been taken to address this. Nowadays most of the decals are designed by Jonathan Mock, who recently wrote a book about Airfix. Airfix had contracted the company, which was considered to be the best decal producer, to produce the decals: this was Cartograf, and since around 2010 all Airfix kits have the Cartograf logo on the box, which ensures that the kits are no longer let down by less-than-perfect decals. It is another reason why the new Airfix is so highly considered in the modelling world.

2012

2012 was the seventieth anniversary of the Battle of El Alamein, and several existing kits were recorded in the catalogue as being suitable for that important battle. The sinking of the *Titanic* was also prominent. It was also the thirtieth anniversary of the Falklands War, and that would provide the impetus for one new tool. Several of the previous year's new tools were announced as new for this year, and a few of them were allocated different, higher catalogue numbers. Nineteen new tools were actually announced, and they consisted of the following:

A01004	NA P-51D Mustang	1:72
A01008	Messerschmitt Bf 109E-4	1:72
A02033	Supermarine Spitfire Mk 22	1:72
A02047	NA F-51 Mustang	1:72
A02062	Messerschmitt Bf 109E-Tropical	1:72
A03029	Douglas A-4 Skyhawk	1:72
A05006	Swordfish Floatplane	1:72
A65000	Valiant B.1 Sprue Set	1:72
A05301	Supacat HMT400 Jackal	1:48
A06302	Supacat HMT600 Coyote	1:48
A65001	Land Rover Photo-etch Parts	1:48
A65002	Jackal/Coyote Photo-etch Parts	1:48
A03702	British Vehicle Crew	1:48
A75009	Afghan Single-Storey Dwelling	1:48
A75010	Afghan Single-Storey House	1:48
A75011	Narrow Road Bridge, Full Span	1:76
A75012	Narrow Road Bridge, Broken	1:76
A03110	King Tiger Tank	1:76
A03413	Ford Fiesta RC WRC 2011	1:32

Gift Sets

A55105	Red Arrows Gnat	1:72
A55106	Messerschmitt Bf 109E	1:72
A55107	NA P-51D Mustang	1:72
A55108	Cromwell Cruiser Tank	1:76
A55202	Red Arrows Hawk	1:72
A55203	Douglas A-4 Skyhawk	1:72
A55302	Ford Fiesta RC WRC	1:32
A55303	Tiger Ausf.B 'King Tiger'	1:76
A50124	British Forces Forward Assault	1:48
A50143	Aircraft of the Aces	1:72
A50146	RMS *Titanic*	1:400
A50149	RAF Benevolent Fund Hawk	1:72

Dogfight Doubles and Classic Conflicts

A50014	Bf 109F v. Spitfire Vb	1:48
A50134	A-4 Skyhawk v. Sea Harrier	1:72
A50135	Spitfire Mk Ia v. Bf 109E-4	1:72
A50142	King Tiger v. Cromwell Tank	1:76

Re-Releases

A01013A	DH Comet Racer – Green	1:72
A02005A	Red Arrows Hawk	1:72
A05101	BAe Sea Harrier FRS.1	1:48
A05102	BAe Harrier GR.3	1:48
A07870	Four-Stroke Petrol Engine	N/A
A08870	Maudslay Paddle Engine	N/A

In the 1970s, Airfix had moulded a new Mustang and a Bf 109E kit, both of which were good models and based on work done for the 1:24 kits. Both were replaced in this year by new CAD models. The level of detail was very good, and much as I liked the old kits, I had to admit the new ones were stunning.

They were both available in Series 1, from where the bulk of sales would come, but were also available in Series 2 with two sets of decals and a few extra parts. It was Airfix policy now to release small aircraft in Series 1 with only one decal choice; pocket money modellers, whom Airfix was trying to attract, did not want to pay for extra unnecessary decals. Serious modellers, however, would also buy the Series 2 version as it gave them more choice, and they would probably buy two or more.

That is how Airfix had made its name, by offering inexpensive kits to youngsters. The old Woolworth's sales motto had been 'Pile 'em high, sell 'em cheap', when it came to its range of products. When it came to Airfix kits, the 'two-bob' kit was easily affordable by youngsters, who would go on to later become keen adult modellers and buy the bigger and more expensive kits. Ask any man over fifty or so and he'll say he made Airfix kits as a boy!

Hornby realized that it had to get that young market back. The grown-up boys who nowadays bought Hornby's expensive trains had started off with a simple train set when they were younger. Unfortunately for Airfix, for the last thirty years or so the youngsters had been buying computer games instead of making Airfix kits, and the only steady market it had was the older guys who had made kits as boys.

Making available inexpensive kits of small aircraft was now seen as a priority. Airfix was also attending and sponsoring many model shows throughout the country. At these venues, the latest kits and test 'shots' were put on display to excite the older and dedicated enthusiasts who attended these events. Then in a side room or a section of a marquee, Airfix set up an area for a 'make and paint' activity. Here, youngsters with a parent can make an Airfix aircraft kit. Pots of acrylic paint, glue and brushes are provided, along with plenty of Series 1 kits in polythene bags. At the end the youngster is given a simple folded box, resembling a hangar, in which to put their 'pride and joy'. For many it will be their first attempt at following instructions, and some of the finished paint schemes can best be described as 'exotic'! But if it arouses their interest then it is certainly worthwhile.

The kits chosen are usually end of runs, where sales have dried up. One of the first was the new Spitfire IX kit. The first run of that kit revealed that the fuselage halves were made symmetrical (there was a cockpit entrance door on both sides) so the mould had to be corrected for production. The large number of 'faulty' kits was then used up at the early 'make and paint' venues.

Afghan diorama from 2012: Coyote and Jackal vehicles, and single-storey dwelling. HORNBY

Having initially relied on releasing older kits and 'polybagging' ones from other manufacturers, Hornby had made the decision, within the next few years, to have a range of kits of the principal World War II aircraft that was composed of new, state-of-the-art models. The Mustang and Bf 109E were the latest examples of that decision. Also the use of other manufacturers' moulds was to be largely curtailed: they had served their purpose, and if it was considered important enough to sell, then Airfix would rather tool it. One or two kits, such as the *Titanic*, would still be 'borrowed' as it was probably not worth the expense to tool it for a short run.

Airfix's love affair with the Spitfire resulted in a lovely little kit of the Spitfire Mk 22, previously modelled in 1:48 scale. Hopefully the Seafire FR.46/47 will get the same treatment in the future.

The Douglas A4D-1 Skyhawk was an early kit from 1958, and was very simple with rather crude detail; but despite other manufacturers making newer and vastly better detailed models, it continued to sell. So with the thirtieth anniversary of the Falklands War looming, Airfix released an excellent replica of the aircraft. It was sold in US markings in a starter set, but one of the options in the single kit was for an Argentine aircraft, and it was paired with the new Sea Harrier kit in a Dogfight Double set for that conflict.

Two of 2011's much longed-for kits were the Valiant and Swordfish models. Both were released in new versions but were tackled slightly differently. Extra runners that catered for the new parts needed, were moulded, but the approach differed when it came to selling them. The Swordfish was boxed in Series 5, but included the new runners and two decal options.

However, when it came to the Valiant, a novel approach was tried, and the extra parts were put into a smaller box and sold with two sets of decals to make photo reconnaissance or 'buddy' refuelling tanker variants. You still needed to buy the basic kit, but it did mean that Airfix did not need to package another kit, which would not be popular with modellers who only wanted to build the original bomber.

The market for the two new variants was a lot smaller than that for the main bomber version, but it enabled Airfix to cater for this market without upsetting the main market. Sooner or later one of the 'cottage industry' manufacturers would provide 'short run' parts to make these

versions, so Airfix was providing all the parts, decals and plastic in one kit.

Airfix continued the expansion of its Afghanistan range in 1:48 scale. The Jackal and Coyote were in fact one vehicle but with four or six wheels, the latter achieved by 'bolting on' a two-wheeled unit to the main vehicle. Airfix did exactly the same, moulding the four-wheeled Jackal and then providing another runner to make the Coyote. A separate set of vehicle crew figures was made available, which could fit into the two new kits as well as the earlier Land Rovers.

Airfix also announced they were to sell sets of brass photo-etched parts for those modellers who wished to superdetail their Afghan kits. Previously, Airfix had left advanced detailing and obscure versions to 'after market' companies. This suited Airfix as it enabled these smaller companies to thrive, and promoted extra sales of its main kits which the modeller would buy to make the different versions. For years companies had been producing decals for those wanting more exotic choices.

The principal company for 'superdetailing' parts was Eduard, and Airfix contracted Eduard to make the photo-etch parts for them, which could be considered to have access to a larger market in an Airfix-branded package.

Airfix expanded its resin building range with four new buildings, two in 1:48 for

the Afghan range, and two more in the standard range at 1:76.

The final two kits were a new kit of the World Rally Car Ford Focus in 1:32 scale to join the new Mini. In 1:76 a lovely model of the King Tiger tank was made, which would be paired up with the new Cromwell Tank introduced the year before. The size difference between the two tanks was considerable!

At this time Airfix returned, much to some modellers' chagrin, to producing flexible tank tracks again. Actually Airfix had very little choice, because the design of the tank tracks was such that they could not be moulded sideways on without losing the detail on the tank track. There were at least two variants of the King Tiger Tank with different turrets, so that provides a possibility for the future.

Many of the older sets were dropped, and seven of the starter sets with older kits in were now shown as of 'limited availability'. Most of the new sets utilized the new releases. The new Gnat was released as a Red Arrows Gnat, and the Red Arrows Hawk was upgraded to the latest markings.

A 1:48 Dogfight Double was produced; it was produced for sale in the Modelzone group of model shops. A little while later Modelzone went into administration and it was sold in normal shops and appeared in the catalogue.

North American P-51 Mustang from 2012.

ABOVE: *2012's RMS* Titanic *model.*

RIGHT: *King Tiger tank from 2012.*

The 'Aircraft of the Aces' set used the three new tool kits of the Spitfire Ia, Bf 109E and Mustang, with decals for three aces. The sinking of the *Titanic* was celebrated, or perhaps commemorated, with the issue of a 1:400 kit made by another manufacturer.

The Hawk kit got yet another outing, this time in RAF Benevolent Fund colours. By now the majority of the sets were composed of new tools.

There was the usual number of re-releases with new paintings and decal options. Interesting re-issues included the elderly Comet Racer with decals to make the green-painted aircraft from the 1930s.

There were not so many deletions in this year, but the 1:400 battleships all went. Re-releases tended to be for the various anniversaries.

The Sea Harrier and Harrier GR.3 in 1:48 returned to join the Falklands War collection. Finally, the two remaining steam engines from the old 'Museum Models' range joined the earlier two engines.

An oddity was Project R, which aimed to provide 'rockers' for children's play areas!

The range for the following year had now become very much a guessing game for modellers. We knew that old 'faithfuls' such as the Beaufighter, Defiant, Typhoon, Me 262 and Blenheim and many other old aircraft kits were almost certainly going to be replaced, but the question was, when? Airfix had a programme of new releases planned for the years ahead, so we would just have to wait and see.

Several other manufacturers had released new tools of the Lancaster,

Mitsubishi A6M 'Zero' model, 2012.

Sunderland, Halifax and Wellington, for example, which in the past had meant that Airfix was unlikely to mould new versions, but now it was inconceivable to imagine that Airfix would not have state-of-the-art kits of these important aircraft in its range. Again we had to wait and see.

2013

The year 2013 would bring answers to several of those queries. Twenty-two new moulds were announced, along with four from the previous year. As well as the 'remoulds' there were several exciting and long-awaited new subjects. The new tools were made up of the following:

A01020	Focke-Wulf Fw 190A-8	1:72
A02041	Hawker Typhoon IB	1:72
A02052	Gloster Gladiator Mk I	1:72
A02058	De Havilland Vampire T.11	1:72
A02063	Gloster Gladiator Mk II and Skis	1:72
A02066	Focke-Wulf Fw 190A-8/F-8	1:72
A02067	Hawker Hurricane Mk I 'Early'	1:72
A02091	Hawker Hurricane Mk IIb	1:72
A03003	Hawker Siddeley Harrier GR.1	1:72
A04054	English Electric Lightning F.2A	1:72
A04055	Hawker Siddeley Harrier GR.3	1:72
A08001	Avro Lancaster BII	1:72
A08012	Stratos4 TSR.2MS	1:72
A09007	Lancaster BIII 'Dambuster'	1:72
A05119	Supermarine Spitfire PRXIX	1:48
A12007	Gloster Javelin	1:48
A04701	British Quad Bikes and Crew	1:48
A07300	BAe Warrior	1:48
A65004	BAe Warrior Photo-etch Parts	1:48
A05330	World War II Bomber Re-Supply Set	1:76
A03414	Mini Countryman WRC	1:32
A75013	Italian Farmhouse	1:76
A75014	Italian Townhouse	1:76

Quick Build

J6000	Supermarine Spitfire	N/A
J6001	Messerschmitt Bf 109E	N/A
J6002	Eurofighter Typhoon	N/A
J6003	BAe Hawk	N/A
J6004	Apache Helicopter	N/A
J6005	F-22 Raptor	N/A

Gift Sets

A55110	Focke-Wulf Fw 190A-8	1:72
A55112	Folland Gnat 'Yellowjacks'	1:72
A55113	'Das Boot' U-Boat Type VIIC	1:400
A55204	De Havilland Vampire T.11	1:72
A55205	Hawker Siddeley Harrier GR.1	1:72
A55206	Gloster Gladiator Mk I	1:72
A55208	Hawker Typhoon Ib	1:72
A55304	Mini Countryman WRC	1:32
A50136	Fw 190 v. Typhoon 'Dogfight'	1:72
A50147	'Channel Dash'	1:72
A50138	Dambusters Lancaster	1:72
A50153	Battle of Britain Experience	1:72
A50154	Ford Fiesta and Mini Countryman	1:32
A50155	RAF Display Team Hawk	1:72
A82013	'Under the Red Star' – Club Kit	1:72

Arguably the best year yet from Hornby, things just kept getting better! Several perennial favourites received the 'remould' treatment, and the most surprising one of these was the Lancaster. The second Lancaster kit was released in 1980 and was an excellent replica. During the Humbrol years it was modified so that a Dambuster and 'Grand Slam' variants could be modelled. Despite other manufacturers recently releasing new tool Lancaster kits that were slightly better than the Airfix model, there were still parts of the Airfix kit that were superior.

We were expecting a new Stirling, Halifax or Wellington, and I am sure they will arrive soon, but not a new Lancaster. Airfix chose the seventieth anniversary of the May 1943 attack on the dams to release its all-new kit. It was very cleverly designed from the outset to make all the main variants of this best-known of all bombers.

The Dambuster variant used a basic tool of the Lancaster, which was incredibly detailed, inside and out. The clear plastic runner included all the turret variations for each model. The wings were designed with large cut-outs for the engines to fit. There was a separate runner with the Merlin engines on to enable that variant to be modelled. Another runner contained all the parts to make a detailed and accurate model of the Dambuster aircraft. Details of the 'Upkeep' bomb had only recently been de-classified so it was now possible to design an accurate replica. It was also released in a gift set.

In July, the basic kit was to be released without the Dambuster or Merlin parts. A new runner was added to make a Hercules-engined BII variant. It was no secret that a Merlin-engined standard BIII would follow in the next year. Thus if Airfix wished to release a 'Grand Slam' variant, then very little work would be required.

It was sad to see the old Lancaster go, but it was still available in the Battle of Britain Memorial Flight set.

Another late Airfix kit was the Focke-Wulf Fw 190A released in 1977, and a very good model it was, enabling one to build the 'A' and 'F' models. Now it was to be replaced by a new tool which would follow the new Airfix practice of releasing a Series 1 version with a Series 2 version, having extra parts and decals to make a choice of the two variants. Much as I liked the old Fw 190A, I had to admit this was better.

To fight the Fw 190, Airfix moulded a new Typhoon which would also make a 'Dogfight Double' pairing. The new Typhoon would be ready for the following year's D-Day celebrations. It was very detailed with separate gun access panels in the wing so it could be modelled being re-armed – in fact it almost seemed too detailed for a small aircraft, but at Scale Model World at Telford in November 2013 we realized why!

The Gloster Gladiator had been Airfix's second aircraft kit, produced in 1956 and still going strong despite being a very basic kit. Its replacement came in Series 2 and was to be sold in two variants. The

BAC 'TSR.2MS Stratos4' kit, 2013.

basic kit contained more exquisite detail, with a full cockpit interior, a new way of fixing the struts accurately, tiny holes for those wishing to add rigging, and a beautiful representation of the fabric detail. The second of the new kits would contain an extra runner with the ski parts on and two further decal options.

Airfix had moulded a Hurricane Mk I back in 1979, and now a very early Mk I was announced, with all the parts needed to make the early pre-war Hurricanes.

Airfix now replaced the original Harrier kit with a new GR.1 and separate GR.3 kits. The baseline kit was the GR.1, and then extra parts were added to make the later GR.3 variant. The original Harrier kit was designed as a GR.1 and later modified to a GR.3. Now one would be able to make any of the 'first generation' Harriers.

Another early Airfix jet was the English Electric Lightning F.1A, which had, like the Harrier, been altered to a later F.3 variant. Now Airfix would release a new F.2A, opening up the prospect of an F.6 variant later. Also, like the Harrier kit, the cockpit and intake assembly would be a mini kit in its own right.

Airfix had not neglected subjects it had not previously modelled, because a lovely little replica of the Vampire T.11 joined the range. Apart from using the Heller model earlier, a Vampire had always been a noticeable omission from its range.

Airfix had also not ignored 1:48 aircraft kits, because a lovely model of the Spitfire PRXIX was released. So the PR variant could now be modelled in both main scales. The other new subject was a beautiful model of the Gloster Javelin. The internal and external detail was so fine that some modelling publications suggested it might be the best Airfix kit of all.

Aircraft modellers were obviously in for a treat that year. Other ranges were not neglected, however, with a new set of

British Quad Bikes with Crew, and a model of the BAe Warrior armoured vehicle released in the Afghan range. A set of photo-etch parts for the Warrior was announced.

A model of the Mini Countryman was released, which would find its way into a pairing with the New Ford Focus.

The 'ruined' buildings moved south, so that military modellers could fight the Italian campaign.

Probably the best received new release and arguably the most wanted was a magnificent set enabling modellers to make a World War II Bomber Re-Supply Set. For years modellers had wanted Airfix to make a separate tractor and bomb trolley for use with the earlier airfield sets: it could work out expensive to keep buying Stirlings just to get the bomb trolleys included in the kit. The new kit included not only the David Brown tractor and bomb trolleys with a selection of bombs, but a motorbike, fuel bowser, maintenance stands and two trucks much used by British forces. The set had been cleverly designed so that in the following year the two trucks could be released in a single set, which would help modellers considerably.

Other manufacturers, such as Revell and Italeri, were releasing new moulds to a high standard, but they all seemed to lack the coherency of Airfix's release programme. Airfix was fortunate that historically it had covered more ranges than any other manufacturer, so it was possible to build on those ranges without them looking like an isolated choice.

The various gift sets were added to by inserting the new moulds. The only oddity was the inclusion of a 1:400 submarine which had previously been manufactured by Mirage. The remaining 1:400 ships having been withdrawn, it did seem a somewhat unusual choice as there was nothing left for it to torpedo!

Most of the 'old model' gift sets were withdrawn, as was a large number of single kits. The 'Channel Dash' set comprised a Swordfish and Spitfire Vb kits, which featured in the dash by the *Scharnhorst* and *Gneisenau* battleships through the English Channel. The Airfix Model Club Kit for 2013 was 'Under the Red Star', and featured a Spitfire, Hurricane and P-40B in Russian markings. Not advertised was the fact that the Hurricane kit contained a previously unreleased runner of new wings to make a IIB variant and was listed as A02091.

About two dozen kits were reissued, most with new decals. The 1:24 Spitfire Vb, P-51K/RF and Fw 190A returned with Adam Tooby paintings, and gave the whole range a consistency previously lacking. The three fast patrol boats and the lifeboat all made a comeback, along with 1:48 Hawker Fury.

1:32 figures sets saw the Japanese and Ghurkhas return to fight again. The rarely issued SAS figures also returned. Monty's Humber and Rommel's Half-Track came back, along with the first two clip-together buildings, Strongpoint and the Desert Outpost.

Airfix also announced a 'Design a Hawk' colour scheme competition, the winner of which would be issued as an Airfix kit next year. The 1:1 Project R Rocker announced last year was noticeable by its absence in this year's catalogue!

The only 'bought-in' kits remaining in the catalogue were the small *Titanic* and the

ABOVE: *English Electric Lightning F.2A kit from 2013.*

RIGHT: *2013's bomber re-arming set.*

U-boat. Airfix was now no longer reliant on other manufacturers' kits to bolster its range.

One completely new range was revealed. For years Airfix had been introducing Heller-designed kits for junior modellers. Now it designed its own range, called 'Quick Build'. The new range won 'The Toy of the Year' prize, and was a range of snap-together aircraft which were very Lego-like in their build. The original Airfix company had produced a range of building sets that were very similar to Lego, and were as old as Lego. Called Betta Bilda, I choose to believe that it was the source of inspiration for these new kits!

More importantly, they were to be manufactured in the UK in Sussex.

1:72 DASSAULT-BREGUET SUPER ETENDARD

2013 model of the Dassualt-Breguet Super Etendard.

ABOVE LEFT: *World War II British infantry: a 2013 re-issue of a kit from 1980.*

ABOVE RIGHT: *'Make & Paint' Gazelle Helicopter set, 2013.*

RIGHT: *Two 'Quickbuid' kits from 2013.*

Recently well over half of the Humbrol production had been returned to the UK, where it was believed the quality could be better controlled. Whether we shall ever see Airfix kits being manufactured in the UK again, I cannot say. The problems that Hornby Railways has experienced lately with its Chinese suppliers has not so far affected Airfix. The tools are made in China, and after the first run the kits are moulded in India. It seems to be working well, and I don't think British companies can be competitive at the moment.

2014

The 2014 range was revealed on 18 December 2013, although a couple of announcements had been made at Scale Model World in November. Twenty-four new kits were announced along with four more quick-builds.

New Moulds

A01010	Hawker Hurricane Mk I	1:72
A01024	DH Tiger Moth (Military)	1:72
A01025	DH Tiger Moth (Civil)	1:72
A04003	Supermarine Swift FR.5	1:72
A04016	Bristol Blenheim Mk I (Bomber)	1:72
A04017	Bristol Blenheim Mk IV (Fighter)	1:72
A05010	Dornier Do 17Z	1:72
A05042	EE Lightning F.6	1:72
A08013	Avro Lancaster BI (FE)/ BIII	1:72
A08014	Douglas C-47 A/D Skytrain	1:72
A08015	Douglas DC-3 Dakota	1:72
A09008	Douglas Dakota Mk III and Jeep	1:72
A05123	Folland Gnat	1:48
A05124	Red Arrows Gnat	1:48
A05125	Supermarine Spitfire Mk Vb	1:48
A19002	Hawker Typhoon Mk Ib	1:24
A02339	Willys Jeep, Trailer and 6-Pounder Gun	1:72
A02340	Higgins LCVP	1:72
A03311	RAF Vehicles	1:72
A75015	Polish Bank	1:72
A75016	Czech Restaurant	1:72
A75017	European City Steps	1:72
A75018	European City Fountain	1:72
A55114	*Mary Rose* (only in starter set)	1:400

Quick-Build

J6007	Lamborghini Aventador	N/A
J6008	Bugatti Veyron	N/A
J6009	BAe Harrier	N/A
J6010	Challenger Tank	N/A
J6011	Spitfire – Desert Version	N/A
J6012	Bf 109E – Desert Version	N/A

Reissues

A01013B	DH 88 Comet Racer – Red	1:72
A02029A	Messerschmitt Bf 109G-6	1:72
A02065A	Supermarine Spitfire Mk IXc	1:72
A03050	Fouga Magister	1:72
A03082A	NA F-86F Sabre	1:72
A03083	Canadair Sabre F.4/ F-86E(M)	1:72
A06008A	HP Halifax BIII	1:72
A05120A	Messerschmitt Bf 109E-4/ E-1	1:48
A05122A	Messerschmitt Bf 109E-Tropical	1:48
A07112	DH Mosquito PRXVI	1:48
A04177A	Boeing 727-200	1:144
A04178A	Boeing 737-200	1:144
A05171	Boeing 707-420	1:144
A06382	Bamboo House	1:32
A06383	Frontier Checkpoint	1:32
A05701	D-Day Gun Emplacement	1:72
A05702	D-Day Coastal Defence Fort	1:72
A03301	LCM III and Sherman Tank	1:76
A04301	Churchill Bridge Layer	1:76
A04207	RMS *Mauretania*	1:600
A06201	RMS *Queen Elizabeth*	1:600
A06443	1910 'B'-Type Omnibus	1:32

Starter Sets

A55111	Hawker Hurricane Mk I	1:72
A55115	DH 82a Tiger Moth	1:72
A55305	EE Lightning F.2A	1:72
A55306	Jaguar XKRGT3 Fantasy Scheme	1:32
A55114	*Mary Rose*	1:400
A55207	VW Beetle	1:32

Dogfight Doubles

A50160	Spitfire Mk Vb v. Bf 109E	1:48

ABOVE: *2014 releases: Blenheim and Spitfire.*

RIGHT: *World War II RAF vehicle set from 2014.*

Gift Sets

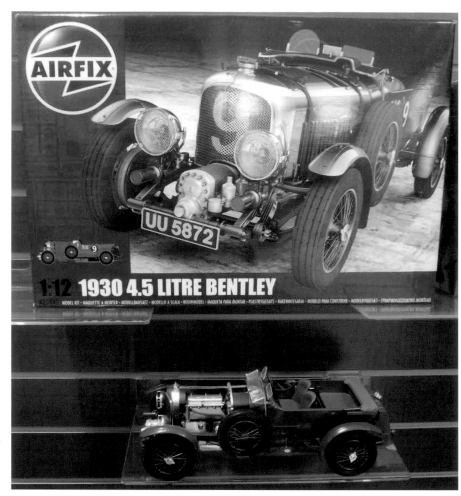

RIGHT: *2014 release of the 1930 Bentley car kit.*

BELOW: *2014's D-Day landing set.*

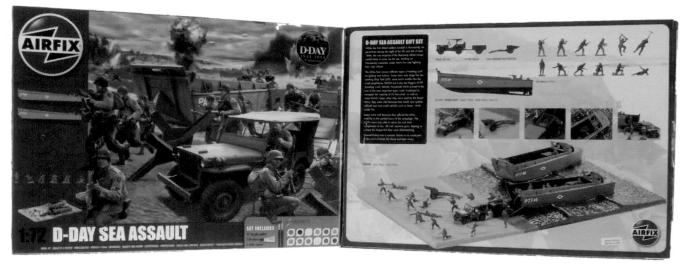

RAF Benevolent Fund Sets

Club Limited Edition Kits for 2014

The big surprise to be revealed at Scale Model World was the release of a 1:24 Typhoon Ib. Sales of the big Mosquito had prompted Airfix to look again at new 1:24 aircraft kits, and the choice of the 'chunky' Typhoon was a brilliant one as it fitted in with the seventieth anniversary of D-Day and provided more scope for internal detailing.

The level of internal detail was incredible, and it was possible to make the aircraft 'ready to fly', or undergoing various levels of maintenance. Now we realized why the small Typhoon was so well detailed internally. Clearly this kit was in a class of its own and a fitting subject to celebrate Airfix's seventy-fifth anniversary. Its catalogue number of A19002 seemed slightly odd, but we were told by Airfix that A19001 was reserved for an early 'car door' Typhoon. We could now look forward to further 1:24 kits being moulded.

Interestingly, Hornby received a boost to its income in July and August, when it was revealed that sales of 8,000 Typhoon kits had been made!

Overshadowed, literally, by the mighty Typhoon at Telford was news of a brand new Tiger Moth kit. The original kit was

ABOVE: *Models of the ships HMS* Victory, Cutty Sark *and* Vasa *from 2014.*

LEFT: *2014's English Electric Lightning kit.*

released in 1957 and seems to have been in every catalogue, in one form or another, ever since. It is a testament to the power of the Airfix name and the quality of the Roy Cross artwork that such an old and basic model could continue to enjoy robust sales when competitors' newer and better models have long since been retired.

It was moulded as one kit with extra parts included and would be sold in Series 1 as two kits, one civil and the other military. A starter kit using a similar colour scheme to the original was released as a starter set.

Like the Gladiator, the fabric effect was beautifully rendered and it employed the same novel method of attaching the wing struts. Float- and ski-equipped Tiger Moths are a possibility in the future.

The 'early' Hurricane Mk I was released as a standard Mk 1 in Series 1, and the new EE Lightning was announced as an F.6 in Series 5. An F.1a could be modelled in the future but it would require a totally new tool.

Airfix continued its programme of replacing old kits in its catalogue. The Bristol Blenheim IV was the subject of a

heavily riveted kit in 1968, when Frog issued a 'smooth' Blenheim I kit. Now Airfix released a new Blenheim kit that was cleverly engineered so that both versions could be made. It was released as the Mk I or bomber version and the Mk IV or fighter version. As with all new Airfix kits, the amount of detail and the fineness of moulding was superb.

In 1960 Airfix had released a good replica of the famous DC-3 Dakota as a paratroop transport and a civil airliner. The main fault with that kit was the lack of dihedral on the outer wings. In 1973 it had been altered, irrevocably, to an AC-47 gunship variant, and enjoyed a few years of life before eventually retiring. In recent years and as late as 2013, Airfix had relied on 'polybagged' kits from Italeri to meet its Dakota requirement.

To commemorate the D-Day and Arnhem seventieth anniversaries a new tool C-47 was released. Like the Blenheim, it was cleverly engineered so it could make the most of the original versions. The first to be released was a C-47 transport as used on D-Day. Later a Dakota with a Willys Jeep was released, and a civil DC-3 was released in wartime BOAC colours and post-war Dan-Air colours.

One of the earliest Airfix kits was a nice replica of the Dornier Do 217E-2,

ABOVE: *1:32 Bamboo House kit from 2014.*

BELOW: *Starter Set kit of HMS* Victory *from 2014.*

and this year Airfix released a new tool of the Battle of Britain Do 17Z model. The only surviving Do 17 had recently been raised from the seabed off the Kent coast, so this model was very topical. It was another excellent kit from the young team at Margate.

For its final 1:72 kit Airfix modelled the Supermarine Swift, a much requested aircraft kit that had not been in the range before.

In 1:48 scale Airfix moulded the Folland Gnat, the RAF's advanced fighter / trainer from the early 1960s. Airfix had just released a 1:72 tool of the Gnat, and in 1:48 scale it is available as a trainer plus, of course, the Red Arrows Gnat. It is also available with the recent Hawk in a gift set celebrating the fiftieth anniversary of the Red Arrows.

Finally, the first of the 1:48 aircraft, the Spitfire Vb, was retired and replaced by a new Spitfire Vb kit. This model was designed to the latest standard and included several extra parts to make different variants of the Mk V aircraft. According to the designer, Matt Whiting, it has been designed so that any number of early Spitfires can be modelled based on this tool.

To celebrate the seventieth anniversary of D-Day, Airfix released three new kits in its AFV range. The Bomber Re-Supply Set, introduced in 2013, was designed so that the two RAF vehicles were moulded on separate runners to the tractor, bombs and trolleys. So this year the two trucks,

the Standard 'Tilly' and the Bedford Truck, were released as the RAF Vehicles Set, which meant that those modellers who did not want the bombing supply equipment could just buy the vehicles. You could still build the two options of the water bowser and lorry with the Bedford, but at least you didn't have to buy the complete set just to model the option! The BSA motorcycle was included in this set. The set was also released along with the RAF Personnel and new Typhoon in the 'D-Day: Air Assault Gift Set'.

The other two kits were a surprise, as Heller had moulded a Jeep and LCVP 'Higgins' boat for Airfix in 2004.

However, I was told that using these kits in sets could prove problematical, and it was considered cheaper in the long run to mould new kits. So Airfix has released a new LCVP boat. The Willys Jeep was also moulded and it now included a trailer and an air-portable six-pounder gun.

Two LCVPs and a Willys Jeep, trailer and gun were included in the 'D-Day: Sea Assault Gift Set'. The Willys Jeep by itself was sold with the Dakota Mk III and Willys Jeep kit.

Airfix continued its programme of releasing resin buildings for use with OO/HO AFVs and figures, and this year a Polish Bank and Czech Restaurant were added, along with a set of European steps and a fountain. It is now possible to make dioramas covering most of the European campaigns, and presumably many of these buildings would also be suitable for World War I.

Finally, and surprisingly, Airfix released a new tool of the Tudor warship the *Mary Rose*. Ever since the ship was raised from the seabed in the 1970s, it has been a much requested subject for a sailing ship kit. The recent opening of the new *Mary Rose* Visitors' Centre in Portsmouth where the remains are displayed is timely. Airfix has chosen to model the ship at 1:400 scale, which means it fits in with the company's other eight small sailing ships. It is interesting that the Airfix kit range was launched with a series of small-scale sailing ships, and just over sixty years later we have come full circle!

The new kit is being sold only in a starter set. The painting used on the kit box was executed by Geoff Hunt for the *Mary Rose* Trust. Hunt painted several ship pictures for Airfix in the late 1970s before making his name illustrating all the covers of the Patrick O'Brien novels.

The new quick-build range of clip-together kits had two new 'supercars', a Harrier jump jet and a Challenger tank added to the earlier six kits. Also the Spitfire and Messerschmitt were given different markings to make desert versions to add to the existing ones.

Several of the new moulds were released as starter sets, and the old VW Beetle returned in a starter set.

The Dogfight Double pairings had the new Spitfire Vb kit paired with the recent Bf 109E kit to make a 1:48 set. All the Dogfight Doubles now contained new tools.

Several new sets were added to the larger gift sets. Two anniversaries for 2014 were celebrated. Three sets were produced for the D-Day landings, and included the new tools of the Typhoon, RAF vehicles, LCVP and Willys Jeep. Arguably, Airfix made the biggest effort of any kit manufacturer to celebrate this important event.

For the upcoming 100th anniversary of the beginning of World War I a major upgrade of Airfix's World War I models was expected. To launch the new range, four sets were released: two combined the German Infantry with the British in the Trench Warfare Set and the French in the First Assault Set. These three-figure sets were all based on the uniforms used

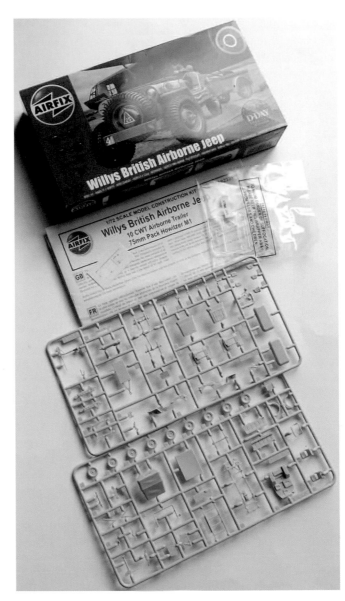

Willys Jeep kit, 2104.

2014 1:24 kit of the Hawker Typhoon. HORNBY

in 1914. The 1:32 kit of the 'Old Bill Bus' returned to the catalogue after a long absence. Airfix had proposed 1:32-scale versions of its small figures back in the late 1970s, but they were not proceeded with; it will be interesting to see whether new 1:32 figures will be moulded.

The most intriguing set was the World War I Artillery Barrage Set, as this kit contained new tools for a British and a German artillery gun. Hopefully they will be the first of many new tools of models for this important war.

The new BAe Warrior Tank kit was released in a set with the British Army Troops in what may be the last kit from Airfix's 'Operation *Herrick*' Afghan range.

The new 1:48 Red Arrows Gnat was paired with the Hawk to celebrate the fiftieth anniversary of the team. A new Battle of Britain Memorial Flight Set was issued, which used all the new tools.

Three of the range of 1:32 multipose figures were released. They had been proposed in 2008 but in the end were not released. A range of World War I multipose figures would be much appreciated!

Two new RAF Benevolent Fund sets were added. The Bomber Command Gift Set included the new Lancaster BIII kit and the Bomber Re-Supply Set. The winning entry, by fourteen-year old Heather Morien in the 'Design a Hawk Scheme' competition, was issued as a set.

The Club Limited Edition kit for 2014 combined the new Swordfish and Sea Hurricane kits to make a set entitled 'Operation *Torch*'.

As always, several existing kits were re-released. Several new tool aircraft kits came back with new decals, as did the old Comet Racer, Fouga Magister and Halifax kits. The Boeing 707-420 kit contained new decals, as did the Boeing 727 and 737 kits.

Two old 1:600 liner kits returned just after most of the 1:600 warship kits had been deleted. The two remaining 1:32 clip-together military buildings made a comeback. The Frontier Checkpoint had not been sold by Airfix since the late 1970s. The two Coastal Defence Forts were reissued for the D-Day range.

Hornby Hobbies Ltd, which owns Airfix and Humbrol, had issued a couple of profits warnings, largely due to supply problems in China affecting Hornby Trains. Also, Corgi Toys was suffering from the intense competition from other die-cast manufacturers. However, Airfix was, and is, doing well. The ambitious programme

of new tools and replacing old kits meant that now the Airfix range was composed of a large number of new moulds, particularly aircraft. For too long Airfix had not been releasing enough new models, and many modellers had turned elsewhere to satisfy their needs. But the aggressive new mould policy of Hornby Airfix had at last borne fruit, and once again modellers are eagerly looking forward to the next Airfix catalogue.

Many are now asking when they are going to get a new Sunderland, Beaufighter or Halifax – and the answer is, wait and see! Airfix can only re-tool so many old kits a year. Also it is in a different position to where it was in the 1980s and 1990s, when if a major kit company such as Tamiya produced a kit, then it meant that the others could not viably produce one. Now, given Airfix's return to the front rank of the modelling world, it would be inconceivable to imagine that Airfix would not have a new Sunderland or Halifax in its range because someone else had released a new tool.

Airfix has improved out of all recognition since its acquisition by Hornby in November 2006. CAD design means that the new tools can be designed and tooled for less than was possible many years ago, and the time taken to recoup the development costs has fallen dramatically. By utilizing Cartograf decals, Airfix has, arguably, the best decals on the market. The instruction sheets are being continuously improved. Many modellers have noted that the aircraft kit designer's face is now usually superimposed onto the pilot figure in the instructions – a nice little touch. The new and vibrant packaging with the excellent digital artwork is attracting many more purchasers, who are finding the contents to be exceptional.

In the late 1950s and 1960s, every boy made Airfix kits, some carrying on into adulthood. During the 1980s and 1990s most youngsters had abandoned kit building for the attractions of computer games and the availability of rapidly improving personal computers. It seemed as if the art of 'hands-on' kit building would wither away and be replaced by the virtual world of the PC.

It must seem, therefore, to be the supreme irony that kit-making may once again become a popular pastime because of computers. Airfix has employed those young men who have spent their youth playing on computers, to use their computer skills to design the new

generation of Airfix kits. These young graduates, who had little knowledge of, or interest in the wars and the aircraft that fought in them, are now very knowledgeable about them and enjoy modelling them. Airfix is steadfastly introducing the joys of kit building to a whole new generation of youngsters, who are re-discovering the joys of putting together something with their own hands and getting covered in glue and paint in the process!

You may be able to do seemingly magical things on a computer, but you cannot pick the up finished item and say, 'I made that with my own hands'. Airfix is once again making that possible.

2015

At the IPMS 'Scale Modelworld' show at Telford in November 2014, Airfix revealed details of its new LIDAR – light radar scanning – process, which it intends to use on most new models. In this system the actual subject, be it aircraft or car, is scanned, so that even the most complex of shapes is accurately reproduced, within of course the limitations of the moulding process. This will lead to unprecedented levels of accuracy being achieved.

Two new tools were announced, for which the new process was used: a Heinkel He 111 P-2 and a Westland Sea King HCIII.4. The main announcement concerned a new tool of the Boulton Paul Defiant Mk I in 1:72 scale.

The rest of the new models for 2015 were announced just before Christmas. Publication deadlines mean it is not possible to comment further, but it is another excellent year for modellers.

The models for 2015 are as follows:

A02069	Boulton Paul Defiant Mk I	1:72
A02070	Grumman F4F-4 Wildcat	1:72
A03087	Junkers Ju 87B-1 *Stuka*	1:72
A04019	Bristol Beaufighter Mk X	1:72
A04056	Westland Sea King HC.4	1:72
A04057	AV-8A Harrier	1:72
A04058	Nakajima B5N2 Kate	1:72
A06014	Heinkel He 111 P2	1:72
A08016	A.W. Whitley Mk V	1:72
A11004	Avro Shackleton MR.2	1:72
A05126	Supermarine Spitfire Mk I	1:48
A05127	Hawker Hurricane Mk I	1:48
A04072	WWII RAF Ground Crew	1:48
A03312	Albion AM463 3-point fueller	1:48
A03313	Bedford MWD Light Truck	1:48

Quickbuild

J6013	McLaren P1	N/A

DOGFIGHT DOUBLES

1:72 DORNIER Do17z BOULTON PAUL DEFIANT Mk.I

A50170 MODEL KIT • MAQUETTE À MONTER • MODELLBAUSATZ • MODELLO À SCALA • BOUWMODEL • MAQUETA PARA MONTAR • PLASTBYGGSATS • RAKENNUSSARJA • MODELO PARA CONSTRUIR • MODELBYGGESÆT • ΣΥΝΑΡΜΟΛΟΓΟΥΜΕΝΟ ΜΟΝΤΕΛΟ

Humbrol Set includes
12 Acrylic paints
2 Brushes
2 Poly Cement

LEFT: *Boulton Paul Defiant Mk I & Dornier Do 17Z 'Dogfight Double' set, 2015.*

BELOW: *2015's Albion AM463 3-point fueller in 1.48 scale.*

J6015	VW Beetle (Classic)	N/A
J6016	NA P-51D Mustang	N/A

Starter Sets

A55213	Boulton Paul Defiant Mk I	1:72
A55214	Grumman F4F-4 Wildcat	1:72

Dogfight Doubles

A50169	B6N2 Kate & F4F-4 Wildcat	1:72
A50170	Defiant Mk I & Dornier Do 17Z	1:72
A50171	Beaufighter Mk X & Fw 190A-8	1:72

Battle of Britain - 75th Anniversary Sets

A50172	B-o-B Ready for Battle (4 kits)	1:48
A50173	B-o-B 75th Anniversary (4 aircraft)	1:72

Re-issues, Sets & New Series

Airfix Challenge

A76508	Sopwith Camel	1:72
A76509	Fokker Dr.1	1:72
A76510	WWI Male Tank	1:76

Sets

A50174	Battle of Waterloo Set	1:76
A55308	Ford 3-Litre GT	1:32
A55309	Maserati Indy	1:32
A50031B	Red Arrows Hawk Set (Revised)	1:48
A55202A	Red Arrows Hawk Set (Revised)	1:72

Kits

A02005B	Red Arrows Hawk (Revised)	1:72
A09179	EE Lightning F.1/F.1A/ F.2/F.3	1:48
A25001A	DH Mosquito FB VI	1:24
A03171	Vickers Vanguard (BEA/Invicta)	1:144
A04176	DH Comet 4B (Airtours/Olympic)	1:144
A04301	Churchill Bridge Layer	1:76
A06361	17-Pdr Anti-Tank Gun	1:32
A08360	Crusader Mk III Tank	1:32

The 1:24 'Car Door' Typhoon and 'Bomber' Mosquito are not yet in the catalogue. With the exception of the 'Old Bill' Bus, the new World War I items from 2014 have been quietly dropped; presumably they could not compete with World War II for modellers' money. However, three old World War One kits are included in the 'Airfix Challenge', which is similar to 'Project Airfix'. Similarly, the Battle of Waterloo 200th Anniversary sees only the return of the Gift Set so far.

There are the inevitable deletions, mainly of old tools to make way for their

Battle of Britain Ready for Battle gift set, 2015.

2015's Bedford MWD Light Truck.

replacements. There are several longed for re-moulds, such as the Defiant and Beaufighter, plus some exciting new subjects like the Whitley and Shackleton. We also see the first of the 1:48 vehicles to support the growing range of 1:48 aircraft, though the withdrawal from Afghanistan means we have probably seen the last of the modern AFVs for the moment. Several older kits make a welcome return, suit-

ably refreshed. All in all it is a good year of new releases for aircraft modellers but perhaps not much for ship and car modellers. Airfix is also a step closer to its aim of having a catalogue of new-tool aircraft that will be the envy of other kit manufacturers and is once again at the cutting edge of kit development.

In Airfix's sixtieth year of producing aircraft kits, which started with the

original Spitfire, BT-K, we have a totally new Spitfire Mk I, which promises to be the most accurate and detailed Spitfire anywhere. Airfix kits have come a long from the little *Golden Hind* over sixty years ago. The catalogues today may not show the huge range of Airfix kits that enabled Airfix to proudly proclaim in the 1960s and 1970s that it had the 'Largest Range of Construction Kits in the World', but with its vast tool bank largely intact and a steady stream of new moulds and re-releases appearing, it can once again make that proud boast.

Looking Ahead to 2016

In summer 2015, Airfix revealed six new aircraft models, two of them World War I aircraft, for release in early 2016:

A01086	Fokker E.II (Late) Eindecker	1:72
A02101	Royal Aircraft Factory BE2c	1:72
A08017	Boeing B-17G Flying Fortress	1:72
A05128	Boulton Paul Defiant Mk I	1:48
A09182	Gloster Meteor F.8	1:48
A06304	USAAF Bomber Re-supply Set	1:72

It looks like perhaps the expansion of the World War I range, proposed in 2014 but largely dropped in 2015, may now be going ahead!

CHAPTER SIX

Packaging

Over the sixty years or so that Airfix has been producing its famous construction kits, the style of packaging has changed considerably.

Before we look at the various packaging 'types', here is a brief overview of Airfix packaging. The first proper Airfix kit, the *Golden Hind*, was offered to Woolworth's in a box with a suggested retail price of 5s (25p). When Woolworth's stated it was overpriced, Ralph Ehrmann and John Gray came back with a simpler packaging and a retail price of 2s (10p). This entailed putting the kit in one of the then new transparent polythene bags stapled to an illustrated header made by folding a rectangle of paper into four. Thus was born the famous 'two-bob' (slang for one 'old' shilling – 5p in current coinage) bagged kit which reached its zenith in the glorious Type 3 packaging (*see* later). Series 1,

Type 1

Type 2

Type 3

Type 4

Type 5

Type 6

The evolution of Airfix packaging demonstrated by kits of the Junkers Ju 87 Stuka down the years.

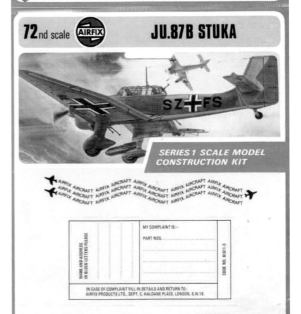

and for a few years Series 2, kits would hang, tantalizingly, in their polybags in front of our eyes in the shops until the arrival of the short-lived 'blister' pack.

The innovative blister pack was introduced in 1973. This overcame the main drawback to the bags, which was that the bits could get broken if the bag were roughly handled before it was opened. It also meant that a few kits migrated to Series 2 because they wouldn't fit into the blister! Although Airfix no longer use these two types of packaging for single kits, many other goods are still sold in them, and Airfix was an innovator in packaging developments (this is not surprising in that Airfix Plastics was a leading company in packaging design).

Series 3 and above, plus Series 2 after a few years, were all sold in boxes. When the style changed, Type 2 to Type 3 and so on, the box size was often increased: it was made slightly longer, wider or deeper, or a combination of all three. If you compare a late Series 2 box with one of the first, you'll see what I mean. This change was mainly due to the increased number of parts in the kits, plus a change in the runner design.

Initially the kit parts ran off a single, usually bent, runner such as 'pig iron'.

Later, the runner formed a rectangular, hexagonal-section runner, with all the kit parts inside it. Periodically the runner sizes were increased, thus necessitating a slightly larger box. Like this, kit parts were now much better protected.

Apart from the very early 1950s, Airfix kits were sold in a standardized packaging style. Within each type there would be variations, but the logo and basic design would be compatible with that type. Thus, for example, the early 1:24 cars and original 'museum models' are Type 3. Where, however, the basic design was altered slightly, but significantly, it was designated a sub type, such as Type 3a to 3d. Generally though, a new type would be denoted by a change in the Airfix logo style, which would bring a new box design with it. However, in the last couple of years of Humbrol's tenure we had a basic box design from Humbrol-Airfix, but with three variations on the logo!

The original classification for early kits was compiled by the founding members of the Airfix Collectors' Club in the late 1990s. It has been updated since, and now covers all the main styles, and is the one that most modellers use when classifying kits.

Type 0

The first type lasted until 1956/57: there were several variations, but they are all generally referred to as Type 0. All had the 'Airfix Products in Plastic' logo on the front. Apart from the *Southern Cross* and the Tractor, there were no boxed kits.

The first few sailing ships, the first six Trackside kits, the Lancaster, Wellington, Superfreighter, Ferguson and *Southern Cross* are all considered to be Type 0.

Type 1

In Type 1, the design became more standardized; the illustrations were still basic line drawings but with more colour and background scenery. They lasted for a couple of years. They are not particularly rare, because the kits were being produced in the tens of thousands and many were not assembled! The first ones are referred to as Type 1A, but later ones are usually known as Type 1B. The Series 2 kits with Type 1A headers were more detailed and sophisticated than the earlier ones. In fact the drawings were more accurate than some of the later Airfix illustrations! They began to be replaced by Type 2 around 1959/60.

FAR LEFT:
Type 0 packaging.

LEFT:
Type 1 and 2 versions of the Beaufighter and Swordfish packaging.

Type 2

In Type 2 a much more uniform style was introduced, and the 'Airfix Products in Plastic' logo was replaced by the standard 'Airfix' logo. The header or box top was split down the middle by a vertical coloured stripe (in three colours in the case of the AFVs). There was generally very little background, but the aircraft, tank or ship was particularly well drawn, and for the first time there was consistency across the whole range. There were, however occasionally two variants of the same header, with very minor detail differences, probably when a fresh production run was made or a different printer used.

Boxes were of the old folded and stapled variety, but were soon replaced by the newer, glued variety, which could be folded in to lie flat.

Types 1A and 1B packaging.

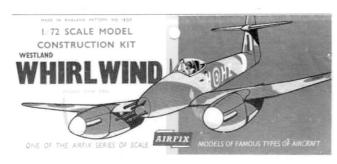

ABOVE: *A variety of Type 2 boxes.*

LEFT: *Type 1, 2 and 3 headers.*

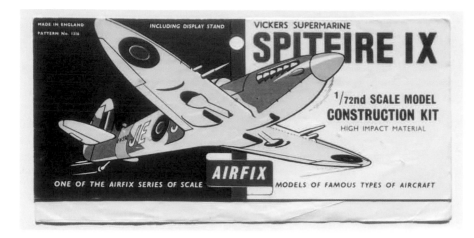

ABOVE: *Type 2 (top) and 3 packaging.*

RIGHT: *(Top to bottom) Type 3a, 3b and 3c versions of the Tiger tank header.*

Type 3

Type 3 is arguably the most popular, and probably the style which lasted longest. It is best remembered for the magnificent artwork of Airfix's new illustrator, Roy Cross, and when this was combined with the lovely figure and sailing ship artwork of Brian Knight, the resulting illustrations achieve what I believe to be Airfix's most consistent period for the design of the whole range.

Type 3 was introduced in the autumn of 1963; the first kit to receive the Type 3 treatment was the Prairie Tank Locomotive in Series 3. The early ship and aircraft pictures were done by Charles Oates and William Howard Jarvis, but Roy Cross, Brian Knight, Kenneth McDonough and Geoff Hunt later redid most, if not all, of these.

Basically Type 3 consisted of a full colour illustration that covered the entire header and wrapped round the side of the boxes. In one corner, usually the lower right, was a white strip. The red stripe at the end of the strip was the remnant of the Type 2 stripe. Along the sides of the boxes were rectangles illustrating other kits in the range, with, once or twice, kits not announced appearing on the side! The ends of the boxes were white with the new scroll-style Airfix logo and a smaller version of the box-top artwork, although sometimes they were separate pictures.

There are four distinct variations of Type 3; these are described below in the order of their introduction.

Type 3a

Type 3a is the earliest Type 3; some came with rather simple drawings reminiscent of Type 2, others with illustrations by Charles Oates and Roy Cross. The subject of the kit was printed on the picture, with *AIRFIX – OO* or *AIRFIX – 72* printed on the white strip, with parallel lines running through *AIRFIX*. They represent the first moves towards Type 3 packaging.

Type 3b

In Type 3b the simpler illustrations disappeared, and the kit name now appeared below *AIRFIX – 72 SCALE,* for example. The *AIRFIX* still had parallel lines through it. On some of the early Type 3a boxes the full name of the kit also appeared on the illustration (e.g. Wildcat & Airacobra) but on most of them it only appeared below *AIRFIX – 72 SCALE.*

Type 3c

Type 3c is virtually identical to Type 3b but without the parallel lines through *AIRFIX*. The quality of the illustration was also much improved. It was quite subtle, but the pictures were clearer and sharper, with richer colours. These are arguably the best of the Type 3s, and most Airfix *aficionados* consider them to be the best of all Airfix packaging.

The final stage of Type 3 was Type 3d, which did not affect those kits sold with a header, but only boxed kits.

Type 3d

Towards the end of the Type 3 era, boxed kits began to appear with the Airfix scroll logo on the box ends, painted light blue or yellow, for example. Otherwise the box was unchanged. The colours were:

Series 2: Yellow with white lettering
Series 3: Blue with white lettering
Series 4: Green with yellow lettering
Series 5: Red with white lettering
Series 6: Yellow with red lettering
Series 7: None issued?
Series 8: Crimson with white lettering
Series 9: Purple with white lettering

Throughout this period Roy Cross gradually repainted most of the original Type 3 subjects, though sadly not all.

Type 4

In mid-1971, the Airfix logo was redesigned. The famous scroll logo had been appearing in the middle of a red circle, and it was decided to completely redesign the logo to make it circular. The new logo appeared on the 1971 'Summer Reprint' leaflets, and has largely remained the same, apart from its 'oval' period.

The HO/OO figures in the Type 3 'blue' boxes started to receive the new logo on the end and sides, although the front still bore the old scroll logo. Certain kits, such as the Playforts, stayed in their Type 3 packaging and do not appear to have been updated. Before long, however, it was decided to use the new logo on all the models, and so Type 4 was born. Basically it was Type 3 amended: a white border was put around the picture, and the title strip was given a round end to accommodate the new round logo.

The box end logo was red and white, except for the first few, but most of the title and box side logos were in two colours to reflect the two main colours used on the

LEFT: *(Top to bottom) Type 3a, 3b, 3c and 3d boxes.*

BELOW: *Roy Cross' dramatic painting of a Junkers Ju 88A-4 from 1964, on a Type 3b box.*

BOTTOM: *Type 3c packaging.*

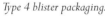

Type 4 blister packaging.

TOP: *Type 4b packaging.*

ABOVE: *Type 4a (top) and 4c versions of the Britten-Norman Islander packaging.*

rest of the box. Series 1 headers appear to be all red and white because there were no sides for other colours. A few kits had only one colour, and this was on the first few (for example, the first issue 1:24 Bf 109 and 1:12 Bentley kits). The three mainstream variants of Type 4 are described below.

Type 4a

The first releases in Type 4, Type 4a included the Islander with its all-yellow logo on the front, the sides and the ends of the boxes. They were rapidly replaced by Type 4b.

Type 4b

Very similar to Type 4a, these Type 4b boxes had the red and white logo on the box end with a two-colour logo on the box sides and front, using the predominant colours from the painting.

Type 4c

Towards the end of Type 4, new releases and reissues started to receive a modified Type 4 packaging. A coloured background to the title was added, and all the logos were red and black. Some of the Type 4c packaging had the same box sides as Type 4b, but some had a side view of the aircraft on the side. Interestingly the blister packs were Type 4c at the top but with a Type 3 bottom! The Collector's Series with the all-white logo are just Type 4. The Series 1 figure kits are best described as Type 4 card header (earliest) and the rest 'blister'.

Since the majority of kits were in production, either continuously or once or twice a year, most kits soon appeared in Type 4. Then in 1975, the figure kits, museum models and Collectors' Series started to appear in a revised style, which had all the writing superimposed on the picture and did away with the white title

frame, the boxes being largely white. Since these still retained the Type 4 features of rounded rectangles they are simply Type 4. They would lead on to Type 5.

Type 5

In Type 5 the logo was now always red/white/black, and the boxes had single colour sides with the kit name written across the picture. Additional wording described the kit: for example 'The RAF's Greatest Wartime Bomber', or 'Advanced Carrier-borne Swing-wing Fighter/Bomber', and so on. The 'blister' packs for Series 1 were replaced by boxes. We were also informed that as well as being a 1:72 scale model kit it was also a 1:72 'Modele Reduit': the beginnings of multi-lingual boxes?

The second edition 1977 price list revealed a new, italic-style logo, which ran through the 1978 catalogue; however, I don't remember any models being released using this logo. In 1979, we saw the introduction of the oval logo. Palitoy also used an oval logo in 1982, which seemed to bear a resemblance to the earlier US logos.

Type 6

In Type 6 the oval logo was used. One reason for the oval was, we were told, because it allowed narrower titles, but a larger logo. The box was now full colour with no border, and many of the aircraft appeared without background and consequently any scenes of fighting, or had the 'action' airbrushed out to satisfy certain countries. Much of the surviving artwork comes in 'violent' and 'non-violent' transparencies. 'Feathered' propellers were even restarted because they obviously hadn't been shot at before! This was a very costly exercise for Airfix, particularly as we seem to have now gone back to the 'blood and guts' originals! Boxes and instructions were now multi-lingual.

Type 7

A very short-lived design, Type 7 was intended for the 1981 releases and appeared throughout the rare 1981 catalogue. The logo was once again circular, but now bore the legend 'Precision Model Kits' around its edge. Most of that year's intended releases bore the new logo.

LEFT: *Top to bottom, Type 4a, 4b, and 4c packaging.*

BELOW: *Type 5 packaging.*

BOTTOM: *Type 6 packaging.*

There was a full colour picture or photograph of the model on the front with 'SNAPnglue' or 'SNAPfix' in a white band also on the front. This style did not last long after the take-over, and was superseded by Palitoy's new design.

In January 1981, Airfix called in the receivers, and modellers throughout the world waited to see whether Airfix would survive, and if so, who the new owners would be. A proposed management buyout was rejected in favour of a purchase by General Mills, which put Airfix under its Palitoy division in Coalville, Leicester.

Those moulds at Wandsworth were shipped out to the Miro-Meccano plant in Calais, owned by General Mills, and the archives were relocated to Coalville. The 1981 Airfix catalogue seems to have had a very limited release (were they all pulped, or had only a few been printed by the time of the Toy Fair?). Most of the new releases for 1981 eventually came out, and in 1982 we had the first Palitoy catalogue.

The early Palitoy kits were obviously in Type 7 packaging, and soon began to appear with 'Made in France' ('Fabrique en France') on the box, or with white labels with 'CPG Corp.' printed on them. By 1982, Palitoy had begun to stamp its mark upon Airfix, and two new logos appeared. One was a short-lived variant of the oval design and was, I think, used on some of the American car kits and on the cover of some issues of Airfix's *Railway Magazine*. The other was a return to the Type 4 style logo but with a small 'r' after Airfix – to show it was a registered trademark of Palitoy. This logo lasted for several years

Type 7 SNAPnglue packaging.

into the Humbrol age, and appeared on Type 8.

Type 8

In Type 8, the round logo featured prominently on the front, sides and end, but instead of a painting, a made-up model of the aircraft sat on what appeared to be a blueprint, with the top edge fading into blackness. All very uninspiring, particularly as the models were not painted to the highest standard and frequently showed that the actual model did not look much like the real thing, whereas the Roy Cross paintings did! It also meant that models were no longer instantly recognizable because they all, at a glance, tended to look the same.

Certain series in the range did retain the original artwork, such as the OO/HO figures, and these were actually an improvement over the final Type 7 boxes (Italians and British infantry).

We were led to believe that this style of box-top design was produced to comply with laws relating to the contents of boxes matching the box top. However, in the *Boys' Book of Airfix*, Arthur Ward reveals that

an early 1983 presentation document to Palitoy states that new 'strongly branded artwork, colour coded and in eight languages' was needed. This could be achieved by 'model photography'!

It is worth remembering that by the early 1980s, Airfix was no longer releasing new models every month, and very few kits were in continuous production or even in production! Therefore, a run of a particular model could easily outlast the life of a box type. In the 1960s and early seventies all the kits were in production, and as soon as stocks of a kit ran low, another run was made. Thus a kit such as the 'Tiger' Tank would appear in Type 3a, 3b and 3c packaging because as each new run was made the packaging was modified to the then current style of that type. So with Type 3 and possibly Type 4 it may be necessary to identify the Tiger you are selling as, say, a Type 3b, but with all the other kits generally to say 'Panther Tank – Type 9' is sufficient.

By the mid 1980s Airfix was on the market again, this time to be bought by Borden UK, the owners of Humbrol. The design offices moved to Hull and home of the Humber Oil Company, but the moulds remained in France. These were moved to Heller's (also owned by Humbrol) plant in Trun.

Initially kits were released in Type 8 packaging, but with Humbrol printed on the side, and for a couple of years Humbrol concentrated on getting a lot of the kits back into production. The catalogues of this period are somewhat slight, and some were almost flyers (for example, 'Forty new models for the Airfix range').

Then in 1987 we saw the first decent catalogue released, with Roy Cross paintings as well as new ones by Anthony Sturgess and James Goulding. This marked the birth of Type 9.

Type 9

The now standard Airfix logo with its small 'r' was retained, but the boxes were now mainly white with a large painting

SNAPfix packaging for 1983.

on the front. Down the left-hand side was the logo with a series of coloured (yellow or blue) bars beneath. They were the first Humbrol-designed box style. The nearly all-new Series 3 'Buccaneer' S.2B appeared crammed into one of these boxes before being elevated to the roomier Series 4!

Since most of the range was now aircraft, tanks and warships, there were few other ranges to warrant a modified Type 9 design. In addition to James Goulding and Anthony Sturgess, several of the Geoff Hunt warships appeared with Type 9.

Type 10

The change to Type 10 took place around 1990. The boxes were still predominantly white, but the logo tended to be larger and there was a wide border round the illustration. The Collector's Series and multipose figures were issued in this type rather than a variant of Type 9. 'Aircraft of the Aces' were released in slightly modified boxes but are still clearly Type 10.

Type 10 lasted into the mid 1990s, and several new kits (virtually all aircraft) appeared first in these boxes. Quite a lot of new artwork was commissioned (the photographer no longer having to nudge the model around on the blueprint).

The 1:48 naval Buccaneer kit was released in a new style – Type 11.

RIGHT: *(Top to bottom) Type 8, 9 and 10 packaging compared.*

BELOW LEFT AND RIGHT: *Type 10 packaging.*

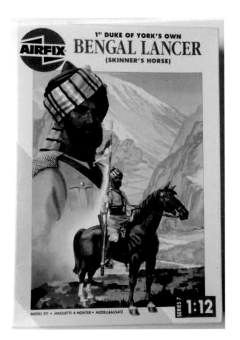

Type 11

Type 11 was a return in some respects to Type 5 with its full colour box top with logo and titles superimposed. The blue sides also harked back to the lighter blue of Type 8. It also introduced a new logo, Type 10. The italic design of the 1970s was introduced with yellow shading. The packaging remained largely unaltered into 2002. The main alteration has been to the logo, which has gone through three very similar variations. While the logo has altered slightly the main box design has

not, and so they can be considered to be one basic type, but with three variations – shall we say Type 11a, 11b and 11c?

When used with a striking Roy Cross illustration (for example, Short Sunderland and Douglas Dauntless) they were real eye-catchers. The only real criticism concerned the blue sides, which was virtually the same blue as used by Revell – so when scanning the shelves in a model shop it was not always easy to see where Revell ended and Airfix began. This is, however, a small point, but one Airfix was aware of.

Concurrent with Type 11 was a new design mainly used for the kits in the starter sets, but also used solely on some of the cars and motorbikes. This was Type 12.

Type 12

Type 12 boxes are blue, red and yellow in colour, and feature the model's photograph or painting posed against the three-colour background. On some, the rear features details of the Airfix website. Several non-car kits appear in this box as

Naval fighters of very different eras, both in Type 11 packaging.

well as Type 11. It was apparently not a replacement for Type 11.

Also in 2002 we saw a return to boxes with lids – even for the figures! This was, I felt, a great improvement and made the boxes much more rigid and easier to keep the kit components in.

Type 13

In 2003, most kits were being issued in Type 11 and 12 packaging. Although the Type 12 packaging seemed at first to be reserved for those kits in the starter sets, several were issued as separate kits in this packaging without being issued in the Type 11 style. Then mid-year we had two new releases in a modified Type 11 packaging style. But this proved to be a 'blip', because in late December and in January 2004 we had another new style of packaging, and it was this that was the new packaging. All of the kits released so far that year were in the new packaging.

The two mid-2003 kits, the Honda RC211V (02485) and Subaru Impreza WRC'02 (01421), were sufficiently different to warrant a new type number, so I suggested Type 13. I have never been keen on missing out the number 13 because of bad luck, although I appreciate that many people regard it as unlucky. So since we have only two kits we can call them Type 13 and need never worry about sub-types. In fact, one may call it an unlucky designation as only two kits were issued in it!

Type 14

The new releases for 2004 became Type 14. It would appear that the boxes were colour co-ordinated according to type of

Type 12 packaging.

Type 13 packaging.

Type 14 packaging.

kit. Thus the main colour around the sides and on the box front seemed to be in a particular colour for each range of kits. For example, the two 1:72 motor launches have light green as their predominant colour with a red strip (common to all Type 14s) running round the base.

The colours used so far, and their co-ordinated kit group, appeared to be as follows:

Aircraft	Dark blue
AFVs	Olive green
MTBs	Light green
Vintage cars	Light grey
OO/HO figures	Black

The Footballers were in a totally different style and I suspect don't warrant a separate designation.

Type 15

In late 2004, Airfix had been experimenting with silver/grey boxes for many of their aircraft collection sets, and a modified version was to emerge for the main ranges, which became Type 15. In 2005, the new style was introduced. It overcame the two problems of the blue box ends being confused with Revell kits, and the difficulty in reading the sides and ends from any distance.

When Hornby purchased Airfix in late 2006, the decision was taken to keep the box style, with one or two small revisions (such as the Hornby logo on the sides). Thus Humbrol-produced kits are Type 15A, and Hornby's are Type 15B. The later boxes are also sturdier and have a glossier finish. OO/HO figures have been put back into boxes with end flaps, as originally sold.

Type 16

Shortly after Hornby purchased Humbrol and Airfix in late 2006, it was decided to move towards digital artwork for the new releases and re-releases. At the same time, Type 15 packaging was replaced by a new style, which was predominantly red.

The new style, Type 16, featured red sides and front, with dark red 'runners' superimposed on the front. The new Airfix Type 13 logo was on the front and all four sides. The box tray was also red, with details of the club and website on the back, with modelling tips around the side. These trays were standard for all kits. A couple of years ago the club information was updated, so we can describe the early ones as Type 16a and the latest as Type 16b.

In Summary

So in the sixty years since Airfix's first true kit, the *Golden Hind*, in 1952, we have had sixteen different box styles for the mainstream ranges, and thirteen logo designs. Hopefully the current style, Type 16, will remain, as it seems to be one of the best.

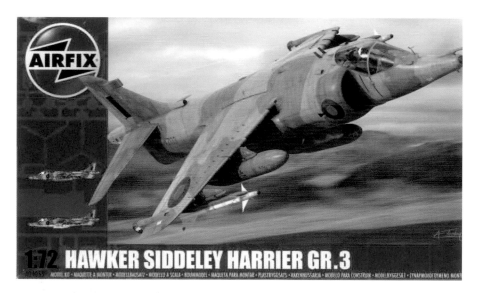

Type 15 packaging.

The front (top), and back of Type 16B packaging.

CHAPTER SEVEN

Logos

Possibly one of the most important elements of product awareness is the product(s) logo. One only has to look down a crowded street or alongside a busy road and see the BP or Shell signs to instantly know the identity of the fuel being sold. Similarly, when you see a superstore, the sight of the logo immediately identifies the company that is supplying it – though of course a striking logo is only useful if you recognize the company or product that it represents.

There are many toy companies out there, but only a very few that the general public associates with a particular product. Mention Hornby and Scalextric and everybody immediately thinks 'trains and racing sets'. However, mention Hasegawa or even Tamiya and many people would probably have to be prompted to reply. When it comes to construction kits, excellent though these two companies are, there is only one company (certainly in the UK) that virtually everybody recognizes, and that is good old Airfix.

There are very few companies whose name is generally regarded as the generic name for that product. One almost invariably says that someone is *hoover*ing upstairs, when in fact they are more likely today to be *Dyson*ing, but we all call a vacuum cleaner a 'hoover'. The same is true of Airfix. The famous kits were only a part of (and a later addition to) a prominent plastics company, but they would come to take over the name in the public's perception, and also be the only part of the group that would survive intact after 1981, and still be eagerly sought after today.

Long before the kits were thought of, Airfix was probably only well known to a few people, and then for toys. However, if you'd mentioned Airfix to a 'spiv' in the late 1940s he'd have instantly whipped out his comb! So, therefore, every company, whether a household name or not, needs a recognizable logo, and Airfix is no exception – and its logo has evolved into one of the most recognizable ones, certainly in the toy and hobby trade. Without the famous kits, it is likely that most people would hardly remember

Airfix today: it would be a barely remembered name from their youth.

Logos Until 1981

Type 1

The earliest known logo is 'Airfix Products in Plastics', and is the one which probably lasted longest. Later the 'Products in Plastics' would disappear as the brand became better known. The logo was originally based on a scroll with the two ends unrolled or turned back. In essence it has remained a scroll, but later was incorporated into a circle: thus the logo adorning the new Gladiator kit is still recognizable as a scroll with the ends turned back, albeit stylized. If we are to give logos 'type' numbers then this is clearly Type 1.

The Type 1 logo reigned supreme throughout the early days at Airfix up until Type 2 packaging was first used around 1959 – about twenty years! Not only was a new box/header style introduced, but the logo was also modernized to suit it.

Type 1A logo.

Type 1B logo.

Type 2

In the Type 2 logo, 'Products in Plastics' was dropped and 'Airfix' was enlarged to fill the scroll. The font was changed to probably Arial, and italicized; in fact the whole scroll was 'italicized' and sharpened up. The turnbacks now met in the middle and were generally left white, while the background to the main part was usually coloured with the word 'Airfix' left in

white. Sometimes the 'Airfix' was in black, with or without the other colour.

AIRFIX without the scroll background was sometimes used on catalogues and leaflets. When the motor racing sets were introduced, the turnbacks were lengthened slightly and black and white squares were added, presumably to resemble the 'chequered' flag waved at the winner! Later *AIRFIX:MRRC* would be inserted into the logo.

This new logo should be referred to as Type 2, and it lasted until Type 4 packaging was introduced in late 1971.

Type 2 kit logo.

Type 3

However, two subtle changes occurred with the introduction of Type 3 packaging in 1963. Firstly, the Type 2 logo was placed inside a coloured circle (usually red), and on the kit boxes/headers, details of the scale were added, for example 'AIRFIX-OO SCALE' or 'AIRFIX CONSTANT SCALE'. Some of the 1:24 American cars used a blue circle. Although it is not strictly speaking a new logo design, I shall refer to it as Type 3, because it keeps us in step with the packaging. It also represented a transitional style to Type 4 and introduced the concept of the round Airfix logo. A circle is considered to be the perfect shape, which is why the likes of BMW, Mercedes and Audi all have circular logos.

The 1971 eighth edition catalogue and leaflet both used the red circular Type 3 logo. However, the 'summer reprint' leaflet displayed a new, Type 4 logo that was clearly an update of the Type 3 logo and was to form the basis of all subsequent logos.

Type 3 logo.

Type 4

Oddly, although the new logo appeared on the leaflet in its final form, the ninth edition catalogue showed it with the turn-backs in red, and the first Type 4 packaged kits (Type 4a) showed the logo in one colour (for instance Islander was yellow). Type 4b packaging used the two prominent colours from the box illustration, and it was only on Type 4c packaging that we get the red, black and white logo used exclusively. Some Type 4 boxes (the Collector's Series) used an all-white logo.

Although red was the standard colour, some other ranges, such as Arts and Crafts, used orange or blue/green for the background colour.

Type 4 logo.

Type 5

When Type 5 packaging was introduced, the Type 4 logo was still used. However, on the front of the second edition 1977 leaflet and the first edition 1978 leaflet a revised 'italicized' logo was shown, but not on the back! It also featured throughout the fifteenth edition catalogue alongside the standard Type 4. I'm not aware of it

being used on any kit boxes. It was used on the 1977 Toys and Games catalogue, and was used by Airfix MRRC and Airfix Motor Ace. Since it was around at the time of Type 5, this makes it also Type 5.

Type 5 logo.

Type 6

In 1979 there was a further alteration to the Type 4 logo. Apparently many boxes were getting longer, and to incorporate a reasonably sized round logo with similar-sized titles would result in a greater incursion into the box-top illustration. The answer was to 'flatten' the circle to make an oval. Now a much larger logo could adorn the box top because it was wider rather than deeper. It was used on Type 6 packaging and was the basis for the GMR logo on the rebranded trains of the same time. It thus becomes, conveniently, Type 6.

Type 6 logo.

Type 7

In the last few months of Airfix Products Ltd, a new logo was devised and it adorned the short-lived 1981 catalogue, although very few of us got to see one! It seemed to hark back to all the earlier logos, combining bits of each to produce a logo that was instantly unrecognizable. With hindsight it does seem strange that if money was so tight in 1980, a considerable amount should be expended on a costly redesign of the boxes and logo to seemingly little effect. Perhaps I am being unfair and there were sound commercial reasons for doing this. So what about the logo?

It returned to the circular shape of Type 4, using the red circle of Type 3, only now smaller. AIRFIX was written in a font similar to the original Type 1, and the 'Precision Model Kits' reminded us of 'Products in Plastics'. On the catalogue, these words were replaced by 'New Kits for 1981'. Boxes using this logo with paintings or photographs of the model are referred to as Type 7, so the logo becomes Type 7 also.

Thus far the logo has more or less coincided with the box type, but following the 1981 buyout by General Mills, they began to diverge.

Type 7 logo.

Logos Post-1981

Type 8

When Palitoy, like Humbrol and Hornby later on, took over Airfix, initially they would use the existing designs and logos, including Types 6 and 7. Then in the 1982 catalogue two new logos appeared. The first and main one was a modification of Type 4, where the black and white were reversed. The red was the same. A small 'R' in a circle was added after 'AIRFIX', presumably to indicate 'registered' as in registered trademark. It first appeared on Type 8 packaging and so is a Type 8 logo.

Type 8 logo.

Type 9

The second was a modification of the Type 6 logo without the turnbacks and with stylized lettering for Airfix. It also had the small R. It mainly seems to have been used on US-originated kits and two issues of Airfix's magazine *Model Trains*. It should probably be referred to as Type 9.

When Humbrol acquired Airfix in 1986, the Type 8 logo was used for several years. In the 1990 catalogue it was used in modified form to indicate the contents of the page.

Type 9 logo.

Type 10

A modified logo was introduced in the 1995 catalogue to coincide with the introduction of Type 11 packaging. 'AIRFIX' was now outlined in yellow and the turn-backs were italicized as per Type 5. It has remained as the standard logo ever since, with a couple of minor variations, and becomes Type 10.

Type 10 logo.

Type 11

In 1999, the logo was given a 3-D effect complete with shading and highlights, making it reminiscent of the old enamel badges often worn at school to denote certain responsibilities such as 'prefect' or 'librarian'. Although it is the same layout as Type 10, I shall refer to it as Type 11, as it is different enough to warrant a seperate type number.

Type 11 logo.

Type 12

In 2001, however, it was modified again when it lost its 'enamelling' and the red parts were given a raised, shaded effect which looked almost plastic. The little R was also dropped, which made it a much clearer and more satisfying logo, although it has recently been added to new Hornby releases. Its use was initially continued by Hornby, although the little R was put back. It is, by my reckoning, Type 12, so we have Types 12a and 12b, to be pedantic.

Type 12a logo.

Type 12b logo.

Type 13

Around 2009, Hornby introduced its new Type 16 packaging, which is predominantly red. To go with it is a modified logo, which becomes Type 13. It is an amalgam of several earlier logos and drops the yellow around 'Airfix'. It is not an unlucky logo, since many of the finest Airfix kits have been released beneath it.

Type 13 logo.

In Summary

Hopefully, the accompanying artwork will make the above descriptions clear. I have tried to produce an example of every variation. There may have been one or two minor variations not mentioned above, but on the whole I believe the list is fairly comprehensive and allows us to roughly date a kit release.

One logo which has not, so far, been mentioned is the corporate logo. This was used to represent the main company of the Airfix group, Airfix Industries Limited, and was used on company stationery, financial documents and even lorries! It was a stylized 'A' and was in use until Airfix called in the receivers in 1981; it is illustrated below.

Airfix's corporate logo.

CHAPTER EIGHT

Airfix Artists

Over the sixty or so years of Airfix kit production, numerous artists have been employed to illustrate the kit boxes. Some were employed freelance through art studios while others were employed directly. Nowadays the freelance artists are the hardest to track down, as much of their work was unsigned, or the art studio is listed as the painter.

Many artists had successful careers before and after their time with Airfix. Some, despite illustrious careers and fame in the art world, are remembered by the man-in-the-street because they painted the box tops of the Airfix kits he bought as a child. Roy Cross, for example, has published several books showcasing his artwork, and when you see his Airfix paintings in their original format you realize what beautiful paintings they were – and all to sell a 'two-bob' toy!

If these paintings had been 'dashed off', as many were for cheap toys from Hong Kong, for example, we would not have looked twice at them and they would have gone straight from obscurity into obscurity. Instead they were executed with such skill and dexterity that they could still be used fifty years later, and we still marvel at them.

The artwork was always very important to Airfix; it was the artwork, after all, that sold the kits. Airfix kits were aimed primarily at the 'schoolboy pocket money' market. When we went into Woolies or our local newsagents fifty years ago, we were always pleasantly surprised to see a new box top nestling amongst the trays or racks of Airfix kits. We may not have recognized the aircraft, but the guns firing and bombs exploding told us all we needed to know. By the time we had made it, painted it and put the transfers on, we considered ourselves to be 'experts' on the Sturmovik, Boomerang or Airacobra. Now, half a century later, we tend to forget the shortcomings of these models, but we never forget that beautiful artwork, which at the time seemed to suggest our latest pocket money was burning a hole in our pockets and shouted out to us 'Buy me'!

As a teenager in the mid-1960s I was not keen on the early Type 3 paintings that were used to illustrate the new style packaging introduced in 1963. I felt that the aircraft and ship paintings were flat and lacking in perspective and detail. Much later, I would appreciate that many of the ship paintings were in fact remarkably good pieces of artwork, being painted by a renowned marine artist, William Howard Jarvis.

The appearance in an early Type 3 boxing of the Dornier Do 217E-2 was a revelation to me. Here was a painting that depicted an accurate shape of the aircraft combined with good perspective and a bright sunny background, with lots going on. It was almost 'photo-like' in its execution, yet was clearly a painting. Then over the next few months many of the Series 1 aircraft started to appear with this artist's paintings. I remember seeing the Spitfire IX in Woolies and feeling that the picture caught the subtle shape of the Spitfire. Needless to say, I had to buy one to get the header! How many of us have done likewise?

For the next ten years the artist, Roy Cross, plus Brian Knight, would go on to create the most memorable of Airfix artwork, which still to this day most modellers feel has not been surpassed.

In this section I have tried to list all the known Airfix artists. Some only painted one or two models, whilst others were the 'in-house' artist(s) for a period. Arthur Ward in his various books has given detailed biographies of many of them, so I do not propose to repeat that information, but will include more on the lesser known artists I have been able to talk to. I have not been able to track down many of the freelance artists, so can only suggest when they worked for Airfix, and include just some of the paintings they did.

Airfix artwork is like all other art, it is subjective. Each artist will have his enthusiastic supporters, and also those who do not particularly care for his style. And even amongst his devoted followers, there will be differing opinions as to which piece of his artwork is the best. Roy Cross, having the largest body of work for Airfix, is generally considered to be the favourite Airfix artist, but there are those who consider that other artists should wear the crown. At the end of the day, it is all down to personal taste.

Those who wish for a more complete listing of the various artists' box tops might refer to my recent seventy-fifth anniversary publication *The Complete Airfix Kit and Artist List*, published in 2014.

The rest of this chapter lists all the known Airfix artists, in roughly chronological order.

Charles Oates

The earliest known artist for Airfix kits was Charles Oates. He had painted many works for television and other companies, and in 1958 became art editor for the magazine *Model Railways Constructor*; he often used Airfix Trackside kits in his

Charles Oates' Douglas Boston III artwork on a Type 3a box, 1963.

articles. I have been unable to find any surviving records of his paintings for Airfix in the archives, except for a 'rough' he sent in, which he hoped Airfix would use for the 'Old Bill Bus' released in 1966; this was subsequently painted by Roy Cross. He is generally credited with painting all, or nearly all, of the pre-Type 3 headers and box tops. He is believed to have been in poor health in the mid-1960s, which explains why Airfix was eager to employ Roy Cross.

He painted several of the Type 3 rolling-stock kits and one or two aircraft kits before Roy Cross took over. Fortunately, several of his and Howard Jarvis' paintings are now held at the Bethnal Green 'Museum of Childhood' in London.

William Howard Jarvis 1903–1964

William Howard Jarvis was a renowned marine artist, and painted most of the early ship kits and several Type 3 aircraft.

He was born in Liverpool on 6 February 1903. He studied at Liverpool and Naples, and trained aboard HMS *Conway* from 1918 to 1920. He served as a Lieutenant RNVR from 1939 to 1946. In 1953 he designed the canopy of Her Majesty's state barge. He worked in the Walker Art Gallery, Liverpool, and Great Yarmouth Municipal Gallery, and was elected to be a member of the Royal Society of Marine Artists in 1947. (All this material is by courtesy of the RSMA's own book *A Celebration of Marine Art*.)

He probably painted for Airfix from around 1963 until his death in 1964, when Roy Cross joined. The large part of the surviving original artwork from the pre-1981 period is the very early artwork that was given to the Bethnal Green 'Museum of Childhood' by Palitoy. These paintings formed the bulk of the pre-1981 artwork on display at RAF Hendon from June 2013 to May 2014, where many of Jarvis' originals were displayed.

His aircraft paintings are very similar to Charles Oates' paintings, but his ship paintings were very good. Most measured about four feet by three feet, and some of the detail was incredible. A close study of HMS *Tiger* reveals details of the face and uniform on the sailor standing by the front turret: this cannot, of course, be discerned on the box top, but it is good to know it is there.

His aircraft paintings were mainly repainted by Roy Cross and later Ken

This Type 2 artwork is probably by Charles Oates.

William Howard Jarvis' HMS Victorious artwork.

George Schule's Panther tank artwork.

Dick Miller's Churchill tank artwork.

McDonough, and his warship paintings were redone by Geoff Hunt. His initial large sailing ships were repainted by Brian Knight.

In the couple of years that Roy was establishing himself and Brian Knight was joining Airfix, at least four artists were used to repaint existing box tops and headers for Type 3 releases. G. Schule's signature appears on three of the 1:76 AFV headers – the Panther, Sherman and Assault Gun – and he possibly painted four more unsigned ones, as they are all very similar in style: the Tiger, the Bren Gun Carrier, the German Armoured Car and the Centurion Tank. The Churchill Tank, however, was painted by Dick Miller. Roy then took over painting the AFVs.

Two ship box tops, HMS *Nelson* and RMS *Mauretania*, were painted by Jack Avery. Again, Roy took over painting the ship kits. Another artist was Andrew Prewett, who painted the first issue of the

HMS Nelson, *portrayed by Jack Avery.*

Fort playsets in 1966 and 1967, prior to Roy Cross repainting these and subsequent sets.

I cannot find any information about these four artists, and assume they were probably studio artists.

Roy Cross

Roy Cross' life has been well documented by Arthur Ward in his various books. He was born in 1924, and during the war produced technical drawings for various aviation companies. In the 1950s he was a

technical illustrator for Fairey Aviation, and produced 'cutaways' for the *Eagle* and *Swift* comics. He approached Airfix in 1964: having seen the artwork on their box tops, he was not very impressed by it, and felt he could do better. The two incumbent artists were in poor health and Airfix liked the quality of his artwork, so he was quickly signed up. The first painting he did for Airfix was the Dornier Do 217E-2 for a Type 3 release in 1964, and for the next ten years he painted the majority of Airfix box tops, the remaining ones being painted by Brian Knight.

Roy's paintings were mainly done in gouache and were smaller than the previous artwork. However, the detail was incredible. He managed to capture the shape of the subject, apply panel lines and rivets, and add a suitably detailed background. The great majority of modellers, if asked which box tops encouraged them the most to buy the kits, will say that it was those with the brilliant paintings of Roy Cross.

The paintings were generally painted in a rectangle that was almost square, but the subject would have to fit into the 'letterbox' shape of the box top or header. Roy found this 'letterbox' constraint annoying, but he always managed to deliver the goods: the Fokker Dr.1, for example, fitted perfectly. It was only much later that we were able to see the rest of the painting that had been excluded by the 'letterbox' dimension.

Roy would be supplied with copies of technical drawings by Airfix, as well as a pre-production kit that he could assemble and then 'pose' for his initial drawings. He usually submitted two or three pencil 'roughs' to John Gray, who then returned them with 'No' or 'Yes, this one' written on them. He would then prepare a colour rough with a clear overlay showing the box-top shape, and when that was approved, painted the final artwork. One or two kits, such as the 1:24 Mustang and Harrier, actually featured a second final painting rather than the one shown in the catalogue, but all the rest used his final artwork.

LEFT: *Hurricane IIb artwork from 1972, by Roy Cross.*

BELOW: *The 1975 Airfix calendar, mostly illustrated by Roy Cross.*

ABOVE: *Fokker Dr.1 artwork by Roy Cross.* AIRFIX

BELOW: *Roy Cross' final ship artwork for Airfix: 1975's* Prinz Eugen.

Roy and Brian would both take their completed artworks to Airfix. These were immediately sent to the photographic studio where they were photographed on to transparencies for ongoing use. Usually three photos were taken: one for the box top, the second for the box sides and ends, and a third for use in the catalogue. The original artwork was then carefully stored. Any alterations, such as the removal of any violent action, were made using the transparencies, often by other artists.

Roy's tenure at Airfix was the period of greatest consistency, with Brian Knight painting the sailing ships and figure sets and Roy painting everything else. Most of the memorable artwork comes from this period. His fine painting of the Lancaster coming in to land with an engine on fire was so popular that in 2005 Humbrol released a model of 'G for George' just so the painting could be used!

By 1974 the workload was tailing off, and Roy left Airfix to pursue his career as a marine artist. His final paintings for Airfix were for the A300B Airbus and *Prinz Eugen* kits. Before he left, he recommended Ken McDonough as his replacement.

There has been much speculation over the years about the fate of the original artwork, everything from the paintings being thrown into skips to them lying on the factory floor and being walked on! Peter Allen states that all the kit artwork was successfully transferred to Palitoy's offices in Coalville, Leicester, in 1981. It seems that the bulk of the artwork went missing in the period between General Mills announcing it was to sell Airfix and Humbrol buying Airfix in 1986.

Peter Allen, who had left Palitoy by then, offered to travel up to Hull, unpaid, for a weekend to supervise the transfer of the Airfix archive. Unfortunately Humbrol refused his generous offer, and consequently it has not been possible to say what actually went to Humbrol!

Peter says that Palitoy considered all the playforts and polytanks to be 'toys' and ordered the artwork for them to be dumped in skips. Peter managed to save several, and these were recently sold at auction. The moulds for all these playforts did, however, remain at Palitoy and are today much used by Hornby!

This is probably the origin of the rumour about artwork being thrown out. Apart from the early artwork given to the Bethnal Green Toy Museum by Palitoy, the whereabouts of only half-a-dozen Roy Cross originals, at most, are known. The owner of one of these paintings states that when Palitoy was clearing out the offices in Coalville, the staff and employees of associated companies were offered anything from a waste bin to a painting for a fiver (£5); not surprisingly he chose to spend his £5 on a Roy Cross original

rather than a stapler or an office chair! Whether all the rest went that way cannot be confirmed, but it is surprising that more artwork has not reappeared over the last thirty years. It is likely that senior employees may have been given several artworks, but again this cannot be confirmed.

Fortunately all the artwork was still stored on transparencies, and it is the transparencies that are used to this day for any box tops or catalogues. Having been through the transparency files I can confirm that Airfix has all but a dozen or so of Roy's and Brian's paintings in this format. In Roy's books about his Airfix artwork, the most recent being published in 2014, the vast majority of the paintings reproduced therein came from transparencies kindly loaned by Airfix. The Humbrol artwork is largely intact but is also, sensibly, recorded on transparencies. The modern digital artwork is, of course, stored on computer.

Brian Knight, 1926–2007

Brian Knight had been painting pictures for Revell and FROG for some years, when he came to the attention of Airfix. Following the death of William Howard Jarvis, Airfix had a need for a sailing ship artist and Brian was asked to repaint the *Endeavour*. With the exception of the *Great Western*, painted by Roy Cross, he painted all the other large sailing ships, the final one being the *St Louis* in 1972. The two later ships were painted by Geoff Hunt.

For a couple of years after Type 3 was introduced, Airfix continued to produce its OO/HO figures in Type 2 boxes, but wanted to put them into Type 3 boxes with full-colour paintings. They were also just starting to produce the 1:32 scale range of figures. Since the sailing ships were only being released at a rate of one

LEFT: *Brian Knight's* impressive Royal Sovereign *artwork.*

BELOW: *'Washington's Army' artwork by Brian Knight.*

a year, Brian was hardly overworked and he was approached and asked whether he was any good at painting figures; Roy had never been keen on painting figures. He produced 'roughs' for the Bedouin Arabs and British Paratroops to replace the existing Type 2 paintings in use, and promptly got the job. He then repainted all the earlier box tops and, from the 1968 World War I Royal Horse Artillery, he painted all the new boxtops as they were released. His last OO/HO painting was probably the Waterloo British Cavalry released in 1972.

He also painted all the early 1:32 figure sets up to the Afrika Korps in 1972. In 1972, Bill Stallion was producing the artwork for the new OO/HO and 1:32 releases, so it is likely that Brian left Airfix around that time.

Sadly he died in 2007, having suffered from Parkinson's disease.

William H. (Bill) Stallion, 1925–2008

Brian Knight had been successfully painting box tops for Airfix figures for several years, and it had been assumed that he painted all the figure sets. However, it recently became clear that the later ones and the multipose sets were painted by a hitherto unknown artist, whose style was similar to Brian Knight's: hence the confusion. Following the publication of his book *The Boys' Book of Airfix* in 2009, Arthur Ward was contacted by the son of Bill Stallion, who had painted many of the 1970s figure sets, as he had recognized his father's face from the multipose Eighth Army box top included in the book!

Arthur interviewed Bill's widow and wrote the following biography for his 'Collecting Friends' website and his most recent book *The Other Side of Airfix*, which

he allowed me to reproduce in *Constant Scale* No. 44 in 2011. I am indebted to Arthur for his permission to reproduce it in this book:

As a young man Londoner, Bill Stallion joined the prestigious 6th Airborne Division, serving as a wireless operator in Palestine during World War II. After demob he missed out on the ex-serviceman's grant and ended up working in a brewery. However, he had always been interested in drawing, and found that living in Brixton it was possible to combine evening classes at London's prestigious Slade School of Art.

Before long Bill had the confidence to embark on a career as a freelance commercial artist, and approached agent Dick Browning, who quickly took him on. Bill's chosen vocation was that of a figure artist. Dick Browning also represented well known design team Negus-Sharland, who were well known for their advertising art. They designed some very famous posters for BOAC and also created notable stamp designs for the British Post Office, together with a wide range of other highly regarded designs. It seems that Dick Browning procured similar commissions for Bill Stallion, who soon became proficient at illustrating press ads and posters for companies producing everything from radios to toiletries.

Bill's wife Edna told me that he was pretty adept at amending his artwork to suit different international markets, changing the racial characteristics of foreground figures to suit the requirements of domestic consumers in China, Africa or Asia, whilst retaining the key product details.

Whilst he was scouting for new business in the early 1970s, Dick Browning discovered that Airfix, then at its height and producing a dazzling array of new kits and model soldiers each month, was keen to

add more freelance illustrators to its roster. Consequently Browning managed to get Bill on Airfix's books, and from a period starting around 1972 up until the end of that decade, kept his client very busy indeed. By this time Bill and Edna had moved to Sussex and started a family.

A figure artist, Bill naturally specialized in illustrating the boxes for Airfix soldiers – mostly for their soft plastic 1:32 scale figures (many of the famous 'Target Boxes' are Bill's) but also for Airfix's 1:32-scale figure kits – all of the multipose range, and many from the 54mm Collectors Series.

Interestingly Bill, who worked alone from his studio in his home in Southwater, near Horsham in Sussex, was forced to cast himself as the subject of many of his paintings. I was shown a selection of surviving Polaroids, self-portraits, taken by Bill or his wife Edna, showing him frozen in the classic poses so familiar to Airfix fans.

When the subject was carrying a firearm, which most soldiers were, of course, Bill would fashion a German MP42 sub-machine gun or a Browning .303 SMLE, for example, from offcuts of wood or broomstick handles.

The most obvious self-portrait of Bill can be seen in the box art of the Multipose British 8th Army set. He is the figure in the foreground bursting through coils of enemy wire with his bayonet fixed. To accurately portray the musculature on a figure's legs, and the Desert Rats for example, Bill wore short trousers, or had to be photographed in his underpants!

Bill realized that questions might be asked at Haldane Place if Airfix were presented with box art which repeatedly featured an all-too-familiar face, so to avoid using himself as the model for the model as it were, he enlisted the assistance of his neighbour Steve Brown, a pilot with BEA. I was told of many occasions when curtains twitched in adjacent houses and when other neighbours relaxing in their gardens became aware of two grown men, often carrying prop weapons and wearing makeshift helmets, apparently fighting in the garden of Mr and Mrs Stallion. The couple's children, Greg, Mike, Kate and Helen, soon grew used to such behaviour!

It is because Bill Stallion dealt exclusively via an agent that he has remained anonymous. Airfix's relationship was only with Dick Browning. Furthermore it is only in recent years that when they can, in appreciation of the work of Roy Cross, for example, Airfix have added artist signatures to box art.

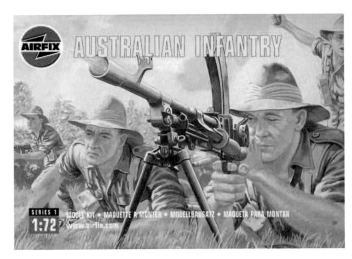

Australian Infantry artwork from 2003, by Bill Stallion.

In fact as every Airfix enthusiast knows, it is very difficult to be precisely sure about the provenance of a great deal of vintage Airfix art. Fortunately because Bill's daughter Helen, herself a professional picture researcher and familiar with the intricacies of the media world, got in touch with my publisher, Ebury Press, that her father will earn his rightful place in that hallowed list of Airfix Artists.

In a second interview Arthur records how Bill went on to a successful artistic career in the British film industry. I have managed to find the signature 'Stallion' on only one transparency so far, and it was his daughter Helen who kindly supplied me with a list of her father's artwork.

Ken McDonough, 1921–2002

Ken McDonough, who died in 2002 aged eighty, was recommended to Airfix by Roy Cross when he retired. For the remainder of the 1970s he was the principal artist at Airfix, with the figures being painted by Bill Stallion.

His artwork style was very similar to Roy Cross' artwork, although to the seasoned eye it was possible to see the differences. He painted the two 1:32-scale Lee and Grant tanks as well as repainting a couple of the small ones. He produced a stirring picture of the German E-Boat, and his masterpiece is probably the 1:24

TOP: *Fire engine artwork by Ken McDonough.*

ABOVE: *Consolidated Liberator artwork by Ken McDonough.*

LEFT: *Ken McDonough's Sopwith Camel artwork.* AIRFIX

Stuka. Geoff Hunt would take over the painting of ship subjects.

Mainly he concentrated on aircraft and finished off the repainting of the early Type 3 box tops, including the Lightning F.1a, Hunter, Liberator, Halifax and Catalina. In 1979, when Airfix introduced its 'New Squadron' programme of kit rotation, a lot of aircraft needed new artwork, most of which Ken would complete. However, several aircraft were repainted by another new artist, Ron Jobson.

HMS Warspite *artwork by Geoff Hunt.*

Geoff Hunt

Following the departure of Roy Cross and Brian Knight, Geoff Hunt was commissioned to paint the 1:600 warship kits. He worked for Airfix until around 1980, but recently he painted the *Mary Rose* for the *Mary Rose* Trust, and his painting features on the 2014 *Mary Rose* kit release. He told his story of his connection with Airfix in *Constant Scale* No. 53 in 2014:

> Even as a child I was fascinated by ships, and was always drawing pictures of them. One of my artist heroes was Roy Cross, whose work I followed avidly, first when he was one of the illustrators for *Eagle* comic – of which I still have many, including Roy's absolutely incomparable double-spread cutaway paintings – then when he worked as the artist for Airfix, of course, and later still as a 'proper' marine artist. When I was growing up, *Eagle* comic and Airfix box-tops were my art galleries: I learned so much about how to paint and visualize from them. My own career followed a somewhat similar course to Roy's, though to begin with I trained not as a technical artist but as a graphic designer and illustrator.
>
> My first box-top illustrations were not for Airfix but for Frog kits, then part of the Lines Brothers/Tri-ang group at Margate. Having first written to introduce myself, I went down to show them some specimen ship paintings, on the strength of which they commissioned me to do two box tops, HMS *Exeter* and HMS *Revenge*. This would have been in about 1975. As it turned out, Frog kits were nearly at an end, and these were the last two ships they ever produced. But arising from that I got a great deal of other business from Margate, working on brands such as Tri-ang Trains, Minic Ships, and much else; while the experience with the box tops gave me an opportunity to approach Airfix, then based not far from me in Wandsworth.
>
> I can't remember how I had discovered that Roy had finished working for them. However, I went along to see Jack Armitage, and he commissioned me to work on the 1/600 ships. I think the first subject I worked on may have been HMS *Warspite*; certainly it was one of the early subjects as far as I was concerned, and I remember it very well for the enormous difficulty I had in getting a sketch approved – I know I did at least fifteen alternative sketches. But no other subject ever gave me, or them, the same amount of trouble.
>
> Over the period 1976 to 1979 I painted all the ship box tops that were issued, after which there was a break because my wife and I sold up house, bought a boat, and went sailing for a year. But we came home for a time in the middle of that period, and in that time – February/March 1980 – Airfix came up with a further two 1/600 ships, HMS *King George V* and HMS *Repulse*, for which I did the box tops. There were to be no more British World War II ships – the last one I remember Airfix considering in research would have been the cruiser HMS *Sheffield* – but there was one more really epic 1/600 ship, the USS *Forrestal*.
>
> Finally, as far as I was concerned, there was one more square-rigger, the *Bounty*, and then the 1/72 RAF rescue launch. At this point Airfix, as I had known it, changed out of all recognition, with little requirement for new box tops, and for the next ten years or so I devoted much of my energy to illustrating book jackets, the highlight of which was the whole series of Patrick O'Brian novels. Like Roy, I became a member of the Royal Society of Marine Artists, and in 2003 its president. Since 2008 I have formed a very close association with the *Mary Rose* Trust, and the new kit painting was done originally for them.

Geoff's only foray into non-maritime artwork was his painting of the T-34 tank for a late 1970s release. Although nowadays he is best known as the artist for the Patrick O'Brian novels, Geoff retains an affection for his Airfix artwork.

Ron Jobson

Ron Jobson was born in Brixton and won a scholarship at thirteen to the Camberwell School of Arts and Crafts, where he studied for three years until the outbreak of war in 1939. He then worked in Fleet Street doing work for wartime magazines and Ministry of Information propaganda. After the war he produced artwork for Sci-Fi magazines and later Matchbox toys and Airfix kits.

He was probably employed through a studio in the late 1970s. His aviation artwork was very similar to Roy Cross and Ken McDonough's in its execution.

He repainted the Panther and Churchill tanks, and for their 'New Squadron' releases he repainted the P-47, Avenger, Pe-2 and Il-28. The aircraft were particularly fine paintings and it was a pity he did not do more, as his aircraft paintings come closest to those painted by Roy Cross.

Panther tank, by Ron Jobson.

Other Artists

Another artist who repainted a few of the early tanks for 1979 releases was Jeremy Banks. He painted the Bren Gun Carrier and probably the Sherman and Assault Gun, although these are unsigned.

The large Crusader Tank painting has the signature of Harrison on it, and he also painted the Bugatti 35B box top. A single artist was Stephen Hipwell, who painted the first box top for the 1:12 Bentley, which was used in the 1975 calendar. Likewise Roy Huxley, who painted a lot of Matchbox kit box tops, painted the Porsche 917 for Airfix. The MG Magnette was painted by a James Dugdde.

The robins were painted by John Barber, and he possibly painted the other birds, but this cannot be confirmed at present. He also painted the box tops for some of the Japanese car kits Airfix bought in the late 1970s. Apparently Airfix did not buy the artwork, but were given several boxes to copy. The rolling stock paintings that appear in the trains catalogues were by husband and wife team, Cliff and Wendy Meadway.

Most did not paint for Airfix again after its rescue from bankruptcy in 1981. One who did was Mike Renwick, who painted the 1:48 Mosquito, and then for Humbrol painted the Swedish Bristol Bulldog and DH Heron.

Ron Jobson's Petlyakov Pe-2 artwork.

RIGHT: *Bentley artwork by Stephen Hipwell.*

James Dugdde's MG Magnette artwork.

LEFT: *15-Ton Diesel Hydraulic Crane artwork, by Cliff and Wendy Meadway.*

ABOVE: *John Barber's Porsche 934-5 artwork from 1979.*

LEFT: *De Havilland Mosquito artwork by Mike Renwick.*

BELOW: *Mike Renwick's Bristol Bulldog artwork on a Type 11 box.*

Post-1981 Artists

Following the rescue of Airfix in mid-1981, Palitoy was using the photo boxes, and there was less need for new artwork. Those kits that did require paintings either used the existing artwork or, in the case of the MPC kits, the US artwork tended to be used.

Initially Humbrol used art studios who provided artists, but later they employed the likes of Gavin McLeod and John D. Jones.

Paul Monteagle

Shortly after purchasing Airfix, Humbrol employed the talents of several new artists. One was Paul Monteagle who was active around the late 1980s to early 1990s. I made contact with him after I noticed his signature on a painting of kittens on a lap tray I was using, and he gave this account of his time with Airfix in *Constant Scale No. 48* in 2013:

I have always had a passion for Airfix. In Tadcaster, North Yorkshire, where I was brought up, Airfix was all we had. I recently built a 1:48 Grumman Widgeon (Paul still models for pleasure – ed.). Why, because of fond memories of my Airfix one built when I was about eight or nine. In fact if you look at most of my builds in 1:48 and 1:35, they all equate to Airfix subjects. It is almost as if that if Airfix didn't produce it in the 1960s it wasn't used in World War I and World War II!

I have most 1980s catalogues as I patched and pasted them as well as worked out the layouts, which is how I met Jeff Robinson and came to do the box art. Unfortunately they were 'art' directed and not done how I would have liked. I even did the stegosaurus. If you look at page 36 in the 1989 catalogue you may notice it doesn't have an artwork:

that is because Jeff realized the 'tranny' and original painting were missing, and I had twenty-four hours to produce an outcome for the printer who needed to proceed.

I did all the Historic Cars' (pp. 32–33) and Vintage Aircraft series (pp. 26–27) at that time, again all in the 1989 catalogue. Sometimes the deadline was so tight I was told to 'copy' existing box art, as they owned copyright – kind of early computer art, I guess. The boxes that I originated fully like the Spad and Pup (p. 27), and I think all the cars, I still quite like but wished I could have done backgrounds. I also painted the portraits in the 'ovals'.

I am an Airfix fan more than any other large kit name. I also did a 1:32 Fokker DVII for Revell-Monogram for the American market, which is on my website, as is other commercial work.

As you (editor) mentioned, I have also done cats and now horses (a new venture), but I love aircraft and I am still a modeller. I did have a regular column in *Scale Models International* magazine for a while (till family and work got in the way), which started in April 1996 with my Blue Max box-art painting on the cover, showing I think what I could have produced for Airfix had I been given 'full rein'!

I have just secured early retirement from full-time teaching and hope to do more book covers for Ray and Angie at Albatros, where I am currently doing a datafile cover for early Avros. Also Colin at 'Freight Dog' (who owns the Blue Max range now) has asked me to produce a cover art, so maybe the story isn't over yet, except for Airfix? Trevor Snowden offered me the 1:24 Mosquito –

Paul Monteagle's Albatros DVa artwork.

ABOVE: *Lancaster BIII artwork by James Goulding.*

RIGHT: *Messerschmitt Bf 109E artwork for the 'Aircraft of the Aces' series by Anthony Sturgess.*

my dream job, but I had to say no because Hornby insist now that all artwork is computer generated.

As a postscript I would like to add that I was once at the nationals and a certain Mr Cross was there signing books. I joined the queue. Without looking up he asked me what name he should make it out to. I politely said, 'Paul, and can I thank you'. 'Why?' he said – and I replied 'Because of you I have painted all my life.' 'I have heard that before,' he replied. 'What do you do'? 'Well I do quite a few datafiles for Albatros.' 'Are you Paul Monteagle'? Well, I was on cloud 9: my hero knew who I was! Now, he must have known Brian Knight who did the other volumes, and I wasn't him, still he knew me and I was (still am) made up with that!

As a further postscript I would like to say that I haven't anything left from those days except for a couple of black-and-white photos of the models of 1:32 cars to help me produce the paintings. I was upset that the 'art' director wouldn't let me paint skies for the aircraft as he wanted the same blue colour for all of them, which resulted in awful and badly done cutouts around the paintings. I didn't do the airliners (which were copies of the Roy Cross artwork – editor), just World War I aircraft and the cars, plus the stegosaurus that I think had my name on. I haven't kept a copy.

Fortunately Airfix did keep his original stegosaurus painting, which I found in the Artwork Archive.

It is ironic that for the 1990s releases, the cars had a rather lack-lustre back-

ground added. Paul's official website is found at www.paulmonteagle.com

James Goulding

James Goulding sadly died in 2010, but from the mid-1980s to around 1990 he painted many of the Humbrol releases. Humbrol was gradually returning the aircraft kits to the catalogue, many with new decals and markings, so they required new artwork. Being an aircraft illustrator he was well suited to the task, and had actually previously painted for Airfix, doing the box top for the 1980 Avro Lancaster.

He is recorded at Airfix as working for the 'Spearhead' Design Studio, and several paintings are attributed to Spearhead but clearly resemble his style. Along with Anthony Sturgess he painted many of the World War II Aircraft of the Aces series, as well as several other re-released aircraft.

He repainted Roy Cross' Spitfire IX, JE-J, and his Hurricane Mk IIb. He painted the much updated HS Buccaneer S.2B, and prepared an artwork for the unfinished Goshawk kit. He painted most of the new and reissued aircraft of the late 1980s.

His style was quite distinctive, and one can easily identify his box tops. Amongst the larger scales he repainted the 1:48 Hawker Fury I and the 1:24 Messerschmitt Bf 109E.

He appears to have finished painting for Airfix around 1990.

Anthony Sturgess

Anthony Sturgess may have been a studio artist; he was certainly a contemporary of James Goulding, and he painted roughly half of the World War II 'Aircraft of the Aces' series. He repainted the Dornier Do 217J in a style more like a 'rough'. His 'Aces' aircraft were of a much finer style and far better than his Dornier. He also painted the modified Mil Mi-24 Hind A/D for a 1988 release.

As with James Goulding, he does not appear to have painted for Airfix after about 1990.

Terry Harrison

Terry Harrison is now a successful painter of landscapes. In 1988 he painted the updated Lynx HAS.3 for a Type 9 release. His signature is identical to the 'Harrison' on the 1975 Crusader Tank and Bugatti 35B, so he is almost certainly the same artist.

The Humbrol Fire, 1989

In 1989, Humbrol suffered a serious fire in a warehouse at Hull. Many kits, including

Crusader III tank artwork, Terry Harrison.

supplies of Arthur Ward's *Model World of Airfix* book and kit combination, were destroyed. It is understood that some of the artwork was damaged by the water used to extinguish the fire. As part of the insurance settlement, Airfix was required to have several artworks repainted.

This does seem a strange exercise, since some of the repainted artwork was never used. Others, such as the Wellington and Sunderland were repainted, in a darker style, by Doug Gray. Gavin McLeod re-did the Me 262 and several others. Gavin would go on to become Airfix's in-house artist until his death in 2003. The repainted pictures were basically copies of the Roy Cross artwork, but minus the background detail for which Roy was well known.

In the early 1990s Airfix re-released, at short notice, three German aircraft, the Hs 126, Fw 189 and He 111, and these were painted by D. Hubert and John Wallis; they were rather lacklustre paintings which did little to encourage the buyer to part with his money. John Wallis also repainted

Serge Jamois' Mitsubishi KI46-II Dinah artwork.

the Bf 109G-6 boxtop, which was used for many years.

Airfix was now working closely with Heller, and some Heller artists would be used by Airfix. The 1:48 Buccaneer S.2D/ SMk50, Grumman Duck and Avenger were painted by Serge Jamois, who also painted the 1994 Coastal Defence Fort set. The Gun Emplacement was painted by Adrien, another Heller artist?

Gavin McLeod, 1951–2003

Gavin McLeod was contacted by Humbrol following the fire of 1989 to repaint some of the damaged artwork. He was employed by Airfix from then until his untimely death in 2003. He is best remembered for his beautiful airbrushed artwork, which featured on most of the box tops in this period; his B-17, Navy Lynx HAM.8 and Mosquito NF.XIX are particular favourites of mine.

I have been fortunate to examine, close up, all the surviving original artwork for the period from 1982 to 2006. Gavin's artwork, when viewed at life-size (often roughly 3 × 2ft), is simply stunning. The colours are vivid and of course the airbrush imparts a smooth finish. There is less emphasis on panel lines and rivets, but these don't really matter when the picture is reduced to box-top size. Detailed backgrounds did not feature on much of

Gavin McLeod's Modern US NATO Troops artwork.

WESTLAND NAVY LYNX Mk 8

SERIES 3
1:72

SKILL 4 3 2 1

MODEL KIT • MAQUETTE A MONTER • MODELLBAUSATZ • MAQUETTA PARA MONTAR
www.airfix.com

4 x DECALS

ABOVE: *Naval Lynx artwork by Gavin McLeod.*

LEFT: *Gavin McLeod's reworking of Geoff Hunt's painting of HMS* King George V.

BELOW: *John D. Jones' Lockheed Hudson artwork.*

LOCKHEED HUDSON I

05034

the post-1981 artwork, and this is true of much of Gavin's work.

In addition to aircraft he also painted the box tops for the OO/HO Modern NATO Troops and Ground Crew, and altogether he painted around 140 box tops for Airfix, making him probably the second most prolific artist for Airfix. His *tour de force*, though, must be his exquisite paintings of the 1:24 cars released by Airfix in the 1990s. He brought his airbrushing talent to bear on most of the range of modern and older cars, including the four 'hi-tech' cars released in 1991. For these paintings the background was non-existent, as the whole painting was of the car. They were perfectly proportioned and the airbrush gave an almost photo-like finish. Most of the cars were painted by him, but the three Scania Eurotruck and Trailer kits released in 1992 and some of the modern performance cars were painted by Allan Croft.

After Gavin's death in 2003, Humbrol employed the talents of artist John D. Jones.

John D. Jones

John D. Jones, known as Dave Jones, took over from Gavin McLeod as the principal Airfix artist. After a dozen years of largely airbrushed artwork, his style returned to painting by brush. He painted some of the new, modified AFV releases, and following the Hornby takeover, did several of the new kit releases, notably

the four Canberra bomber kits in 1:48 scale. Most of the re-released and modified aircraft kits put out by Humbrol from 2004 onwards were the work of John D. Jones.

The decision by Hornby to utilize the digital artwork of Adam Tooby (*see* biographical note below) for its future releases brought to an end Dave Jones' time at Airfix.

Other Artists

Two artists working for Heller before 2006 and who would be utilized by Hornby, were Daniel Bechennec and Vincenzo Auletta.

Daniel Bechennec painted many of the World War II boxed sets, and also the new OO/HO World War II British Infantry. His figure paintings were almost photographic in their appearance. He recently painted the 2014 D-Day sets.

Vincenzo Auletta painted the new AFV kits and the four Hobbycraft Gift Sets in 2010. He also painted the box top for the first World War I Trench Set.

Hornby had embarked on an ambitious programme of new kit releases, many of them replacing the old and 'tired' tools in use since the 1950s. Adam Tooby was contracted to produce the digital box tops for these new Airfix kits. Hornby initially released several 'polybagged' kits from other manufacturers to bolster the range in the first few years. The AFV moulds of JB Models were also acquired by Hornby for release in their initial catalogues. To illustrate these releases, Airfix called on two new artists: Mike Trim and Keith Woodcock.

Mike Trim

Following the takeover of Airfix in late 2006, Hornby, like Humbrol before, was keen to get the basic range back into production. Until the new kits designed by Hornby reached the shops, several kits were 'polybagged' in from other manufacturers, and the moulds of JB Models were purchased. To illustrate these kits several artists were taken on to assist

John D. Jones. One was Mike Trim, who wrote the following article for *Constant Scale* No. 54 in August 2014. He tells us of his brief time at Airfix and, more interestingly, he reveals some of the history of Airfix's involvement in the television sci-fi programmes of the 1960s and 1970s that we all watched in our childhood. I for one will play 'spot the Airfix part' next time I watch a programme such as *Thunderbirds*!

In 1964, having just left art college and uncertain of what came next, my attention was drawn to a small and ordinary-looking advertisement in Dad's evening paper. It simply stated 'Film Company Requires Model Maker', and having always enjoyed making models, I contacted them and secured an interview. I had no idea who these people were or what kind of films they made, but two weeks later found myself outside a very modest industrial unit on the Slough Trading Estate which bore the legend 'A.P. Films' above the door.

The company was run by a man called Gerry Anderson, and their production, *Fireball XL5*, was then being screened on television. Whilst there I was given a sneak preview of their new product, *Stingray*, which, unlike its predecessor, was in colour rather than black and white. It looked very impressive, but the real eye-opener lay in the models used to film it. It was immediately obvious that one of the key components in their construction was the extensive use of plastic kit parts to dress the models, which, along with all the added weathering and so on, created a fairly realistic appearance. This was my kind of model making.

I had made my very first kit, an Airfix Fokker Triplane, when I was eleven, and there then followed a long line of mainly Airfix kits. However, after a while I also began coming up with my own creations using pieces from several different kits to produce something a bit different – and what I was looking at that day at A.P. Films was exactly the same process. A few weeks later I started work there doing just that on their latest project, *Thunderbirds*.

This production, like those that followed, made extensive use of Airfix products, and we regularly received very large boxes filled with girder bridges, footbridges, signal gantries, level crossings and water towers, amongst others. Anyone watching the *Thunderbirds* launch sequence cannot fail to have noticed the very obvious use of the girder bridge, in particular. In time this range increased, and kits such as the early

Daniel Bechennec's D-Day Sea Assault Set artwork.

Chi-Ha Tank artwork by Vincenzo Auletta.

hovercraft, Old Bill Bus, the vintage Dennis Fire Engine, Saturn rockets and the B-29 were added, all of which yielded many useful parts with which to dress our models. Nothing went to waste, even the kit's sprue being used for piping on things such as atomic power stations or oil refineries. Right through *Thunderbirds*, *Captain Scarlet*, *Joe 90* and in the live-action series *UFO*, Airfix remained a major component in our model-making strategy, despite also using kits from Revell, Aurora and Tamiya.

In 1971 our company sadly closed its doors for the last time, and I, like many others, found myself contemplating moving elsewhere. However, with the British film industry in the doldrums, people began drifting into other unrelated areas. For me, I moved into illustration and went freelance two years later, where most of my work concerned aviation or marine subjects. Perhaps the piece most remembered is the cover for Jeff Wayne's 1977 album, *The War of the Worlds*. Here my love of ships was combined with a welcome return to the role of designer, my main occupation in the latter Anderson years, as I had to design the various Martian machines as well as produce the cover artwork.

In more recent years, after leaving teaching, I worked on several sci-fi projects, designing and model making, and once again found myself extensively using reissued kit parts made from old Airfix Trackside accessories moulds.

My recent association with Airfix as one of their box-top artists was a highly enjoyable opportunity, but sadly not a particularly long one. It had begun when a friend of mine, who was one of my first students many years ago and had worked at Hornby's in Margate, and was now freelancing with them, alerted me to the fact that there might be some illustration work required by Airfix. I obviously jumped at the chance, but the advent of digital artwork and the comparative cost of conventional artwork, coupled with the company cutting back its reissues, all too soon brought it to an end.

I had found the redesigned packaging limiting in terms of choosing not only a good view of the subject, but also one that fitted the new format. Given that both ships and rockets are, by their very nature, long thin shapes, the use of narrow boxes, and the inclusion of so much information on them, resulted in much of what one painted being omitted in the final product. Nevertheless, to have found myself painting Airfix box tops somehow seemed a fitting conclusion to my journey with that company

from that eleven-year-old boy, all those years ago, excitedly assembling his first kit. Now retired, it is unlikely that I shall ever be making models again. But if I did, I'm pretty sure Airfix kits would be involved somehow.

For more information Mike Trim's website is www.miketrimart.com

The paintings he did for Airfix since 2007 consist of the Wellington Mk Ic/Mk III, HMS *Victory*, *Golden Hind*, HMS *Warspite*, HMS *Iron Duke*, HNoMS *St Albans*, HMS *Montgomery*, RMS *Titanic* (1:700); also Vostok, Saturn 1B, Saturn V Skylab, Saturn V, Space Shuttle and 'One Small Step for Man'.

Keith Woodcock

Another artist who joined Airfix briefly in the period after the Hornby acquisition was Keith Woodcock. He painted all the ex-JB Model kits for their 2008 release, although today only three survive in the Hornby range. One, the Vickers Light Tank, has been repainted by Vincenzo Auletta to match his other AFVs, although the two Land Rovers were simply modified. His last painting for Airfix was of the Churchill Bridge Layer, but Airfix had decided to go for digital artwork so it was not used. In *Constant Scale* No. 55 in late 2014, Keith wrote this interesting account of his time at Airfix:

My initial contact with Airfix was via Trevor Snowden, whom I had known for some time through my occasional leisure activity of plastic modelling. As he lived fairly close by, although separated by the River Humber, it was very convenient for both of us to meet up and discuss the projects and for him to collect the artwork instead of having to risk the postal services.

Apparently Airfix had just taken over another kit manufacturer, JD, and their box art was in need of revamping and bringing up to the standard of other kits in the Airfix range. However, at that time there was a shortage of available artists who undertook this type of work, so Trevor contacted me to ask if I would be interested, and I agreed to work on the project. As many of my paintings are commissioned with no deadline I could slot these new items between those I already had in progress. They were a little outside my normal sphere of activity, and I don't pretend to be very knowledgeable on such military subjects, but I was given more than adequate information and

photographs, together with test shots of the actual kits. I found the latter to be invaluable for ensuring I was painting the actual subject in the box and not a variation!

Half-tone pencil sketches were completed (*see* attached), then coloured up and submitted for approval, these having to fit the standard kit box format. Once approved, I completed the artworks using my normal method of gouache on heavy watercolour paper, as this produces a very flat surface ideal for reproduction, as opposed to oil on canvas where the weave can show through. I didn't sign any of the paintings as this would intrude on any cropping of the image which might be necessary when planning the descriptive wording on the box.

The last subject I painted was the Churchill Bridge Layer, and I have attached the original pencil sketch for this, roughly showing the possible locations for the logo and title. Around this time I had a call from Trevor to say that there had been a management meeting at which it had been decided that all future artwork would be digitally produced and that there would be no further painted work commissioned.

I had quite enjoyed my short time of working with Airfix, despite the subjects being outside my usual range of aviation and motoring subjects. It is also satisfying to walk into a model shop and see one's paintings adorning the kit boxes. My only regret is that I was not allowed to keep the artwork, apparently a company policy but quite different from many other publishers. I believe these paintings may have been auctioned or sold off at some time, as a few of their new owners have contacted me to confirm that I was the artist.

Like Mike Trim and John D. Jones, he was to find that the move to digital artwork would bring to an end his painting for Airfix. This decision was largely inspired by Adam Tooby, who had showed his digital artwork to Hornby, when it was decided to use digital from then on.

Adam Tooby

I suppose the artist who has had the biggest influence on Airfix box tops since Roy Cross is Adam Tooby. He introduced digital artwork to Airfix, and it was quickly decided that that was the way to go for the new releases, which were predominantly aircraft. The first hint of a move towards this type of artwork was the advertisement for the 1:48 TSR2,

ABOVE: *Land Rover artwork by Keith Woodcock.*   BELOW: *Adam Tooby's Mini Countryman WRC car artwork.*

which was totally different from the other artwork Airfix was using.

The big advantage of digital artwork is that the pictures are made up of layers, so it is possible to move around objects in the background. Some of the adverts for a new aircraft feature other aircraft in the background in different positions, and this gives a flexibility not possible with a standard painting. Also the resulting painting has a 'photo realism' that few brush painters manage to achieve.

Adam currently illustrates all the new aircraft releases, and his box tops, such as the stunning 1:24 Typhoon, are rapidly creating a sizable following of adherents. It is fair to say that his digital artwork, when used with the new Type 16 box design, is largely responsible for letting modellers know that Airfix is back!

Other Digital Artists

With the increased number of new tools being released by Airfix, Adam Tooby was being kept fully occupied, so it was decided to have some of the re-releases painted by another artist. John Fox was chosen to paint the Matilda Hedgehog, and later the Dinah and the second re-releases of the Boeing 737 and 727. Several of the 2014 re-releases are the work of John Fox. His style is similar to Adam's, but the trained eye can tell the difference.

Another digital artist who painted for Airfix around 2009 to 2010 was Jon Plumb. He painted all the small pictures on the back of the 1:24 Mosquito, as well as the box tops for the MiG-15 and Sea Hurricane Mk IIc.

In Summary

Airfix has now stopped using conventional painting in favour of digital and now employs digital artists for its AFV and car kits. Just as the new CAD process has rejuvenated the actual kits, digital artwork has brought about a renaissance to the appearance of the range of kits.

Boeing 737-200 artwork by John Fox.

John Fox's Willys British Airborne Jeep artwork.

Jon Plumb's Sea Hurricane Mk IIc artwork.

CHAPTER NINE

Airfix Magazine

ABOVE: *First six* Airfix *magazines, June–November 1960.*

RIGHT: *First issue and first colour issue, December 1960.*

When I started on the Index for *Airfix Magazine* from 1960 to 1980, I rediscovered a wonderful resource for plastic modellers the world over. Whilst it would run until 1993, the glory years were undoubtedly the first twenty or so, until its owner Airfix Products Ltd went into receivership.

The first issue was published in June 1960. In size and overall appearance the new *Airfix Magazine* was similar to *Meccano Magazine*, and was probably the first magazine to cater for the burgeoning plastic kit hobby. The first six issues were in black and white; colour covers first appeared in December 1960, in Volume 1 No. 7.

Looking back, those first few issues have a certain naïve charm, but one can see the seeds of a future comprehensive and informative magazine being sown. Actual modelling articles were split between railway and aircraft, largely because these models dominated the *Airfix Kit Catalogue*. Much later soldier and AFV articles would tend to dominate. Several articles dealt with news about general subjects, such as 'Shipping Notes' and 'On Road and Track' but these would gradually disappear. There were one or two oddities such as 'Stamps', which seemed to have no connection with plastic kits other than also being a 'hobby'! Also 'Star Personality' was sometimes devoted to profiles of lesser known personalities who were not really connected to the plastic products produced by Airfix.

A far-sighted decision by the owners, Airfix Products Ltd, was to give the editor complete editorial freedom. It may have been *Airfix Magazine*, but it wasn't just about Airfix. The simple fact, however, that Airfix was producing more new kits than anybody else tended to steer the articles towards Airfix products. Practically all the kit conversion articles used the Airfix kit as the basis.

In the 1960s, Airfix had introduced several new ranges into its catalogue, such as OO/HO tanks and figures, and these took the modelling world by storm and created whole new branches to the hobby. In a few years, *Airfix Magazine* was full of articles about converting AFVs and soldiers into a whole host of models to go with countless wars and battles, which were also described in *Airfix Magazine*.

More contemporary modellers may tend to sneer at the Airfix Panther and Sherman and the first little figures, but they were the mainstay of all conversions for the first twenty years, and without them the wargaming and military brigades wouldn't be so healthy.

The magazine carried on in its initial size until August 1963, when I bought my first copy and decided I was going to have it every month thereafter! In that issue, Vol. 4 No. 3, it was announced that a new, bigger *Airfix Magazine* was to be produced. To celebrate the new magazine a new volume was started, and Volume 4 ceased at No. 3.

The new size *Airfix Magazine* adopted red as the predominant colour for the cover. Conversions and modelling articles were becoming more important. Allan W. Hall also started the first of his modelling articles. These tended to require copious amounts of obechi (balsa) wood with a mixture of talcum powder and clear dope to seal the wood for painting. I knew I could never match his degree of skill, but it was nice to lie in bed on a Saturday morning reading my 'just delivered' *Airfix Magazine* and marvel at his skill.

In October 1966, in Volume 8 No. 2, the page count was increased by eight pages. In February 1973, in Volume 14 No. 6, the cover was subtly altered, the previous rectangular title boxes, with the italicized Type 2/3 lettering, being replaced with the new Type 4-style round-edged boxes and lettering. Then in December 1975, in Volume 17 No. 4, it was announced that as from the next issue, the magazine would be A4 size. Also the price increased from 25p to 30p. The new cover featured the

Type 4 logo, the first time an actual logo had been used. The colour photographs were replaced by several separate paintings or photos of articles within. Everything was increased in size, which helped with the clarity of the articles.

This, I think, is my favourite period of *Airfix Magazine*. The covers were brighter and more interesting, and the articles inside were much clearer and better laid out than in the smaller ones.

Then in September 1979, in Volume 21 No. 1, the cover changed again, but this time I don't think for the better. The font was changed, though the Type 4 logo remained. The main colour was now a different one each month, and we saw a return to a large rectangular photograph.

In August 1980, in Volume 21 No. 12, subtle changes were made to the cover fonts and style, although the Type 4 logo

remained. This coincided with a change of publisher, Gresham Books to Kristall Publications Ltd, although I think this may have been simply a name change.

By this time, Airfix Products was in quite a dire financial position, but since the magazine was 'independent' it was not directly affected. However, the cover styles seemed to vary slightly practically every month. In April 1981, it was mentioned in the 'Editor's Notebook' that Airfix had gone into receivership. In June the Palitoy takeover was announced, and in July Palitoy Ltd was now shown as the 'proprietor'. The logo had also changed to the oval Type 6.

The announcement in late January 1981 that the Airfix group of companies had entered receivership sent shockwaves through the plastic kit world. The bitter pill that modellers had to swallow was

Last 'small' issue and first larger issue, September 1963.

Change in cover design, February 1973.

that the Kits Division was still showing a profit, but Airfix had been dragged under by other under-performing parts of the group that were not related to kits. The kits, I believe, were the only products that were produced by the receiver until the takeover by General Mills. Other divisions and products disappeared completely or went back to their original or new owners.

Airfix Magazine continued to be published, and it was not until the April 1981 issue that Airfix's troubles were mentioned, and not until July 1981 that Palitoy was shown as the new owner of *Airfix Magazine*. Volume 23 No. 1, dated September 1981, really marks the commencement of Palitoy's ownership of *Airfix* magazine. The most noticeable difference was that the Type 6 logo disappeared from the front cover (it would reappear in November 1981), although it still appeared on the contents page. Also the cover picture now filled the cover, until January 1982 when coloured bands occupied the top and bottom. Existing series continued inside and new ones started up; it was largely 'business as before'. In the June 1982 issue (Vol. 23 No.10) the new Type 8 logo adorned the front cover, minus the little ®.

The editor was still Chris Ellis, so it was basically the old *Airfix Magazine*. Then Ellis 'retired,' and was replaced by David Taylor from October 1983. This, to me at least, seemed to mark the beginning of the decline, and eventual fall, of *Airfix Magazine*. It seemed to mirror what was going on in the Airfix kit world. We saw the beginning of regular and sometimes lengthy articles on Diecast and Meccano products, which had little to do with plastic modelling. Then in July 1983, the first issue of *Constructor*, the Airfix Model Club magazine, was printed inside *Airfix Magazine*. This ran until June 1984. The March/April issue was a combined one: 'the shape of things to come' perhaps?

The December 1984 issue contained the first of a series of articles entitled 'Tailgunner Ward', written by the young author of the first real book on Airfix. The February 1985 issue contained the slim 1985 catalogue in the middle, which was also available separately, I think. Although I saw the 1983, 1984 and 1985 catalogues advertised in the magazine, I didn't see any in the shops until ten years later, when I finally acquired them from an old model shop that was closing down!

Ray Rimell of 'Windsock' became editor from July 1985, with Vol. 26 No.

First A4-size magazine, January 1976.

ABOVE: *Airfix Collectors' Club Guides.*

RIGHT: *Last cover design before 1981 closure of Airfix Products, 1980.*

11. A new style of cover design, incorporating the Type 8® logo, appeared on the August 1985 issue No. 12. In November 1985, ownership of *Airfix Magazine* was now vested in Kenner Parker Ltd, whose task was apparently to dispose of the various parts of Palitoy that General Mills decided to sell when it extricated itself from toy manufacture in Europe and the UK in 1985.

In May 1986, Albatros Productions Ltd was the new 'owner', but in November

The Palitoy logo was applied in July 1982.   *25th Anniversary issue and new design, August 1985.*

1986 the instruction 'Airfix Magazine is a registered Trade Mark of Humbrol Ltd' was displayed on the Contents page. Presumably this meant that the rights to the name 'Airfix Magazine' resides with the current owner of Airfix. Prior to Albatros, the magazine had been printed for the owners of Airfix, but subsequent publishers, including A. W. Hall Ltd, actually owned the magazine but *not* the title.

I must confess that around this time when I was compiling the contents and index, I began to lose interest. Whereas before it had been a 'labour of love', it was now becoming a chore. This was because the magazine seemed to be moving away from plastic kits, and many of the articles and series had less relevance to the hobby, probably because plastic kits were no longer nearly as dominant as they had once been. The quality of the paper and the photographs deteriorated, and there were breaks in publication. Combined issues and changes of both editors and publishers were more common. *Airfix Magazine* 'disappeared' from newsagents' shelves after the publication of the combined September/October 1987 issue.

It returned to the shelves in September 1988 as Vol. 1 No. 1, now owned by Alan W. Hall (Publications) Ltd. 'Airfix Magazine' was still, though, a trade mark of Humbrol Ltd. I show it in *Guide No. 3* as being Vol. 29, and the cover and layout was very similar to the magazine-sized *Aviation News* also published by A. W. Hall.

There were several gaps in publication, and yet more combined issues, and none appeared between the January/February 1993 issue and the August one. For the October/November 1993 issue, Vol. 4 No. 10, a new editor, Michael J. Gething, was appointed and a new cover design

appeared. It turned out to be his only issue, as *Airfix Magazine* disappeared for good thereafter.

This was a sad end for what was once a best-selling magazine and arguably the richest source of plastic modelling information available. I suppose, like the hobby itself, it had passed its heyday. In the 1990s, kit production, particularly at Airfix, was sporadic and struggling to attract the attention of the younger generation, and we would have to wait nearly sixteen years for the hobby, led by Hornby/Airfix, to be revitalized to such an extent that a well known publisher wanted to put the Airfix name on a new modelling magazine. To be called *Airfix Modelworld*, this new 'Airfix' magazine, which was launched fifty years after the first, seems to be very successful. The monthly published copies are a fraction of those enjoyed by the early

Airfix Magazine and there are many more plastic kit magazines competing for a smaller market than in the 1960s and 1970s. I think it is going to continue being a bestseller because the publishers clearly realize that having the Airfix name and logo on the cover is still the best way to attract purchasers of modelling magazines.

For Airfix, the appearance of its now revamped model club with its quarterly magazine is probably more important than a magazine was to Airfix of old. If you, however, are lucky enough to possess a complete set of *Airfix Magazine* then you will have a unique resource of all aspects of plastic modelling. Recently I produced two small booklets for the Collectors' Club, which were 'contents and indexes' for all issues of *Airfix Magazine*. Not strictly an index, each book helps the reader to find many of the articles.

First A. W. Hall issue and final issue, November 1993.

CHAPTER TEN

Airfix Books

In 1970 the Airfix range of kits was expanding, with many new and interesting models being added to the range nearly every month. *Airfix Magazine* was enjoying record sales with over 40,000 copies printed in July 1970, and roughly two and a half readers per issue, which meant that approximately 100,000 people read it each month! In August 1970, Airfix announced the first of a new series of modelling books that were to be published by Patrick Stephens Limited, the publishers of *Airfix Magazine*. PSL had for some time printed a series of modelling books, many edited or written by former editors or contributors to *Airfix Magazine*. The new range was to be published 'in association with Airfix Products Ltd' and initially would consist of books dealing with conversions or superdetailing of specific Airfix kits.

These books would be subtitled *Their History and How to Model Them*. The first part of each book would contain a brief history of the ship, aircraft or tank, followed by a section on how to improve or enhance the model, and then, where appropriate, convert to different marks. The authors were in most cases well known to readers of *Airfix Magazine* as they had for years contributed to that journal. One, Roy Cross, was Airfix's principal artist and had previously written several books on aircraft, so was no stranger to writing a book.

With one exception the 'history' books all used the kit illustration for the cover, the exception being the book on the Lancaster, which probably lacked suitable Airfix artwork. The first book was *HMS Victory – Classic Ships – Their History and How to Model Them – No. 1*. It was written by Noel C. L. Hackney, who also wrote the other two ship books, and was published on 25 August 1970. The second book, on the *Mayflower*, appeared in December shortly after the release of the kit. The third and final ship book was on the *Cutty Sark* and appeared in 1974.

1971 would see the publication of the first of two new series. The first, the *Airfix Magazine Annual*, would run for eight years; each year contained a collection of articles similar to those produced in the monthly magazine.

The final annual to be released was the *Airfix Magazine Annual No. 8*. It was in fact released as two books, one for aircraft modellers and one for military modellers. Both were paperback, which seemed to suggest an element of cost cutting.

The second new series was entitled *Spitfire – Classic Aircraft No. 1 – Their History and How to Model Them*. It was published in November 1971. The author was Roy Cross. Five further books were published, based on aircraft modelled by Airfix. The final one on the Mosquito was produced after the Airfix collapse and was based on models produced by several manufacturers.

Each book contained a section on the history of the subject, which was followed by a section on 'superdetailing' the kit and converting it into other versions. The first few books devoted much space to detailing the wing interiors, where there was much scope for filling in the wheel well and ammunition trays. The later kits had this detail included as standard. I well remember spending hours cutting out plasticard strips based on the templates in the book and sticking them into the wings. A rewarding 'boxed-in' look followed, but I couldn't help feeling relieved when kits such as the Hurricane had it all done for you!

The Messerschmitt Bf 109 book was printed in a second edition in paperback form, but one does not see it very often. In mid-1974 a new range was announced entitled 'Airfix Magazine Modelling Guides'. They were released two at a time and the range eventually totalled twenty-eight books! They were smaller than the other books and had single colour covers with simple drawings to illustrate the contents. They were released in pairs roughly four times a year. The authors tended to come from amongst those who wrote articles in *Airfix Magazine*, not surprisingly.

In 1976 a final range was announced. Entitled *Classic Armoured Fighting Vehicles – Their History and How to Model Them* it ran to two books devoted to the Crusader and Lee/Grant tanks which had recently been produced to 1:32 scale by Airfix.

The final book to be published under the Airfix/PSL agreement was the Lancaster book in 1979. The smaller modelling section was based on existing Lancaster kits and was published before the new Airfix Lancaster was released. The other books were based on the 1:24 Superkits.

The books have long been out of print and did not make the transition to Palitoy. They can still be found on eBay and are worth buying if one intends to model one of the old, earlier Airfix kits that are still available.

A selection of titles from the three 'Their History and How to Model Them' series – Classic Ships, Classic Aircraft and Classic Armoured Fighting Vehicles.

The first eighteen titles in the 'Airfix Modeller's Guides' series.

PSL had also produced several books that expanded on several series of articles which had appeared in *Airfix Magazine*, such as 'Bombing Colours' and 'Fighting Colours'.

It was a bold venture, which shows the strong position held by Airfix kits in the 1970s. No other manufacturer has come close to producing a range of books about their model kits. In fact in 2011, Airfix lent its name to a series of books produced by SAM Publications entitled *Build and Convert*, which mainly deal with improving early Airfix kits.

Books about Airfix

In addition to the books produced by Airfix in the 1970s, many books about Airfix have been written, most since the Hornby takeover.

The first book detailing the history of Airfix was written in 1984 by a young modeller called Arthur Ward. He approached Peter Allen who had been a designer at Airfix and was now chief designer at Palitoy/Airfix. Peter was impressed by the young man's knowledge about Airfix; most would-be authors wanted Peter to supply the information! So Arthur set to work. He interviewed many of the former Airfix staff and examined much of the Airfix archive that had been transferred to Coalville and was at that time still largely intact. The resulting book, *The Model World of Airfix*, was published in 1985 and sold in a box set which contained a model of the HP42 Heracles and Kamov Ka-25B 'Hormone'. Older modellers, like myself, were already familiar with the range of kits, but

it was the early history of Airfix that fascinated us. Arthur had spoken to the likes of Ralph Ehrmann and John Gray who had unique knowledge of the early years of Airfix before it became the premier kit company in the world.

Until Arthur took up his pen again in 1999, it was the only book about the history of Airfix. Pat Lewarne, an enthusiast who ran a kit collectors' shop called 'Collectakit', had produced a privately published booklet entitled *The Enthusiast's Guide to Airfix Models* in 1987, which listed all the kits produced by Airfix up until the sale to Humbrol. Much of the information, such as year of release and catalogue numbers, came from a careful study of the catalogues produced since 1963.

During the lean years of Airfix kit production during the late 1980s and 1990s, these two books helped to remind us of the size and magnificence that was the old Airfix range. We were literally taken back to our childhoods. Diehard enthusiasts like me already had extensive notes and records accumulated over the previous twenty-five years, but these two books helped to fill in the missing pieces and 'flesh out' the story of Airfix.

Inevitably we would find errors or information that did not 'gel' with the careful notes we had been making for many years previously. However, much of the information had come from primary sources, the original Airfix men and the Airfix archive. Memories are not infallible, however, and dates and the like are easily misplaced. Also a book is the result of months, sometimes years of painstaking research, and eventually one has to commit to publication. Any perceived

errors cannot be amended unless one is lucky enough to publish a second edition.

Nowadays we have the internet, which is a wonderful thing but does produce its own problems. Large numbers of enthusiasts, who previously had little or no contact with others of their ilk, could now, through the medium of the World Wide Web, chat and exchange information and ideas instantly with their fellow enthusiasts. Now one can write something on the internet and in the time it takes to make a cup of tea, several people have already made postings to tell you that you've got it wrong!

Frequently, of course, they are right, but often any comments are merely their personal views and not necessarily always right. In the fifteen years I have been running the Airfix Collectors' Club, I have published nearly sixty quarterly magazines, and some of the information printed in the early issues has been revised in later ones to take account of new information that has been unearthed since. Much of the information in this book comes from research that I did for *Constant Scale*. I feel at least I have a body of work behind me to support what will be written in this book.

In 1999, Arthur wrote his second book called *Airfix: Celebrating 50 Years of the Greatest Plastic Kits in the World'*. It took the story up to 1999, the fiftieth anniversary of the Ferguson Tractor. Now we could read about the Humbrol years, and there was further information on the early years. To the man in the street, who wanted to reminisce about his childhood, this was an ideal book with lots of colour pictures and stories to remind him of days gone by.

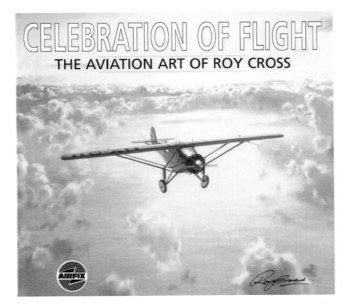

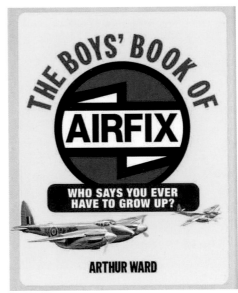

Also in 1999, Steve Knight, who runs the Kitmaster Collectors Club with Marcus Archer, wrote a book entitled *Let's Stick Together* about the history of Kitmaster before it was taken over by Airfix, and the subsequent use by Airfix of the Kitmaster moulds. It contained more details and statistics and helped greatly with our understanding of Airfix in the 1960s. In 2012, Steve printed a greatly revised book that included much new information and was entitled *Let's Stick a Little More!*

Arthur would write three more books before Hornby had got to grips with Airfix. In 2004, he published *Classic Kits: Collecting the Greatest Model Kits in the World* which had sections on all the plastic kit companies. Some only ran to two or three pages, but the Airfix section was naturally the largest. New information was included, particularly about the years up to 2004.

In 2007 and 2008, Arthur wrote two books for Crowood. The first was about television and film toys and had a small section on Airfix film and television toys. The other was about the classic toys of the 1960s and 1970s, and again Airfix featured in a small section.

Meanwhile Roy Cross had published two beautiful books on his aviation and marine art. Airfix illustrations featured in both books to a lesser extent, but it was wonderful to see these paintings as they had been painted. Such was the demand for pictures of his Airfix artwork that in 2009 he wrote a book called *Vintage Years of Airfix Box Art*, which was devoted entirely to his Airfix artwork. Hornby kindly supplied the transparencies for the artwork, and Roy used some of his unseen 'roughs'. This was the book the Airfix enthusiast had been waiting for.

In 2014, to celebrate the seventy-fifth anniversary of Airfix, Roy wrote a second book featuring the remaining artwork. I was privileged to go through the transparencies held by Airfix to select those not previously printed in Roy's earlier

books. About a dozen transparencies are missing, but otherwise all of Roy's Airfix artwork is now available to savour.

In 2004, Paul Morehead, who publishes the quarterly magazine *Plastic Warrior*, privately printed a small booklet entitled *Airfix: The Early Years*, which gave much information on the soldiers and figures produced by Airfix in the late 1940s.

Over half the books on Airfix have been published in the last five or six years since Hornby brought Airfix back to its prominent position in the modelling world. This is an indication of how Hornby has rejuvenated Airfix, because now many people want to write books about Airfix. Some of the books are about specific parts of the Airfix range and have involved considerable research on the part of the authors. A couple seem to be basically abridged versions of Arthur's seminal works and perpetuate one or two of the errors.

Things kicked off in a big way in 2009, when Arthur published his *Boys' Book of*

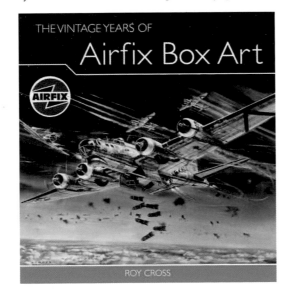

Airfix, which updated and added new details to the Airfix story. It was joined by Roy's book on Airfix artwork, and a book on the Airfix range of OO/HO figures called, aptly, *Airfix's Little Soldiers*. Written by French Airfix aficionado Jean-Christophe Carbonel, it tells the story of Airfix's range of OO/HO figures and is well illustrated.

Three more books were published in 2010. James May, well known for his *Top Gear* and toy programmes, wrote the *Airfix Handbook*, which told the story briefly of Airfix and then went on to to give details of his full-size replica of BT-K, which was built for RAF Cosford. John Bentley wrote a book on the aircraft of the Battle of Britain with numerous references to Airfix kits. Trevor Pask wrote a condensed story of Airfix for Shire Publications, which company produced a series of books on the history of toy companies.

In 2011, Jonathan Mock, who designs most of Airfix's decals, wrote a book called *The Airfix Book of Scale Modelling*, and SAM Publications released the first of a small range of paperback magazines with the title of *Build and Convert*; at the time of writing there are seven books in the series. Each book has a theme, such as military models or aircraft, and the author then

takes an older kit, mostly Airfix, and improves and finishes the model to the current standard. Plans to produce a couple of books devoted to Revell kits do not appear to have been proceeded with.

In 2011, I also printed two booklets for the members of the Airfix Collectors' Club. Listed as *Club Guides* Numbers 2 and 3, they were contents and indexes for *Airfix Magazine*. Number 1 dealt with every issue from 1960 to 1981, and Number 3 covered all the issues up to 1993, when *Airfix Magazine* ceased. In 2010 I had printed *Guide Number 1*, which was a listing of every known Airfix kit and the box-top artist. A greatly expanded and updated version was published in late 2014.

In 2012 Steve Knight published his second book on Kitmaster. Like the first, there is a sizable section on Airfix and its use of the Kitmaster moulds it acquired in 1963, and it has been updated with more information.

Also in 2012, Trevor Snowden, who had recently retired from Hornby/Airfix and was an acknowledged Spitfire enthusiast, wrote *Spitfire Revisited*. In this book he showed how to model every version of the Spitfire. Most of the models chosen were Airfix kits, many of which had been designed by the man himself!

Mark Stanton wrote a book for Crowood about building civil aircraft which used a large number of Airfix kits. Didier Palix, another French Airfix enthusiast had also written a book about Airfix's aircraft kits. Unlike J. C. Carbonel's book on the OO/HO figures, this book was mainly visual. Each page was devoted to all the headers and box tops used in each series from 1955 to 1982. For those who loved the artwork and box styles of the 'golden age' of Airfix aircraft kits, this book will rekindle all those happy memories.

From 2013, SAM Publications produced *Build and Convert* Numbers 3 to 7, again mainly using Airfix kits. Arthur Ward made a welcome return to the literary world of Airfix with his book entitled *The Other Side of Airfix*, which told the story of the non-kit parts of old Airfix, with stories about the arts and crafts, toys and games and other ranges that Airfix was involved with before the collapse of 1981.

Roy Cross produced his second book of Airfix artwork for the seventy-fifth anniversary of Airfix in 2014. So admirers of Roy's artwork can now view virtually the entire catalogue of his artwork through the various books he has published.

Also in 2014, to coincide with the release of the 1:24 Hawker Typhoon kit, a booklet entitled *How to Build: The Airfix Hawker Typhoon Mk Ib* was published by ADH Publishing and also sold by Hornby. Many of the above books are now out of print, but they frequently appear on eBay and are not too difficult to get hold of.

Airfix / PSL Books – All Hardbacks (unless otherwise stated)

Classic Ships – Their History and How to Model Them

90101/0 85059 053 1	No. 1 – HMS *Victory* – 1970	£1.05
90102/0 85059 058 2	No. 2 – *Mayflower* – 1970	£1.05
90107/0 85059 123 6	No. 3 – Cutty Sark – 1974	£1.95

Classic Aircraft – Their History and How to Model Them

90104/0 85059 082 5	No. 1 – Spitfire – 1971	£1.50
90105/0 85059 106 6	No. 2 – Bf 109B-E – 1972	£1.60
0 85059 106 6/0 85059 649 1	No. 2 – Bf 109B-E – reprint – paperback – 1976	
90106/0 85059 107 4	No. 3 – P-51 Mustang – 1973	£1.60
90108/0 85059 124 4	No. 4 – Hawker Hurricane – 1974	£1.80
0 85059 193 7	No. 5 – Ju 87 *Stuka* – 1977	£2.95
0 85059 344 1	No. 6 – Lancaster – 1979	£4.95
	No. 7 – Mosquito – 1980?	

Classic Armoured Fighting Vehicles – Their History and How to Model Them

90110/0 85059 194 5	No. 1 – Crusader Tank – 1976	£2.50
0 85059 269 0	No. 2 – Lee/Grant Tank – 1977	£2.95

Airfix Magazine Annuals – Published Autumn Before

0 85059 077 9	No. 1 – 1972	£1.25
0 85059 095 7	No. 2 – 1973	£1.20
0 85059 134 1	No. 3 – 1974	£1.25
0 85059 166 X	No. 4 – 1975	£1.60
0 85059 214 3	No. 5 – 1976	£1.95
0 85059 266 7	No. 6 – 1977	£2.50
0 85059 264 X	No. 7 – 1978	£2.95
0 85059 294 1	No. 8 – 1979 – Aircraft Modellers – paperback	£2.95
0 85059 314 X	No. 8 – 1979 – Military Modellers – paperback	£2.95

Airfix Modellers' Guides – 1974 Onwards

90120/0 85059 153 8	No. 1 – *Plastic Modelling* – 1974	£1.00
90121/0 85059 154 6	No. 2 – *Aircraft Modelling* – 1974	£1.00
90122/0 85059 177 5	No. 3 – *Military Modelling* – 1974	£1.20
90123/0 85059 178 3	No. 4 – *Napoleonic Wargaming* – 1974	£1.20
90124/0 85059 203 8	No. 5 – *Tank and AFV Modelling* – 1975	£1.20
90125/0 85059 204 6	No. 6 – *RAF Fighters of World War II* – 1975	£1.20
90126/0 85059 210 0	No. 7 – *Warship Modelling* – 1975	£1.20
90127/0 85059 211 9	No. 8 – *German Tanks of World War II* – 1975	£1.20
90128/0 85059 212 7	No. 9 – *Ancient Wargaming* – 1975	£1.20
90129/0 85059 213 5	No. 10 – *Luftwaffe Camouflage* – 1975	£1.20
90130/0 85059 215 1	No. 11 – *RAF Camouflage* – 1975	£1.20
90131/0 85059 216 X	No. 12 – *Afrika Korps* – 1975	£1.20
90132/0 85059 224 0	No. 13 – *French Foreign Legion* – 1976	£1.40
90133/0 85059 225 9	No. 14 – *World War II American Fighters* – 1976	£1.40
90134/0 85059 230 5	No. 15 – *World War II Wargaming* – 1976	£1.40
90135/0 85059 231 3	No. 16 – *Modelling Jet Fighters* – 1976	£1.40
90136/0 85059 232 1	No. 17 – *World War II British Tanks* – 1976	£1.40
90137/0 85059 233 X	No. 18 – *World War II USAF Camouflage* – 1976	£1.40
90138/0 85059 234 8	No. 19 – *Model Soldiers* – 1976	£1.40
90139/0 85059 235 6	No. 20 – *8th Army in the Desert* – 1976	£1.40
0 85059 249 6	No. 21 – *Modelling Armoured Cars* – 1977	£1.60
0 85059 250 X	No. 22 – *Russian Tanks of World War II* – 1977	£1.60
0 85059 257 7	No. 23 – *German Fighters of World War II* – 1977	£1.60
0 85059 258 5	No. 24 – *Amateur Civil War Wargaming* – 1977	£1.60

0 85059 262 3	No. 25 – *Modelling World War II Fighters* – 1977	£1.60
0 85059 260 7	No. 26 – *American Tanks of World War II* – 1977	£1.60
0 85059 261 5	No. 27 – *Modelling RAF Vehicles* – 1978	£1.60
0 85059 259 3	No. 28 – *The English Civil War* – 1978	£1.60
0 905418 71 9	Aircraft Conversions – nine from *Airfix Magazine* – Alan W. Hall – Gresham Books, 1979	£1.35

Airfix Colouring Books

Children's Leisure Products Ltd, 1979:

0 7094 0143 4	*Aircraft – 48 Exciting Scenes to Colour*	£0.35
0 7904 0144 2	*Ships – 48 Exciting Scenes to Colour*	£0.35
0 7094 0145 ?	?	
0 7904 0146 9	*Railways – 48 Exciting Scenes to Colour*	£0.35

Posters

In collaboration with Airfix Products Ltd:

C1182	'HMS *Victory*' – EP Group of Companies – Main illustration Brian Knight – 1973	
C1202	'The Story of Flight' – EP Group of Companies – Main illustrations Roy Cross and Brian Knight – 1974	
90141-3	Datachart No. 1 – 'German Fighter Aircraft, 1939–45' – Roy Cross – Bf 109E – 1975	£?

Books About Airfix

Various authors and publishers:

Bentley, John G. *Aircraft of the Battle of Britain* (Ravette Publishing 2010, ISBN: 978 184161 339 0) £6.99

Cole, Tom *Build & Convert 1: Airfix Military Models* (SAM Publications 2011, ISBN: 978 1 906959 20 3) £19.99

Carbonel, J.C. *Airfix's Little Soldiers: HO/OO from 1959 to 2009* (Histoire & Collections 2009, ISBN: 978 2 35250 089 6)

Cross, Roy *Celebration of Flight: Aviation Art of Roy Cross* (Crowood 2002, ISBN: 978 1 84037 326 4) £25.00

Cross, Roy *Celebration of Sail: Marine Art of Roy Cross* (Crowood 2005, ISBN: 978 1 86126 715 3) £29.95

Cross, Roy *Vintage Years of Airfix Box Art* (Crowood 2009, ISBN: 978 1 84797 076 3) £35.00

Cross, Roy *More Vintage Years of Airfix Box Art* (Crowood 2014, ISBN: 978 1 84797 820 2) £35.00

Grant, Mike *Build & Convert 2: Circuits & Bumps* (SAM Publications 2012, ISBN: 978 1 906959 27 2) £9.99

Grant, Mike *Build & Convert 4: Beyond the Box – More Circuits & Bumps* (SAM Publications 2013, ISBN: 978 1 906959 29 6) £9.99

Green, Brett *How to Build: The Airfix Hawker Typhoon Mk 1B (AH2901)* (Magazine, ADH Publishing 2014) £12.95

Hatcher, Gary *Build & Convert 3: Classic British Jets* (Classic Plastic Series, SAM Publications 2013, ISBN: 978 1 906959 28 9) £9.99

Hatcher, Gary *Build & Convert 5: Classic British Bombers* (Classic Plastic Series, SAM Publications 2013, ISBN: 978 1 906959 30 2) £9.99

Hatcher, Gary *Build & Convert 6: Aviation Classics Part 1* (SAM Publications 2014, ISBN: 978 1 906959 31 9) £9.99

Knight, Steve *Let's Stick Together* (Irwell Press 1999, ISBN: 1 871608 90 2) £13.95

Knight, Steve *Let's Stick a Little Bit More* (Irwell Press 2012, ISBN: 978 1 906919 49 8) £27.95

Lewarne, P. A. *Enthusiasts Guide to Airfix Models* (Collectakit 1987, privately published)

May, James *The Airfix Handbook – James May's Toy Stories* (Conway 2010, ISBN: 978 184486 116 3) £9.99

Mock, Jonathan *Airfix Book of Scale Modelling* (Conway 2011, ISBN: 978 1 84486 126 2) £14.99

Morehead, Paul *Airfix: The Early Years – Plastic Warrior* (2004, privately published) £3.00

Palix, Didier *Airfix: The Golden Age 1955–1982* (Editions Didier Palix 2012, ISBN: 978 2 954207 80 3) 38 Euros

Pask, Trevor *Airfix Kits* (Shire Publications 2010, ISBN: 978 0 74780 791 9) £6.99

Smith, Alec *Build & Convert 7: Classic Warplanes – The Spitfire and Friends* (SAM Publications 2014, ISBN: 978 1 906959 32 6) £9.99

Snowden, Trevor *Spitfire Revisited* (Dalrymple & Verdun Publishing 2012, ISBN: 978 1 905414 17 8) £24.95

Stanton, Mark *Building & Detailing Scale Commercial Aircraft* (Crowood 2012, ISBN: 978 1 84797 428 0) £16.99

Ward, Arthur *Model World of Airfix* (Palitoy 1984, ISBN: 0 947792 03 1)

Ward, Arthur *Airfix: Celebrating 50 years of the Greatest Plastic Kits in the World* (Harper Collins 1999, ISBN: 000 472327 9) £19.99

Ward, Arthur *Classic Kits: Collecting the Greatest Model Kits in the World* (Collins 2004, ISBN: 0 00 717695 3) £20.00

Ward, Arthur *TV and Film Toys and Ephemera* (Crowood 2007, ISBN: 978 1 86126 926 3) £19.95

Ward, Arthur *Classic Toys of the 1960s and 1970s* (Crowood 2008, ISBN: 978 1 86126 926 3) £19.95

Ward, Arthur *The Boys Book of Airfix* (Ebury Press (Airfix No. AH2898A) 2009, ISBN: 978 0 09 192898 8) £20.00

Ward, Arthur *The Other Side of Airfix – Sixty Years of Toys, Games & Crafts* (Pen & Sword 2013, ISBN: 978 1 84884 851 1) £19.99

Index

Models are arranged alphabetically by type with year of initial announcement in brackets. Page numbers in italics refer to illustrations. Abbreviations used: AW – Armstrong Whitworth; AWI – American War of Independence; BAC – British Aircraft Corporation; BAe – British Aerospace; DH – de Havilland; DHC – de Havilland Canada; ECW – English Civil War; EE – English Electric; HS – Hawker-Siddeley; McDD – McDonnell-Douglas; NA – North American; WWO - World War I; WWII – World War II.